Chinese Rules

Also by Tim Clissold

Mr. China

Chinese
Rules

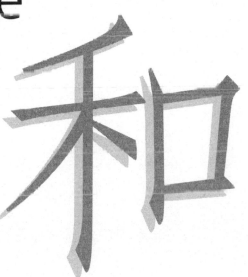

Mao's Dog,
Deng's Cat,
and Five Timeless
Lessons from the
Front Lines in China

Tim Clissold

HARPER

An Imprint of HarperCollins*Publishers*

HarperCollins books may be purchased for educational, business, or sales promotional use. For information, please e-mail the Special Markets Department at SPsales@harpercollins.com.

FIRST EDITION

Library of Congress Cataloging-in-Publication Data has been applied for.

ISBN: 978-0-06-231657-8

14 15 16 17 18 OV/RRD 10 9 8 7 6 5 4 3 2 1

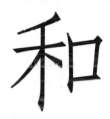

"harmony"

for Lorraine,
for my brothers Oliver and Max,
and for the memory of Lizzie Hicks

To fight and win a hundred battles is not supreme excellence;
the greatest General avoids war and overcomes his adversary
without fighting.

是故百戰百勝，
非善之善也；
不戰而屈人之兵，
善之善者也。

THIRD SECTION, SUN TZU'S *THE ART OF WAR*,
C. SIXTH CENTURY BC

CONTENTS

A Chinese Chop

The events that I describe in the main narrative of this book actually happened, but this is a story of an adventure, rather than an exposé of any particular individual or company, so I have changed the names of some of the companies and the characters that appear. The main events described in the story took place between 2005 and 2012.

Chinese Rules

1

千斤的牯牛也要低頭喝水

EVEN A BEAST LIKE A THOUSAND-POUND OX MUST LOWER ITS HEAD TO DRINK

Traditional peasant saying:
Even the most capable must
sometimes ask for help.

I almost didn't answer the call. I had been gazing absentmindedly out at the hills and the purple splash of heather as the train sped south toward York. But the car was almost empty so I took out the phone and clicked on the button. A voice confirmed my name and asked abruptly if I could go to China. Glancing around me, I whispered, "I can't really take a call right now. I'm in the quiet coach, you see."

"Well, you'd better call me back right away. Didn't you get my messages?" said the voice with a snort. And then the line cut out.

London was still a couple of hours away, so I waited awhile as the stone towers on the minster receded into the distance. The landscape leveled out around York and, farther south, a network of canals stretched out in straight lines toward the horizon; lock gates and brick guardhouses passed by the window. Along the old toll paths, the willows tossed about in the wind, casting long, rolling shadows in the late summer sun. I wandered down to the end of the car and, leaning against the doorway, clicked on the number. The voice that answered immediately launched into a story.

"Okay, so we've got this deal in China," she said, "and we need your help urgently. There's this big factory in Zhejiang—you've been to Zhejiang of course but maybe not to Quzhou."

"Er, yeah, I think I've been to Quzhou."

Another snort. "I doubt it, this must be a different Quzhou. It's miles from anywhere, stuck right out in the middle of the outback, a couple of six-packs from Hangzhou."

"Yeah, that's the one," I said, noticing an Australian accent.

"Really?" She paused for a moment, but quickly resumed the story. "Anyway," she said, "we signed up to buy truckloads of carbon from a chemical factory down there and now it looks like the whole thing's gone belly-up. We found some lawyers in Beijing who said that you'd help us."

"Lawyers?" I asked.

"Haven't they briefed you yet?" asked the voice. "They promised they'd call you. Now the Chinese partner wants to change every-thing." The voice groaned, apparently addressing itself. "This is the biggest deal that's ever been done by private investors," she said, shooting her attention back to me. "We've got fifteen million tons of carbon hanging by a thread, and now they want to change the whole deal!"

"Carbon?" I said, glancing sideways through the window and de-ciding it was time to end the call. "Look, I'm really sorry, but I don't know anything about the chemical industry. You must have got the wrong lawyers."

"Not that type of carbon."

"Catalysts or something is it? Look, fifteen million tons of carbon sounds like a hell of a lot to be moving around in China."

"What?"

"You got transport organized?" I asked. "The railways can be a nightmare," I said. "You know they've still got steam engines running out there?"

"Not that kind of carbon!" said the voice again, shifting markedly upward in pitch. "Credits! Not the black stuff!" There was a sigh and a mumbled comment I didn't quite catch above the clatter of the tracks.

"Oh," I said. "Right."

"Let's just back up here for a minute," she said. "We have a deal to buy carbon credits from a chemical factory in Quzhou. They make stuff used in fridges and air conditioners, right?"

"Oh, yeah? So where does the carbon come in then?" I continued skeptically. This really wasn't making much sense. The connection cut out and the car shook violently as the train roared through a tunnel. She called me back immediately.

"Wait! The chemical plant is chucking out greenhouse gases big-time, so we're helping them put in new equipment, incinerators that'll burn up the gas. That way, we get credits that we can sell on in Europe. Buyers are desperate for this stuff!"

"Uh-huh . . . ," I said, concluding that I was dealing with a nut. "Look, I'm sure this is all really interesting, but I'm quite tied up at the moment. Perhaps you could—"

"No, listen," she interrupted. "This is deadly serious."

She went on to explain that the project was the largest greenhouse gas reduction project ever attempted by private investors. "We just have to make this work," she said. "If we get it right, it could kick-start the whole market." The Chinese factory had agreed to put in equipment that burns up gases from the production line, which they'd been venting out into the air. "It's really bad stuff," she said, "millions of tons of gases just blowing up into the sky and all they have to do is put in incinerators to burn it up."

"So why don't they just put them in anyway then?" I asked.

"There's nowhere in China that makes the equipment; they have to import it from Japan and they don't have the cash. So we agree to buy the credits, and the factory shows the contract to the bank to get loans to buy the equipment. That's the whole point of the CDM, right?"

"Er . . . maybe," I said vaguely.

"CDM. It's part of the Kyoto Protocol for reducing greenhouse gases—Kyoto, right?!" she said doubtfully. "The factory puts in the equipment, burns up the gas, and the UN gives them carbon credits that we can sell on in Europe. Both sides make money, we cut down on greenhouse gases, and everybody's happy."

"Sounds a bit far-fetched to me. You been doing this long, have you?" I added suspiciously.

"Well, yes actually," she said. "I did five years at the World Bank. We did deals all over the world . . . Indonesia, Nepal, India, China, Venezuela. Six months ago I moved to London and joined a carbon outfit here."

The phone cut out again.

"Sorry, I didn't quite catch that," I said once we were reconnected.

"Yeah, I was just saying that I joined a carbon outfit in London but at first no one else here wanted to do this deal—can you imagine it?! The biggest carbon deal on the planet and they got all nervy and started asking all sorts of questions." Another snort. "Anyway, I went right out on a limb and got the Chinese to sign up to sell us the carbon. When I took the letter back to London, man, they were crazy as a snake. There wasn't enough money in the first fund so we went out and raised a syndicate. Wang's just called from China and wants to change the deal. The syndicate is wobbling and it looks like the whole lot's about to go down the chute. Anyway I don't have time for all this. Cut to the point; when can you come out to China?"

"Er . . ."

"We need to get out there as quickly as possible. I've got a flight booked for this evening."

"This evening!? But I don't even get into London till after five . . ."

"The flight's not till eight, so you've got plenty of time to get across town. The guys in Beijing said you'd help us . . ."

"I don't even have my passport with me," I explained. "It's up in Yorkshire."

"We'll send a taxi to fetch it."

"Are you crazy? That's a couple hundred miles! And anyway, I don't have any business clothes with me!"

"Buy some at the airport."

"But I don't know anything about carbon or Kyoto or any of that stuff . . ."

"Read up on it on the plane," she said.

"And my visa's just expired," I said.

She seemed momentarily stumped.

"We'll get you one in the morning. I've got plenty of mates at the embassy. Hang on a moment . . ."

She put her hand over the mouthpiece and there were a few muffled comments before she came back to me.

"Okay, we've got seats out tomorrow," she said. "We're on the four o'clock flight out to Hong Kong."

"But . . ."

"I'll meet you in the business lounge."

"I . . ."

"And by the way," she said, "the name's Mina."

2

樹高千丈 葉落歸根

A TREE MAY GROW TO A THOUSAND FEET, BUT THE LEAVES STILL RETURN TO THEIR ROOTS

Wanderers eventually return to their native soil.

—The Story of a Marital Fate to Awaken the World,
an unattributed Qing Dynasty novel

Behind the Forbidden City stands a hill, which—legend has it—hides a vast reserve of coal for use in times of siege. Each morning, just before dawn, people gather in the park below the hill for exercises. A group of women practice swordplay with their arms outstretched and blades held upright, turning on one heel. An older man shambles past with a battered canvas bag, half running, half walking, toward his usual spot among the flowerpots by the dragon-claw scholar-trees. There he fills a bucket with water, dips in a long brush, and silently practices calligraphy, writing with long, flowing brushstrokes in the dust on the paving stones at his feet. All around, hidden among the bushes, the exercisers stretch and bend and shout to greet the dawn.

I often looked out from the hill as the first rays of sunlight struck the corner watchtowers on the Forbidden City below. In the 1980s it was easy to imagine that Beijing had hardly changed since imperial times. Around the palace complex with its maze of pavilions and passageways, the sloping roofs of a thousand courtyard houses stretched out flat toward the horizon. In the late springtime, a thin layer of mist would trap the smell of fresh leaves in the damp air hanging in the alleyways. Toward the end of the summer, in the main Party compound beside the Forbidden City, lotus flowers poked through the greenery that floated about on the lakes; crooked pathways ran over little stone bridges between the pavilions along the banks. Back then, there was something about Beijing that felt simple and content; the city ran in a daily routine in which everything had its own allotted place and a clear role in life. There was a pattern to the day in the old *hutong* alleyways, a rhythm to the hours and seasons, a closeness to nature that felt unusual in the midst of such a vast city. Up on the hill, it seemed as if the odd honk of a passing Liberation Truck was the only reminder of the turning of the centuries. But when I looked more closely through the haze toward the west, I could pick out the vague and distant outline of factories standing out against the mountainsides. Smokestacks and towers of twisted pipework rose up at the foot of the hills. A trail of smoke drifted from an iron foundry. In the other direction, heaps of coal and ash marked the site of the city's main power station and electrical towers marched off in straight lines toward the south. These were all the early signs of modernization and in those days, I never gave it a thought. But if you were to go back to that hill and look out over the great city today, you would find a very different sight.

I first arrived in Asia in the eighties after I was posted to Hong Kong from London. I'd never been there before, and from the moment I stepped from the plane and through the wall of dense, wet heat, I knew I was in a different world. Giant Chinese characters shone in neon lights from the tops of ten-story buildings. Wherever I looked, there were people hammering in tiny factories, unloading from boats, bargaining in alleyways. Office workers sat crammed into dumpling restaurants between stacks of bamboo steamers. The streets reeked of dried seafood and Chinese medicine and the air was filled with the honking of taxis and clattering of trams. I had no idea that such a concentration of human life could exist in such a state of perpetual motion. The intensity of life in Hong Kong was something completely new to me. Almost immediately, I felt drawn to China.

The following year, I quit Hong Kong and found a place at a university in Beijing to learn Mandarin. It was the year after the tanks had rumbled onto Tiananmen Square and there were almost no other foreigners around. At first the students there sought me out to practice their English, ignoring the bizarre rules about "spiritual pollution" that were meant to keep us apart. But their English was so good that I felt awkward speaking Mandarin with them, and so I started spending more time away from the university, in places where people knew nothing of foreigners. After a while, I could manage simple conversations and slowly grew to recognize the Chinese characters on the shop signs and the notices around me. I found my way more easily through the tangled network of old *hutong* alleyways that spread around the old imperial buildings at the center of the city. I often went back to Coal Hill to find the calligraphy man practicing his characters with his water brush on the dusty paving stones. He would write out characters on the stones at his feet while I tried to catch the meaning of the flowing brushstrokes before they began to fade and disappear.

My student days were short-lived and I soon joined an investment firm run by a Wall Street veteran who was building the first large foreign direct investment business in China. Over the period of a few years, he'd raised $400 million and pumped it into twenty factories across China, ending up with nearly twenty-five thousand employees.

The speed of China's development in those years was difficult to take in; around the Yangtse and Pearl River deltas, shiny new cities rose up out of marshlands in just a few months. Little fishing villages became gigantic container ports, hydroelectric dams choked mighty rivers, and four-lane superhighways were blasted through rock faces. For more than a decade, China existed in a state of supreme upheaval. The government fought to maintain order as it embarked on a program of massive reform, removing the props of the command economy while billions in foreign investment poured into the coastal provinces. As China awoke from a century of slumber, deep within the interior 150 million workers rose up out of the country villages like a tidal wave and swirled toward the coast.

Many of the factories we had invested in were in remote regions of China, where central authority was weaker. "The mountains are high and the emperor is far away," goes the old provincial saying about the distant authorities in Beijing. The country is too big to be controlled from a single center, and unless events catch the attention of Beijing, local interests can often take over. We became embroiled in unequal disputes in far-flung places. Land was transferred out of our joint ventures to prop up loans for other local businesses. Bank transfers and capital investments were made without approval, cash was stuffed into safes in back offices with no records, and contracts were routinely ignored. For a long time, it looked as though we might lose the investment.

It took years to sort out the mess, and during that time, I traveled to almost every province in China. We had strikes and lockouts, sieges and court cases, and had been pursued across the country by officials with writs and freezing orders. But gradually, over a period of several years, the relationships with our Chinese partners smoothed out and the businesses started making money. We got better control of the assets and sales started to grow on the back of the China boom. Most of the investment was saved, together with the jobs of the twenty-five thousand workers, but after nearly seven years in the combat zone of Chinese investment, I was exhausted. I needed some time-out to think.

Several years earlier, I'd married my old college classmate—*ou duan si lian*, as the Chinese would say of a reconnected love affair: "Lotus roots may snap but their threads stay attached." When Lorraine came to live in Beijing, life's possibilities multiplied overnight. She had arrived with two small boys—my stepsons, Max, aged five, and Christian, who was three—followed a year or so later by our children, Sam and Honor. Weekends were taken up by trips out to remoter parts of the Great Wall, scrambling up the Ming Tombs with a couple of dogs, or splashing about on Kunming Lake at the Summer Palace. The foreign community was small in those days and there was still a sense of adventure about a posting to Beijing.

Around the time I was thinking about moving on from the investment business, Lorraine came home one day with news that she had found an old courtyard home for rent about a mile or so east of Tiananmen Square. Hidden in a backstreet, it had been part of the former residence of a Qing Dynasty official; I didn't need much persuading to move back to the old alleyways.

The courtyard had a large south-facing hall behind a row of red lacquered columns. It stood on a stone terrace looking out onto a garden where an old wisteria climbed up into the carved woodwork under the eaves. The alleyway outside was named after the old imperial grain warehouses. Farther down, clouds of steam rose from a line of shabby street restaurants. At lunchtime, they were packed with laborers from the provinces. Oil drums stuffed with red-hot coals lined the street; cooks in white hats threw handfuls of Sichuan peppercorns into their woks as they shouted out for customers. At the end of the street, there was an old Buddhist temple with big bronze studs on the doorways and glazed black tiles on the rooftops. Inside, a drum tower stood next to a huge cherry tree that burst into blossom in springtime. During festivals, there were concerts in the temple and the air was filled with the smell of incense and the strange chanting of monks. For me, it felt completely natural to be back in the *hutong*s and connected to the old way of life. On our first night, as I sat in the courtyard with the children, a storm rolled across the city and chunks of ice fell down among torrents of warm water. But after the downpour, the skies quickly cleared and the familiar smell of stir-fry drifted over the wall from next door. The stars came out and, high above our heads, a kite tugged a long trail of candlelit lanterns across the sky, tiny red dots dancing about against a backdrop of darkening blue.

After we moved to the *hutong*, I took a few months off from work to try to make sense of what happened to the investment business. The prospect of losing so much money and the lessons learned in the fight to recover it had forced me to dismantle entirely my ideas about dealing with China. I had been made to rethink some of my most basic assumptions. One thing was for sure: if you stuck by Western rules, you were finished.

I'd learned my hardest lesson after we'd been hit by a fraud in the southern city of Zhuhai, which sits next to the old Portuguese colony of Macau, far away on China's southern coast but not so far from Hong Kong. We'd invested about $8 million in a brake-pad factory down there but a few months after we wired in the money, the factory director went on a trip to the United States to attend a trade fair in Las Vegas—and he didn't come back. We discovered subsequently that he had gone to Hong Kong with four letters of credit—like unbounceable checks drawn against our account—with a face value of $5 million. There he exchanged them for cash and— carrying what the police described as "a large suitcase," presumably containing the banknotes—he boarded a plane for America. That was the last that we heard of him. In the seat beside him on the way out was the deputy bank manager of the branch that had opened the letters of credit. It was obviously a scam.

Our response to the news had been catastrophic. When I tried to explain what had happened over the crackling phone lines to New York, there had been an instant, knee-jerk reaction. The directors there immediately ordered a highly sophisticated legal operation involving hordes of expensive lawyers all waving worldwide Mareva injunctions, which were aimed at freezing the bank's assets on the basis that the branch officials must have known about the scam and that the bank was therefore liable. The case ended up in China's Supreme Court and, after two years of pointless arguments, we lost. It was a disaster—I remembered bitterly that when the factory director had disappeared from Zhuhai, our cash was still in the account because the letters of credit had not yet been presented. One of our other Chinese factory directors had looked at me with a slightly puzzled expression and asked, "Why did you go to the court? You could have just transferred the cash out in small amounts without the bank noticing and when the documents arrived, they'd be left with the bill." We'd done the opposite; the board had metaphorically marched up to the city gates, announced a full frontal assault, and then assailed the bank with highly sophisticated legal weaponry that was completely useless for dealing with the actual problem. As soon as the bank realized what was going on, they took one look at the court papers, made a quick call to the local government, and froze all our accounts. We never recovered a cent.

Those seven years on the front lines of Chinese business taught me that foreigners had no way to impose their ideas on China from the outside; I'd learned the hard way that if you wanted to survive in China, it had to be on Chinese terms. I had been forced to think through new ideas as basic as how society, business, and government could be organized and how to compete on foreign terrain. There seemed no option but to abandon some of the basic assumptions I'd brought with me from the West. I could see that China had its own modes of behavior, its own conventions, and accepted ways of doing things that were different from our own. China's way of working seemed difficult to pin down, but every country, every society, has its own internal logic; it may not be obvious from the surface but I felt there must be some overarching rationale, some consistent narrative to how China worked. Perhaps it was something in my background that made me seek a more ordered explanation to the chaos I had found around me; perhaps it came from studying physics in college, where universal laws are used to explain diverse and seemingly unconnected observations. I found myself searching for an underpinning to the Chinese universe, reference points or clues to a larger framework that might help me navigate these foreign waters, something that might reveal how it all fit together. China's special logic was elusive and hard to define precisely, but I knew I'd never be satisfied if I didn't at least make an effort to uncover it.

In the southwest of Beijing there is an area of winding alleyways around Tile Factory Street where, in the fifteenth century, ornate ceramic ornaments were fired in charcoal kilns for the rooftops of the great Ming Dynasty palaces. Three hundred years later, the area around the factory had grown into a cultural center, where scholars, poets, and artists gathered to exchange ideas and practice calligraphy. Today the narrow streets are lined with shops piled to the roofbeams with books and scrolls; local painters come there to find paper, brushes, ink stones, and seals. I often visited the bookshops, with their rickety staircases, dusty display cases, and the burnt, earthy smell of Chinese calligraphy ink. At the back of one of those bookshops, there was a room lined with battered bookcases devoted to Chinese history and ancient theories of war. I had heard about Sunzi, but had never really taken *The Art of War* too seriously; tales of battle plans from the sixth century BC had seemed too remote to be of much use in the modern age. But I found the shelves there lined with piles of clothbound books I had never heard of, like the *Book of Qi* and the *Records of Tan Daoji*. I discovered an enormous volume of historical records covering power struggles, plots, and intrigues stretching back well past the time of the European Dark Ages. At first I couldn't understand the antiquated Chinese language, with its ancient, recondite characters, so I sought out translations, trying to put the Chinese and English together to look for the deeper meaning. I dipped into an old collection of battle plans called the Thirty-six Ruses. There I found set-piece strategies, with strange names like "The Beauty Trap," "Take the Wood from Under a Cauldron," and "Kill with Borrowed Knife." Elsewhere, I found a Han Dynasty strategy that set out the "Five Baits for Enticing Foreigners." I sensed an obliqueness in the approach that contrasted with the direct assault favored by Westerners. I found more emphasis on timing and surprise, on harnessing external conditions rather than just relying on firepower, and on ways of deceiving a more powerful enemy. There were unexpected twists: in Sunzi's world, the supreme general avoids war altogether and overcomes without fighting. "Overcomes without fighting," I thought. "What did that mean?" I bought several of the books and found ideas that helped explain things that had happened at our factories. I was wondering whether they could all be collated into a more coherent pattern when I was suddenly contacted by some investors in Hong Kong.

At the turn of the millennium, as China prepared to join the World Trade Organization, the government realized that the banking system was crippled with uncollectible loans and they decided to do something about it. I found myself tempted by the idea of helping to clear up the mess, so I went to work for one of the big American investment banks that had just entered the new market for "distressed debt" in China.

During the forty years of the planned economy, Chinese banks had given money to factories and work units under the central state plan rather than on the basis of commercial logic. Many of the borrowers had no hope—or even intention—of making repayments. The result was a mess of truly astronomical proportions, with about $700 billion worth of uncollectible debts—known as "nonperforming loans" or "distressed debt"—clogging up the banking system. Faced with the prospect of a complete financial meltdown, the Chinese government started restructuring the banks and selling off tranches of these nonperforming loans to foreign investors at reduced prices. An American bank had bought up several of these portfolios and I was hired to retrieve something from the wreckage.

Over the coming six months, I traveled across China visiting factories that owed amounts under these bad loans, often meeting with the local governments in charge of the area. Many of the loans had been in arrears for years and the relationship between the lender and borrower had broken down completely. Just having a new face to negotiate with often unlocked a knotty situation. At first I felt that the work could bring a lot of benefit to local communities: the factories could be released from their debts for a partial repayment; clearing out the backlog might open up the possibility of new loans; the restructuring assets could make them useful again; and management teams might get an infusion of new talent. But some of the cases were much murkier. I heard that one of the borrowers had been held under house arrest; at another, there'd been riots when a local bank had tried to seize machinery. After a while I became uneasy about the effect of some of the settlements on the local community or the individuals concerned.

During those months, as I worked in the plush offices at the bank during the day and returned to the *hutong* in the evening, I noticed the city beginning to change, gradually at first. When we moved into the courtyard, even though we were in the midst of an enormous city, we felt somehow connected to nature and aware of the turn of the seasons. In winter, it was so cold that the children sometimes wore coats in bed; by summertime, it was sweltering and flash thunderstorms flooded the courtyard, sending us retreating up the steps to listen to the rain splashing on the clay tiles above our heads. In the local vegetable markets, pots of pickled vegetables or white cabbage lined the stalls throughout the winter, and in the late summer, we'd find cut flowers, lotus root, and ginger. But the changes around us gathered pace as the city began to modernize. I'd often notice that an old restaurant had vanished and a mobile phone outlet had appeared in its place, or that a corner shop had been demolished to make way for a wider road.

In the early days I hardly noticed, but the pace became more rapid. Suddenly a long line of shops had gone; then the whole side of a road would disappear. I heard rumors about an old woman in Xicheng District, on the west side of Beijing, who had chained herself to a tree inside her old courtyard as an official read out the eviction order. She'd lived there for sixty years and had nowhere else to go. Grabbing my bicycle, I rode over to see what was going on and found a sea of rubble with the odd solitary tree standing where the old courtyard gardens had been. Window frames and roofbeams lay scattered on the ground; broken saucepans and smashed pots sat among the heaps of shattered tiles.

Once Beijing won the hosting of the 2008 Summer Olympics, there was an inevitability to the fate of the old city. Twenty billion dollars had been set aside to upgrade the capital, and for several years large sections of it vanished behind the perimeter fences of construction sites. Huge areas of the ancient city disappeared forever. Miles of old alleyways and winding backstreets fell beneath the hammer. A hundred thousand workers poured in from the countryside and swarmed over the old buildings, uprooting ancient wisterias from courtyard houses and dumping them on the heaps of broken bricks outside. Ornate doorways were torn away; tiles were pulled from roofs. I sank into a kind of siege mentality and shut my mind to what was happening. All around, the air shook with the roar of bulldozers and I could feel the distant pounding of pile drivers through the ground beneath my feet. I heard that more areas of old *hutong*s in the north had disappeared, but I couldn't bear to go and look. All around us, an ancient way of life was dismantled brick by brick.

One day, we came back to find that a character I had seen written inside a circle on hundreds of other courtyard walls was now painted on the wall of our own.

The character means "demolish," "strike down," "strip," or "tear apart." It was the only notice we had that the bulldozers were about to move in. At first I put up a fight; a famous author had owned the courtyard in the 1930s, but of course my argument that the old building should be preserved because of its historical value fell on deaf ears. Then I told them we'd refuse to move out. *"Wo bu zou le!"* I said. I'm not going anywhere! But the old woman at the Street Committee just shrugged and squinted at me briefly before adjusting her glasses and turning back to her newspapers. *"Hao ba! Xingqi san ting shui le!"* she said. Okay then! Wednesday the water will stop! So I sat in the courtyard as the workers climbed onto the roofs around me with their hammers and picks, and bits of old tile and plaster fell down onto the lawn beside my feet.

Nowadays, the view from the top of the hill behind the Forbidden City is often obscured by smog; the air of the Beijing summer is opaque. Down below, the traffic snarls and tempers fray. Cyclists clutch at their mouths and turn their faces away from the fumes. In my mind's eye, I fly westward across the mountains, out toward the dusty orchards, the country villages, and the crumbling loess soil on the plains of central China. Beijing is a vantage point from which to survey all the desperate activity across China; inland, millions toil in search of a better life. Miners descend in black cages; workers hack at rock faces and dig tunnels for the next intercity highway. Engines roar and sirens scream; the rivers inland have run completely dry, their beds a mass of smashed rocks covered with thornbushes, and there are no trees. Dead fish float about in filmy water. Plagues of river rats ravage the crops, deserts devour the fields, and acid rain falls across the land.

On Beijing's old foundations, a new metropolis of vast proportions has been thrown together in a few years. Glass spikes rise skyward and elevated highways dominate the landscape now. In a few small areas of Old Beijing, around the lakes and drum towers of the Ming Dynasty city, the government preserved the ancient courtyards, but they cower in the shadows of high-rise apartment blocks. The alleyways there are clogged with rickshaws full of shouting tourists. China has moved on as it prepares to assume its new role in the world. Beijing had become less foreign, less different, and consequently—for me—less interesting.

I had begun to feel doubts about whether I was doing the right thing at the bank. Besides, the children were growing up so quickly. I felt a growing sense of inevitability about a move back to England. But it was with a heavy heart the following summer, after nearly twenty years in China, that I called a shipping agent and we started the journey back.

We had found a place in a small rural village tucked in among the hills at the foot of the Yorkshire Dales. It was close to the place where I had grown up, and at first I enjoyed the familiar sight of the stone walls arching across the fields as they rolled up the dales, the grass clipped short by the sheep, the smell of bracken and heather. Lorraine seemed relieved to be back in the fresh air and countryside and quickly gathered a menagerie of animals around her. She stocked up the vegetable garden and left grain in the little dovecot. The children threw themselves into the outside life, racing in horse shows, falling out of trees, and galloping through the mud in the hills and in other people's gardens. Three cats and an indeterminate number of horses joined the two dogs we brought back from China.

Stupidly, we chose an old house that was far too big for us and needed an enormous amount of work. The place was so infested with field mice that even the cats despaired; the window frames were rotten; and after poking around in the cellar, we saw that parts of the foundations were propped up with stacks of newspapers dating from the 1960s. I discovered a row of buckets in the attic for collecting the drips, and throughout the interminable damp of the first Yorkshire winter, the rain cascaded through the roof and ran down the walls, short-circuiting the electrical outlets and providing impressive blue sparks around the light switches. Downstairs, the coal fires barely took the frost off the carpets and the wind howled through the shutters. After nearly twenty years in China, it was tough to adapt to such a different life. I found it difficult to reengage and fit in.

Over the following months, I took long walks in the countryside in the drizzle, musing about China and slipping about in the mud with the two dogs from Beijing. My mood recovered slightly with the onset of spring, when the banks along the country lanes were scattered with snowdrops and then daffodils. But I still found it difficult to reorient my thinking to the old English ways. How do you explain to one of the local farmers that if your dogs strayed onto their land just to enjoy chasing the odd sheep, they would only respond to instructions in Mandarin? I'd often end up yelling at the dogs outside the village post office; they'd cock their heads and look at me in bemusement if I said "Sit!" but were instantly responsive to "*Zuo!*"

Lorraine hardly fared any better as she tried to make new friends, and was regarded as eccentric by the locals. She had kept up her Chinese diet and once, when she went to buy eggs early one morning, the postmistress sniffed and asked—quite rudely, I thought—whether she'd had garlic for supper the night before. In fact, Lorraine ate a kind of Chinese boiled rice porridge for breakfast each day, flavored with spring onions and spices. So she eyed the group of nosy customers who had gathered at the end of the wooden counter and said, "No, I just had raw onions for breakfast."

In the early summer, the trees awoke and birds filled the hedgerows. On my daily run through the woods, I'd often pause by an old rickety stile and watch the wild deer jumping through the cornfields or the rabbits diving through the thickets. But my mind always flew back to the dusty skies and congested cities, the dry riverbeds threading across the plains, the persimmon orchards out by the Ming Tombs, and the ancient rice terraces on the hillsides where generations of farmers toiled in the squelching mud. I felt stranded at the opposite end of the earth, so I was in a restless, searching mood when I suddenly received that call in the quiet coach, asking me to go back to China.

3

馬臨懸崖收繮晚
船到江心補漏遲

WHEN THE HORSE HAS REACHED THE EDGE OF THE CLIFF, IT'S TOO LATE TO DRAW ON THE REINS;

When the Boat Has Reached the Midst of the Stream, It's Too Late to Plug All the Holes

—Traditional peasant saying

On the same day that I'd received the call from Mina, Rufus Winchester had driven his hybrid-electric car across Hyde Park toward Mayfair in the perfect summer sunshine. Tall, regimental, uptight, and buttoned-down, this former British Army officer was an energetic and blustering serial entrepreneur who had survived a string of botched business start-ups. Things had never quite come right for Captain Winchester. But now, he thought to himself, we're about to hit the big time.

His company, ECF, had finished its first fund-raising and had signed up nearly €100 million from investors. Together with his partners, an assortment of earnest, well-meaning, and moneyed Englishmen, he had rented a large Georgian mansion in Mayfair as an office and set about hiring a team. Just like an Old Boys Club, the new headquarters had a ballroom on the first floor with high, corniced ceilings, but all the real work took place in cramped attic rooms where the juniors toiled behind computer screens hedging carbon credits in the City. Downstairs, the founders floated about between oak-paneled meeting rooms with the effortless self-confidence that comes from a good public school education. Excitement about carbon credits had just taken hold of the financial markets and ECF's fund-raising had been splashed across the front pages. Winchester took in a deep breath, pushed back against the steering wheel, and smiled. He was in the right place at the right time and he knew it.

Immediately after the first hundred million euros rolled in, ECF had turned its attention to China. Winchester knew that over the past two decades, thousands of new businesses had sprouted up along the coast of China, and that, together with the old state-owned factories in the rust belt cities of the north, they were cranking out greenhouse gases like there was no tomorrow. It was fertile ground for Winchester's new firm and in a couple of months his team had found several big projects in China. By the summer, they'd initialed their first transaction. It was a landmark deal to buy a big tranche of carbon credits from a chemical factory in Quzhou, the biggest ever attempted by private investors. There wasn't enough money in their first fund to cover the contract so they had to go out and find more. Eventually they managed to syndicate the deal with their chums in the City.

It had been three months of exhausting and stressful work, but they'd finally lined up investors. Deutsche Bank had agreed to underwrite the financing and they were ready to sign the contracts. It was a real coup; a big chunk of the first hundred million would be invested well ahead of schedule and the investors were happy.

But much more exciting was that they had "circles" around another €500 million from some big European pension funds to put into a second, much larger fund. "Just close that deal in Quzhou," Winchester thought to himself, "and the money'll come rolling in. If we get those Dutch pension funds signed up, we could end up with a billion and we'll be the largest carbon fund on the planet!" It looked as though the last pieces were sliding perfectly into place just at the right time. But then they got a message from Quzhou. Chief Engineer Wang had called unexpectedly from the chemical factory and said that he wanted to change some key terms of the deal.

When they heard about Wang's last-minute demands, the investors in the syndicate started to waver. It seemed as though the entire financing structure would collapse. The millions that Winchester had lined up from the Dutch pension funds started to crumble in his hands. It looked as though they might lose everything. A few hours later, I got the call from Mina.

At the end of the conversation in the railcar just outside York, Mina had insisted that I drop by at her offices as soon as the train arrived in London. I could see from the address that ECF was located in one of the most expensive areas of London, so I had hesitated; I'd come down to London to see friends and hadn't expected to go to a meeting. I was covered in stubble and in need of a haircut. My glasses were twisted out of shape from one of the children standing on them and I was wearing a pair of torn jeans and a thin cotton jacket that was a bit ragged about the elbows, but I had an hour or so to spare so I took the tube over to Mayfair. ECF's offices were in a long row of handsome merchant's houses near the American embassy; ornate iron railings ran around the first-floor balconies and a row of Grecian urns stood out along the roofline. Underneath a white portico, a flight of stone steps led up from the pavement toward a highly polished black door. I'd heard that Condoleezza Rice was in town that day so the roads around Bond Street were blocked off and snarled with traffic. I was glad I hadn't taken a taxi.

I grasped the brass knocker and, after a few moments, there

was a click and the door swung open. Inside, a hallway led toward a pair of tall double doors of elaborately inlaid mahogany. There was a marble fireplace on the left with vases at each end. Pale gray paneling reached up toward ornate plaster moldings on the ceiling. I sat down next to a low glass-topped table strewn with magazines— *Country Life* and *Horse & Hound*—crossed one leg over the tear in my jeans, and waited.

After about ten minutes, the double doors burst open and a tall blond woman bounded in. "How you doing? Thanks for dropping by," she said, pushing back her hair with one hand and balancing an armful of files on her hip with the other. "This week's been a nightmare!" she said, shaking her head. "Let's grab a coffee and I'll fill you in on the details."

We walked through the doors, up a wide staircase toward the back of the building and out onto a terrace, where we settled on a stone balustrade overlooking a garden. There were neat flower beds and clipped box hedges and a lawn that spread out under the shade of an enormous plane tree. Overhead the skies had cleared; the sun's fading light fell across the leaves with the familiar sharpness of early evening at the end of a perfect summer's day.

"Right," she said, folding her arms on top of the stack of papers in her lap. "We've got a bit of a tricky situation here." She paused, drew a breath, and looked rather intently at me. "It's like this. We signed up to do the carbon deal I told you about in Quzhou. It's about a hundred miles inland from Hangzhou. Hangzhou is down on the coast, just south of Shanghai near—"

"Yeah, I know where Hangzhou is," I interrupted.

She paused and glanced at me briefly before continuing with the story.

"Okay, so we found this big chemical factory out in the sticks," she went on. "It's enormous—you wouldn't believe it—something like eighty thousand people stuck in the middle of nowhere. The factory's behind these big walls and no one can get in or out except through the gates at the front. I think most of the workers live inside. The factory makes solvents, plastics, that kind of thing, and right in the middle, there's a reactor that makes coolants, you know, for air conditioners, fridges, and the like. The waste product from the coolant line is really bad; it's a greenhouse gas that's thousands of times more potent than CO_2 and they're just venting it all into the air."

"Well, can't they get rid of it somehow?" I asked.

"That's the point; they can use incinerators to burn up the gas, but they're only available in Japan. We've signed up to buy carbon credits so the factory can use that income to get loans to buy the equipment. We both initialed the deal a month ago, but it's huge. Our first fund wasn't big enough to cover it so we organized a syndicate to come up with the rest of the money. We ended up with about twelve other investors. I can tell you," she said, rolling her eyes, "getting them all to agree at the same time has been like herding cats!"

"But why would anyone want these credits?" I asked.

"There's a huge new market for them in Europe and Japan. Under the Kyoto Protocol, governments have capped the amount of greenhouse gases that businesses can emit; if they go over the cap, they have to go into the market and buy up extra permits. Prices are expected to rise as the caps on emissions get tighter. Anyway," she said, reverting to the story, "they were all about to sign the formal documents, but Wang just called our rep in China and told us he wants to change the terms. Now the syndicate is wobbling and the whole thing looks like it's about to go belly-up." Her nose wrinkled. "Fifteen rounds of negotiation, everything was agreed, and now he wants to change the deal."

"Sounds familiar."

"I was hoping you might say that," she said. "We've been working with a law firm in Beijing and when this all blew up, they gave us your number and said you might help."

"Any clues why he suddenly wants to change the terms?" I asked.

Mina was stumped. Wang was the chief engineer of the chemical plant in Quzhou and seemed to be leading the negotiations even though he had no legal background. But there were others involved as well. She told me that there was a Mr. Tang, who seemed to be deputy manager; Mr. Yang, who looked after contracts; a Fang, who was in charge of the factory; and a Zhang, who did the accounts. "This is ridiculous," she sighed, pulling her hair back again, rubbing her eyes, and fumbling around with some name cards. "It's just all so confusing."

"Anyway," she went on, "it's Wang who's just called and he wants to change a whole bunch of clauses. Wouldn't normally matter, but some of them require changes to the financing. You can imagine—as soon as Wang said he wanted more changes, Winchester went ballistic. There've been so many different deals along the way that everyone completely lost it when they heard Wang wanted more changes and that they'd have to go back to the syndicate; they're all terrified that the Chinese side will just walk away from the deal, find another buyer, and leave us stuck with commitments to the banks and nothing left in China."

"Well, I can understand that," I said. "But what do they want to change? Price? Delivery? Any other of the key terms of the deal?"

"We just got a message from Cordelia in Beijing saying that they want to change the volume under the contract—the number of credits we have to buy—and the investors are all wobbling. There have been so many changes that they're all starting to think that nothing will stick."

"Cordelia?" I asked. "Who's that?"

Mina explained that Cordelia Kong was a Chinese broker who had introduced her to the project. It seemed that she had established a strong position in the new markets out there. She'd been one of the first movers in the carbon space and had a network of contacts in the ministries in Beijing. But Mina found her to be erratic; after making the initial introductions and running a brief auction for the factory, she seemed to lose interest. She would disappear for long periods without leaving contact details and then suddenly burst back on the scene without warning. Now it looked as though she'd gone down to Shanghai on business but no one could find her.

"She just sent a message telling us to speak to the Chinese party directly," Mina continued, "and now her mobile is off. I've been calling her office, but they can't find her, either. I can't believe it! We're paying Cordelia a ton of money and she just disappears right when we need her. I heard some Japanese buyers are visiting the factory in a few days; they might even be there already," she groaned. "If we lose this deal, I'm stuffed!"

"Okay," I said, "so we just need to slow everything down, put everything on hold. Try to freeze things where they are now and buy some time till we get out to Quzhou."

We talked it through for a few minutes and figured that we should send a message out to the factory immediately. If we told Wang we were coming to visit him in a few days, it might stop him from making any final decision to go with one of the other buyers. But it was nighttime in China so we couldn't just call him. I figured the best thing to do was type out a message in Chinese and fax it over. That way, Wang would find it first thing in the morning. So we trooped upstairs into one of the attic offices. It was crammed with people squinting into computer screens, with electric fans on each desk trying to blow the heat out of the tiny windows.

Mina introduced me to her boss, a pale, wiry New Yorker who tugged at an unruly mop of black hair as he talked about Wang. "There's a standard way of doing these deals," he said, shaking his head. "I've done it a hundred times at Merrill. Just stick to the term sheet, keep the lawyers on a tight leash, and the deal'll get done. The Chinese just don't seem to get it!" he said.

"I'm not sure it works quite like that over there," I said.

"Why not?" he replied blankly. "It does everywhere else."

I sat down at Mina's desk and pulled over a computer but there was no Chinese software to write up a letter. It wouldn't look right just to send a handwritten message and anyway I hadn't brought a dictionary. I was stumped. I suggested sending a draft in English to Cordelia's translator but there was no way Mina was going to agree to that.

"She's hopeless!" Mina said. "Last time she dealt directly with Wang, it took a week to sort out the mistranslations."

"Okay, so I'll write it in English but use Chinese-style sentence structures," I explained. "I've done it plenty of times before; that way the translator knows exactly how to put it into Mandarin and we'd be sure that a clear message gets through to Wang by the morning. We don't have a minute to lose."

Mina was skeptical but there didn't seem to be much alternative, so I started typing and two minutes later handed her a piece of paper.

"I know this looks a bit odd, but it'll go straight across into Chinese, no problem. The translator won't be confused by it. Just put it on company letterhead, get your CEO to sign it, and send it over to Beijing. The translator can add in the Chinese in these gaps and you can get her to fax both versions down to the factory first thing in the morning. It'll be fine."

"Er . . . perhaps you should explain this to Winchester," she said after reading the note. "I don't think he'd sign this for me."

She took me down to Winchester's office and left me outside the door. I knocked hesitantly and a voice from inside barked, "Come!" Inside, there was a couple of worn leather-backed chairs arranged around a fireplace, with a table strewn with teacups and a plate of half-eaten scones. On the sideboard, a decanter and some glasses stood on a tray next to a couple of old sherry bottles, and over the mantelpiece there was a photograph with rows of men in uniform graduating from Sandhurst, Britain's equivalent of West Point.

"I hear Mina called you in for a recce," said a tall man, folding up a copy of the *Daily Telegraph* and rising stiffly from the desk. Behind him, a set of French windows opened out onto the garden and the breeze ruffled a few papers on the desk. On the wall, there was a large map of Eastern Europe, a sign, perhaps, that the Cold War was still in full swing in Mayfair. "Jolly good," he continued. "Jolly good. Tiresome business, this—the old girl seems a bit down on her chinstraps so it's good to have you on board. There's a lot hanging on this mission, you know." He paused and looked at me more closely. "In muftis today are we?" he said, raising his eyebrows and peering at my clothing as if over a set of imaginary spectacles.

"Er, well sort of," I replied weakly, scratching the stubble on my chin and trying to cover the holes in my trousers. "Let's just see what they want first, shall we?" I said, trying to sound more cheerful. I handed over the letter.

Respected Chief Engineer Wang: Hello!

My side, at the day in front of now, received your valuable side's telephone and felt ten-out-of-ten happy. We straight through believe, through twin sides' effort and sincerity, our project fixedly will succeed. Now, if your side, amongst a hundred busy things, pulls out a length of time, my side shall grasp fully empowered representative Project Director Mina and send her respectfully to visit your valuable factory for friendly negotiations on top of the spirit of mutual benefit and equality also. According to my side's arrangement, Project Director Mina arrives at Hangzhou at the day behind tomorrow.

Ask valuable side to confirm that arranging.

Ten thousand things just as you please!

Delivered from,
Winchester

Winchester didn't get much beyond the bit about "receiving your valuable side's telephone and feeling ten-out-of-ten happy" before he swelled to a purplish hue, and I found myself abruptly dismissed from the room. I heard later that as soon as I left, he called Mina over an intercom and exploded. At first he refused to sign the letter, ranting that it looked as though it had been written by a six-year-old and demanding to know how she could have contemplated asking such a disheveled-looking halfwit to represent the company in China. But eventually peace returned to the offices; the letter was rearranged into a more recognizable form, Winchester signed it, and it was sent over to Beijing. Wang replied the next morning. By the following evening, only a few months after arriving back in England, I found myself on a plane out to Hong Kong.

4

上有天堂　下有蘇杭

UP IN THE SKY THERE IS PARADISE, BUT DOWN ON THE EARTH WE HAVE HANGZHOU*

—from Illustrious Words to Instruct the World,
by Feng Menglong, c. AD 1620

As I threw a few things together for the trip out to China, I knew that I was dealing with an explosive mixture. On one side, Winchester seemed nervous and volatile. He was under tremendous pressure, knew little of China, and was working through a harassed and exhausted negotiator. The syndicate was fragile and he wasn't in control. On the other side, Mina's descriptions suggested that Wang was a wily and experienced operator with a number of different options to choose from. The project could be worth a lot of money and other buyers were already circling. On the surface, it looked as though Winchester had a lot more to lose than Wang. I knew that a good Chinese negotiator would sense that and know how to extract maximum value. Finally, Cordelia was lurking unpredictably in the shadows. I knew almost nothing about the carbon industry and had none of the specialist vocabulary even in

*And Suzhou.

English, so I felt unsure of myself. When I arrived at the airport
with an hour to spare, I found the business lounge and pulled up
a computer. I was searching for websites with the technical terms
in Chinese when Mina came bounding up behind me. Later she
admitted to me that her heart had sunk when she found me there.
Winchester had already concluded that I was a halfwit and now
she'd seen from my Web search that I didn't even know the Chinese
for "carbon credit." With more than €150 million of carbon hanging by a thread and one last chance to recover it, she knew that her
job was on the line.

As the plane flew over Russia and on into the night, I could see from
the bundle of papers that Mina had dumped on my lap that ECF had
agreed to buy carbon credits from the chemical factory in Quzhou
for a period of five years. At the back of the files, behind bundles
of contracts and spreadsheets, I found some background information on the carbon industry. It explained how there was a growing
demand for emission allowances because the European Union and
Japan had agreed to impose strict limits, or "caps," on big greenhouse
gas emitters, including power stations, steelworks, chemical factories, and cement plants. If any of the plants failed to meet the cap,
they had to go into the carbon market and buy emission allowances,
which were expensive. The system was known as cap-and-trade and
had some similarities to the system that had been used in the United
States to cut back on gases that cause acid rain. The idea was to force
businesses to pay for emissions they made in order to create an incentive to reduce them. The emission allowances came mainly from
the EU and Japanese governments, but the United Nations was also
involved and could issue equivalent allowances, called "international
offsets" or "carbon credits," from projects that reduced greenhouse
gases in developing countries. ECF intended to buy carbon credits
from the chemical factory in China and sell them in the European
markets to companies that needed additional allowances in order to
meet their caps. From the figures included in the investor proposal,
it was clear that carbon trading in Europe had taken off in a big way.

In the previous three years, the market in Europe had grown from a few hundred million to around €60 billion.

The documents were full of jargon and acronyms that were difficult to follow but I figured out that the UN could issue carbon credits under something called the Clean Development Mechanism, or CDM. Over the past decades, emissions had soared in China, India, Brazil, and parts of Africa as these countries began to industrialize. The CDM aimed to encourage the use of low-carbon technologies in the developing world by providing an opportunity to make money from the sale of carbon credits. If a project based on low-carbon technology was too expensive and wouldn't make returns by itself—as was often the case—developers there could apply to the UN to generate credits and boost their profits so they became financially viable.

On the surface, the CDM seemed like an imaginative way to help reduce the carbon footprints of the vast new infrastructures being built in the developing world. It didn't just apply to chemical plants; cement factories, coal mines, ironworks, and steel mills could all apply for credits if they led to lower emissions. The most important area seemed to be the power sector, which was encouraged to move away from coal, but by far the largest number of credits seemed to come from projects aimed at cutting industrial greenhouse gases from chemical plants in China. While I still wasn't clear about the technical details, it was obvious that ECF thought they could make a fortune from the deal.

We changed flights in Hong Kong and by late morning, we had arrived in Hangzhou under clear summer skies. Hangzhou was the capital of China for a time during the Song Dynasty and the ancient city lies around the shorelines of a lake immortalized over the centuries for its spectacular natural beauty. As the car sped along the embankments, I could see the peaks of little islands jutting out of the water. In the far distance, the powdery blue silhouette of mountains rose up above the canopy of trees on the opposite bank. Reeds and rushes lined the water's edge. On the stone-flagged pathways that meandered around the lake, women in high-collared jackets prac-

ticed *tai chi* between clumps of rustling bamboo. Sunlight flashed on
the ripples that trailed from little wooden boats. Nearby, from the
tops of the sloping temple roofs, the faintest trace of smoke drifted
up from the incense burners inside. I caught a glimpse of a pagoda
rising up through the sandalwood trees on the hill behind the lake
and commented to Mina on how beautiful it all was. "Too right,
mate," she said, looking across the water. "If I had me swimmies
with me, I'd be right in there!"

Just after lunch, we drove over to meet Wang. He was staying near
Hangzhou's main railway station in a hotel owned by the factory.
It was one of a string of hotels left over from the days of China's
planned economy, when everything was owned by the state. In
those days, everyone belonged to a work unit that provided schools,
hospitals, housing, and, in this case, even hotels, where the factory
managers could stay during the long and tedious meetings with the
province's Chemical Bureau.

Bundles of laundry hung from the upstairs windows of the rows
of shabby shops around the station. Long loops of wires sagged between telegraph poles and the narrow streets were congested with
traffic. The whole area was dilapidated and the heat was oppressive
as we sat in a taxi lined up at some broken traffic lights. On the
cracked sidewalks outside the hotel, hawkers sold bowls of fried bean
curd and chives from under sheets of canvas slung between bamboo
poles. Inside, there was a wooden counter at the end of a lobby, with a
couple of bored receptionists playing games on their mobile phones.
On the wall behind them, the name "Quintessence Hotel" stood out
in gold letters and a line of clocks told the time in London, Moscow,
Sharjah, and Beijing. On the end of the counter there was a stack of
company brochures that advertised paints, dyes, and adhesives, with
photographs of the reactor towers in the factory at Quzhou.

We signed a slip of paper and went up to the fourth floor. Next
to the elevator there was a little pantry where a girl was asleep over a
table with her head cradled in her arms. Enamel mugs were piled up
next to a big water boiler that bubbled gently in the corner with hot

water to make tea. Down the corridor, the carpets were wrinkled and stained and around the doorways the paint was battered and scratched. Everywhere smelled of mildew. At the end of the hallway there was sign in English that read "Holding Talks Room." As we approached the door, Mina held back to let me go in first, but I took her arm and gently pushed her forward. It was important that she lead the discussions. I still knew almost nothing about the business, so I couldn't negotiate with Wang. I planned to spend most of the first day invisible and listening.

Inside we found the familiar scene of a big circular table in the middle of the room with a bunch of plastic flowers in a dusty glass vase at the center. The wallpaper was peeling away at the bottom of the walls and a row of badly fitting windows looked out onto a schoolyard below. The shouts and cries of a children's playground rose up through the air. In the corner, a broken metal coatrack leaned against a huge air conditioner that had a notice pasted across that said "Under Maintenance." The air was hot and damp.

Wang was waiting inside with a couple of assistants. He was plumper than I had imagined, quite short and balding. He leaped to his feet as we walked in and was obviously pleased to see Mina. He didn't bother to ask who I was; I guessed that the team from ECF had changed so much that his curiosity wasn't aroused by just one more new face.

For the next five hours, I sat and listened, occasionally helping to straighten out the odd confusion with Wang's translator. The table was big enough to seat at least fifteen people, so there was plenty of space; I sat away from Wang, near one of his assistants, who chain-smoked his way through the afternoon. Mina and I had agreed beforehand that she should run through the contract, clause by clause. That way we might nail down the differences between each side and start to trade them off. It was tedious work. Throughout the afternoon, there were constant interruptions as people came in, delivering messages and collecting bits of paper. I had to get up several times to clear the waves of jet lag washing over me and I wandered around the corridors outside. As Mina went through the contract, Wang seemed alternately distracted or overfocused on details. After his initially friendly manner, he quickly grew irascible and stubborn. I couldn't tell whether it was because he was under pressure or he was just being deliberately awkward, pretending not to understand issues or dragging up old arguments that Mina thought had been settled months beforehand. He didn't seem particularly interested in discussing price or payment terms but he wanted to increase the number of carbon credits to be covered by the contract. But that was impossible; the syndicate had been put together in London to cover the number of credits that had been fixed at the last meeting and it was far too late to change it. Mina just passed on the point without comment and moved on.

After the first few hours, there were frequent lulls in the conversation. Several times, Wang wandered over to a battered old sofa at the back of the room and stretched out, with his trousers rolled over his calves, slurping tea out of a big jam jar and fanning himself with a copy of the *Hangzhou Daily*. He had a bowl of roasted melon seeds on his lap and, leaning forward against the arm of the sofa, he sat cracking the seeds between his teeth and spitting the shells out into a wastepaper basket at his feet. On other occasions, he'd get up, yawn loudly, stretch, and push his hands deep into his pockets before wandering off down the corridor with a rolling, slouching gait for twenty minutes. By ten in the evening, the room was insufferably stuffy; my head was aching from the clouds of cigarette smoke from Wang's assistant and I felt dizzy with jet lag. I moved over to the windows and tried to drag one open, but Mina yelled at me to stop. She had opened one on the first visit and been eaten alive by mosquitoes. Hot, tired, bad-tempered, and hungry, we were getting nowhere so we decided to call it a day. We agreed with Wang that we'd meet up at eight the following morning, hailed a taxi to take us back to the hotel by the lake, and sat dejectedly on the lumpy seats in the back contemplating the day. We had achieved nothing, ended up with more questions than answers, and felt exhausted all at the same time.

Back at the hotel, we made straight for the bar and perched up on a couple of high stools. Through the pine trees in the hotel grounds and reflected in the lake, we could see the shapes of exploding chrysanthemums and shooting stars from an enormous firework display above the distant city skyline.

The hotel was originally built as a state-run training school for the Party cadres, so it occupied a prime position on the hill below the pagoda. It was built like an aircraft hangar, with echoing hallways and drafty corridors. I heard that a Hong Kong property group had taken over the management of the hotel just after China opened up and had tried to spruce it up with yellow wallpaper, thick carpets, and flouncy curtains. There were chandeliers in the hallways and gold fixtures in the bathrooms, but I noticed that sections of the hotel seemed cordoned off by dusty lacquer screens and lines of tired-looking rubber plants arranged in pots across the landings.

After the first beer, jet lag evaporated. I suddenly felt wide-awake. Mina said she thought that the day had been hopeless but I tried to keep our spirits up. "Look on the bright side," I said. "At least they agreed to meet us."

It was true; if they'd reached an agreement with one of the other buyers, Wang wouldn't have agreed to meet. Slowly, as we mulled over the day, the mood brightened. Halfway into the second beer, I began to take the measure of Mina. She told me that she had read law at Melbourne University, snatching the odd moment for study between her commitments to the Student Union, the women's rowing team, and a punishing regime of daily exercise and training. On graduation, she joined one of the big law firms, before moving on to the Sydney Stock Exchange, where she worked on designing forestry credits, one of the world's first financial instruments for environmental investing. By the time she was thirty, she had joined the World Bank. Based in Washington, D.C., she traveled throughout Asia negotiating carbon deals.

She felt passionately about preserving the natural environment and her conversation often reverted to pet topics, such as water conservation, forestry management, or digging wells in Africa. Mina's tall, athletic build, her pale blue eyes, and the distinctive chunky jewelry she wore gave her a striking presence. People remembered her. She had that knack of walking into a room and connecting—of making people she'd only just met feel individual and special. I could tell that Wang liked her even though they couldn't communicate directly. Years later, he told me that the reason that they'd chosen ECF as their foreign counterparty was that they felt comfortable dealing with Mina.

As I got to know her better, I began to realize that Mina's energy levels elevated her above the normal confines of time; strictly vegetarian, she never drank alcohol and needed hardly any sleep. I'd often find out that she had spent several hours before sunrise wading through some turgid documents while doing forty klicks on an exercise bike, or that she'd run fifteen miles before breakfast. Her energy bordered on the inexhaustible; she once mentioned in passing that she'd just completed an Ironman event, which apparently involved swimming several miles before riding a bicycle uphill for about five hours and then blithely embarking on a marathon. I wasn't in the least bit surprised when she broke her hip years later while running two hundred and fifty miles across the Sahara. On top of the almost limitless physical output, she had developed "blue sky thinking" into an entirely new art form; she had a thousand new ideas a minute that used to burst into the conversation unannounced from random angles.

Over the time that she'd been traveling to Asia, Mina had developed an affection for China, which I liked; she felt comfortable there and, like me, she enjoyed its eccentricities. She was easy to be with, that was for sure, and completely focused on the task at hand; but at times it was tough to keep up.

We both agreed that Wang had seemed strangely disconnected and never seemed to answer any of the questions directly. It felt as if he wasn't telling us the real reason for wanting to change the contract; the whole day had been taken up fencing over side issues. We had to figure out his real objective but with Cordelia still impossible to contact, there wasn't much we could go on.

"There's an old Chinese military saying, 'Know yourself and know the other and you'll survive a hundred battles,'" I said. "Trouble is we have no idea what Wang really wants. We need to figure it out and find out who he reports to, what pressure he's under, what other options he has."

Mina grunted.

"That doesn't give us very good odds for winning this particular battle," I said.

"Well, that's all very interesting," said Mina impatiently, "but this isn't warfare, is it!? It's a negotiation."

"Sure," I said, "but the ideas are still useful. That's why Chinese people are so good at all this. Just think, *The Art of War* was written more than two thousand years ago and they still use it every day. Anyway, your lot seem pretty military, too," I added. "I bet Winchester's been reading Clausewitz at bedtime for years."

"Well," she continued, ignoring that comment, "if Wang won't tell us what he wants, how do we figure it out?"

I'd seen from the company brochure that a part of the chemicals group had gone public in Shanghai a couple of years earlier. They were one of the larger manufacturing groups in China, so Wang could easily develop other options; we knew that he was already talking to some Japanese buyers, so that closed off the possibility of threatening to walk away from the deal if we didn't get what Winchester wanted. We had to be smarter than that.

"We can't ask Wang directly," I said, "so we'll have to go around him. Let's try to find someone else to tell us what's really going on. Sunzi always talks about the importance of using spies. That little guy—you know, Wang's assistant, Chain-smoking Chen—he looks as though he might be converted."

We agreed that the next day Mina should continue through the contract with Wang and that I'd start to work on Chen. It was well past midnight by the time we turned in, but at least we had a plan for the next day. I was still wide-awake and only drifted off just short of three o'clock, so I was in a deep sleep when the phone rang at quarter to seven the next morning. "Where are you?" she said. "I've just got back from a run."

Mina and Wang spent the whole of the second day arguing about the timing of some obscure approval documents. I soon lost the thread of the argument, so I started working on Chen.

Chain-smoking Chen was twenty-four and had spent his whole life in Quzhou. Both of his parents worked at the chemical factory. He told me that he had never traveled outside the province, but when Wang assigned him to work on the carbon project, he'd grabbed the chance to come to Hangzhou. He was shy and reserved but he brightened up a little when he saw that I wanted to chat. After his first trip to Hangzhou, he had joined an evening class in English, dreaming of finding a job in a foreign company somewhere along the coast. But his mother and father lived in the factory; Chen was an only child so it looked as though he was struggling with the dilemma between his loyalty to his parents and his desire to break out of this country backwater. He was cautious and I found it difficult to draw him out.

By the second evening in the bar, Mina was becoming frustrated; I'd hardly said a word for two days. I sensed that she was losing patience and beginning to think that Winchester might have been right about me being a halfwit after all. A stream of anxious and distracting messages had been arriving from London all demanding updates on our progress. Meanwhile, Wang frequently revisited parts of the contract that we thought had already been agreed, so it was almost impossible to convey a clear picture back home. Whenever Mina tried to explain that Wang was switching back and forth, the team in London grew even more aggravated, which led to a further cascade of anxious messages. I encouraged her to be patient, but with the drumbeats from Mayfair getting louder and louder, I knew that it couldn't be easy.

Throughout the whole of the morning of the third day, Wang didn't even call us. He kept us cooling our heels at the hotel. Chain-smoking Chen had told us that the mayor of Quzhou was in town so we figured Wang was detained in meetings. That wasn't a good sign; he seemed to be prioritizing routine meetings with a government official ahead of sorting out our contract. By the early afternoon, there was still no news, so we took a long stroll around the edge of the lake, wondering what to do. Suddenly, at about four thirty, Wang called and told us that a car was already waiting for us back at the hotel. He wanted to know where we were. Sprinting back around the lake, we changed into business clothes and were whisked off to another, much smarter hotel in a different part of town. There we were ushered into a large room with low chairs arranged around three sides of a square. Embroidered doilies were draped over the backs of the chairs and between each of them, a ceramic teacup with a lid sat on little wooden tables. After a while there was a commotion outside, and a man in an immaculate black suit strode in and shook Mina's hand.

"*Ni hao!*" she said. Hello!

"*Ey!*" said the mayor, tilting his head back and smiling at Mina admiringly, "*Nide Zhongwen zhen bang!*" Your Chinese is truly marvelous!

Mina stared back blankly, searching around for a translator.

The next thirty minutes were taken up with minor pleasantries: how far we'd traveled to get to China; how the pagodas around West Lake had been famous throughout history; how the scenery had been celebrated in Song Dynasty poetry. The mayor's entourage nodded in agreement and laughed at all the appropriate moments. Next we had a description of the municipal transport systems; the number of Chinese tourists; the delights of the local fresh fish; the esteem in which Hangzhou's dumplings were held throughout China. I could see Mina fidgeting and glancing at her watch. She'd arranged a call back to London for seven o'clock and it looked like we were in for the long haul. Just before six, we were suddenly whisked off to a banquet, stuffed with about fifteen courses, plied with several bottles of beer—each presented with a large white ceramic statue of Confucius—and, less than an hour later, loaded into a car and driven back to the hotel, puzzled by the whole episode. The project had never been mentioned.

When I saw Mina the following morning, she was at her wits' end. She'd been on the phone all night and Winchester was beside himself with impatience. A meeting had been scheduled with the syndicate's underwriters for the next day in the City and the pressure was mounting. Winchester ordered a further teleconference with the whole team in Mayfair as soon as they got into the office, which, given the time difference, was early afternoon in China.

When we arrived at the "Holding Talks Room," Wang turned up late again and the conversation continued for the whole morning without much progress. Just before lunch, Wang wandered off again so I told Mina to take a break downstairs. I took my chance with Chen; there was no time left for subtlety.

I told Chen that I thought it was a pity that progress was so slow on such an important project. Perhaps there was some misunderstanding between the two parties; of course, if he had any suggestions, we would take them very seriously. He was cautious at first and just said that we should continue to talk with Wang. "This is a big project," he said, "so Wang reports directly to General Manager Gao."

"Manager Gao?" I said, "I thought Tang was in charge."

"Gao is the head of the Shanghai listed company and he pays great attention to this project," said Chen.

"So what does Gao think we should do?" I asked.

Eventually Chen came to the point. "It's all about the second line," he said. "Old Gao needs you to take in the second line."

"The second line?" I asked.

"Mina will know what I mean. Old Gao just says that the second line has to go into the contract."

"Well how about price, payment terms, all the other clauses?"

He just pursed his lips and the conversation drifted away. But at least we had the first clue.

I went out to look for Mina and found her sitting dejectedly in the lobby, sipping on a tall glass of chrysanthemum tea. When I told her what Chain-smoking Chen had said, she knew immediately what he meant. Inside the chemical plant at Quzhou, there were two separate production lines. At the start of the negotiations, Mina had tried to get both of the lines into the deal so that ECF would get the maximum number of credits, but Wang had refused point-blank. The second line was huge; Mina told me that every year it spewed out gases with the equivalent warming effect of nearly five million tons of carbon dioxide. There had been weeks of discussions in the spring, but Wang wouldn't be shifted and he refused to put the line into the deal. Eventually Mina figured that the carbon from the second line must have been sold to another buyer, so ECF organized the syndicate to include only the credits from the first line. But now it appeared that Wang needed to reverse his position.

When Wang returned, we raised the issue directly and probed every way we could think of to avoid increasing the number of credits under the contract, but Wang was adamant. His position seemed to have become fixed and he was insistent that ECF bought the credits from both lines. I switched into Mandarin and tried to persuade Wang to be more flexible. Whenever I asked him why he couldn't just sell the second line to another buyer, he just said that it would be too troublesome to separate the two. But this made no sense; only a few months earlier, he'd been insisting on the opposite. Mina tried every idea we could think of—taking an option on the second line, cutting the carbon streams into two parts, taking some now with smaller amounts later—but Wang wouldn't budge. It seemed as if we'd reached deadlock. I became more apprehensive about the phone call to London as the minutes ticked by and we failed to get to the bottom of the story.

At the allotted time, we trooped down the hallway to the little pantry next to the elevators. Mina swore under her breath as she tripped on one of the bumps in the carpet. Bizarrely, the pantry had a fixed line phone with a speaker where we could take a conference call in private. There was no line out, but the phone could accept incoming calls through the switchboard downstairs—but the call didn't come in on time, so we sat there and waited in silence. The water boiler for tea was still steaming gently on a Formica-topped table in the corner, so it was stiflingly hot and as damp as a sauna. On the wall above the boiler, condensation was dripping down the glass frame of a famous photograph of Chairman Mao relaxing with a cigarette on top of Mount Lushan in a large wooden deck chair. As I leaned over the phone, I felt droplets of sweat gathering on the end of my nose. After a few more minutes, I called down to the operator only to discover that a foreigner had called several times earlier but she couldn't understand what he wanted and hung up. I asked her to transfer the next foreign-language call up to our extension and after another few minutes we were connected. It wasn't a good start; the receptionist had already put the phone down on Winchester several times, so he was spluttering with irritation before we even started.

Mina kicked off with a summary of the last few days while I sat on the edge of the table and listened. Once she had finished, I leaned down toward the phone and explained that the Chinese side seemed very fixed on putting in the second line. But Winchester was having none of it.

"We went through all of that in March," he said. "We've closed the syndicate on the basis of this first deal. We can't just go back and ask for more money; it would completely ruin our credibility."

"Well, perhaps we can do something less formal with the second line and get around it that way," I said.

"What does that mean?"

"Maybe we can stick to the existing deal for the first line and do something a bit vaguer for the second."

"Vaguer!?"

"Well, often Chinese parties reach slightly vague agreements while they figure out what they really need to do. It'd buy us a bit of time. We can sign up the first line and do something less formal on the second."

"Less formal! Vague! Have you completely lost your mind?" he raged. "We're dealing with some of the biggest institutional investors in Europe. They're not going to botch together some hare-brained scheme just to keep the Chinese happy. Less formal!" he said with a snort. "The directors would all have hernias!"

After a few more minutes of haggling, we were instructed to go back to Wang and tell him that the deal had to stay the same. But when Mina explained it to Wang, he just replied calmly, "*Bu xuyao tan le*"—no need to discuss then—and quietly gathered his papers. We protested, of course. Why couldn't he just sell the second line to another buyer? We waved our arms in the air and threw papers onto the table; we pleaded and cajoled; we used flattery and promises, threats and excuses, but they were all useless. Wang just stood up and calmly left the room.

When we managed to get through to London to report this latest development, a jumble of voices burst furiously from the speaker-phone in front of us, all demanding that the Chinese needed to go back to the original deal. When the clamor died down, one of them said, "You've just got to go back in there and tell them that they have to go back to the existing agreement."

"But we've already done that three times and Wang won't agree."

"Do it again. Just insist on it. Don't they understand that this sort of behavior will ruin their reputation in the City?"

"What!"

"It'll ruin their reputation in the City."

"Right," piped in a second voice. "Deutsche Bank is underwriting the whole deal!"

"I shouldn't think Wang has ever heard of Deutsche Bank before this deal!" I said.

"What?"

"Yeah," Mina added. "Wang just told me he needs to show a copy of Deutsche Bank's certificate of incorporation to the local Commercial Bureau here in Quzhou. They want to check out they're real."

After a brief moment of stunned silence, a sort of strangulated yell came out of the phone. "Anyone who hasn't heard of Deutsche Bank is a cretin! Don't they realize that Deutsche Bank evolved from the Treaty of Augsburg?!"

After a brief moment to gather his wits, another one said, "They must be out to stiff us. We spent months arguing about that second line in March and they wouldn't put it in. This has to be about price or something."

"Yeah, or perhaps they've closed the factory? I read somewhere last week that everyone's stopped buying fridges in China."

"What?!" I said.

"Or maybe there's been a fire," said another.

"Or perhaps it's exploded!" said a third. "I hear factories are always exploding in China."

"It could have been nationalized!"

"Right," said another. "I saw a report about the government seizing a property business in Shanghai. They'd had riots there about some unfinished apartments."

"Hang on!" I spluttered. "Can we try to get back to reality here? People are still buying fridges in China and the factory hasn't exploded. There hasn't been a fire and the factory can't be nationalized because the government already controls it! No one has ever mentioned price, so why would they want to stiff you? We have to figure out what they really want. Try to look at it from their side. Wang's sitting in a medium-sized town way out in the sticks in China working in some old broken-down chemical factory minding his own business and shuffling bits of paper, and then you all come along and offer him a hundred million bucks if he installs a few incinerators. Why would he want to stiff you?"

"Bunch of yahoos, if you ask me," someone muttered in the background.

"Look," continued another more sharply, "this deal has changed so many times, the syndicate's already wobbling. If we just go back and ask them to double their money, it'll blow the whole thing out of the water."

"Okay," I said, "but something must have happened to change the situation here. We need to take a bit of time to find out what that is. Wang's in a different world; it makes no difference to him personally whether this deal gets done or not, but if you get it right, your investors will make a fortune. Whatever happens with this deal, Wang's salary will just stay the same. But if something goes wrong later, he'll get blamed by his boss. All his housing and his pension and his kid's education are organized by the factory. Wang's never going to risk all that for something where he's got nothing to gain. If we try to put pressure on him, he'll just clam up and do nothing."

"Absolute bollocks!" I heard someone say in the background just before a click as the phone cut off. Then there was silence.

I looked at Mina.

"So where does that leave us?" I asked after a few moments.

"Don't worry," she said, rolling her eyes with a sigh. "We'll get a nasty email in the morning."

5

豈能因爾國王一人之請
以致更張天朝百余年法度

THE FIRST CHINESE RULE:

How Can We Go So Far as to Change the Regulations of the Celestial Empire, Which Are Over a Hundred Years Old, at the Request of One Man—of You, O King?

—*Edict of the Qianlong Emperor to
King George III of England, August 1793*

We were not the first band of foreigners to be kept waiting and given the runaround in China, nor the first to be sent with impossible instructions. For years visitors have felt confused, rebuffed, and bamboozled by what they've found there; and none of them more so than the British.

In the autumn of 1792, while the world was preoccupied by the French Revolution, three ships set sail quietly from the south coast of England. King Louis XVI of France had been deposed and there'd been massacres in the prisons. Guillotine blades skidded down greased runners as carts piled high with severed heads rumbled through the shadows around the walls of the old Bastille; Europe braced for war. So the dispatch by George III of an embassy to China attracted little attention as it cast off with the morning tide on September 26. The expedition was led by a former ambassador to the Russian tsarina, the Right Honorable Lord Macartney, and consisted of physicians, astronomers, painters, musicians, clockmakers, soldiers, and servants, numbering more than seven hundred in all. The purpose of the mission was explained in a letter carried by the ambassador from His Britannic Majesty to the Celestial Emperor as follows:

> *We have taken opportunities of fitting out Ships and sending in them some of the most wise and learned of Our Own People, for the discovery of distant regions. . . . Our ardent wish [is] to become acquainted with the celebrated institutions of Your Majesty's populous and extensive Empire . . . [T]hese considerations have determined Us to depute an Ambassador to Your Court [for] communication with . . . your Sublime Person . . . [W]e rely on Your Imperial Majesty's wisdom that You will allow Our Subjects frequenting the coasts of Your dominions fair access to Your markets.*

> *Imperator Augustissime*
> *Vester bonus frater et Amicus*
> *Georgius R*

This was not the first embassy to tackle China; Portugal, the Netherlands, and Russia had all sent ambassadors on more than one occasion, but they had each returned empty-handed. The gates to the Celestial Empire, it seemed, remained hermetically sealed. France had sent missionaries, and a handful of Jesuit priests had lived in Beijing for a number of years, but none had ever returned. In fact, Macartney's was the sixteenth embassy sent to pry open the gates, but it was the first worthy of the name. Supremely con-

fident, possessed of the world's most powerful navy, and poised on
the threshold of the Industrial Revolution, the British were fixed
upon impressing the ancient Middle Kingdom with gifts that displayed the most ingenious inventions of the modern European age;
but more important—as George III stated in his letter—they were
determined to open the channels of trade.

Macartney's first problem was finding translators; there weren't any.
He eventually recruited two Chinese priests who had been living at
the Collegium Sinicum in Naples. Although they knew no English,
they could communicate with passable Latin. Father Li's teeth had
been ruined by smoking and Father Zhou had that somewhat familiar passion for crunching dried melon pips, which Macartney
described as "a habit not easily tolerated by a gentleman." Impressed
by Li's single-minded commitment to smoking, Macartney was
later less surprised than he might have been to find out that everyone smoked in China—even the children, who came running out of
houses with pipes between their teeth. In fact, smoking was so prev-
alent that if someone was deathly ill and on his last legs, the Chinese
would say, "He's so ill he can't even smoke anymore."

After leaving the English Channel, the embassy was blown off
course in the Atlantic and the ships became separated. They only
regrouped the following March at Batavia—now Jakarta—in what
was then known as the Dutch East Indies. Eleven days later, they
set sail northward. After more than nine months at sea, the embassy
finally caught sight of the Chinese mainland and dropped anchor at
Macao. Terrified of being caught assisting the embassy, one of the
translators skipped ship and disappeared—Macartney had heard
that Chinese were forbidden to leave China and that the punishment for teaching Mandarin to a foreigner was death. The other,
a Tatar whose Chinese was less fluent, took the more imaginative
option of disguising himself as a foreigner.

The embassy, meanwhile, was under strict surveillance by the
watchful mandarins onshore. Prior to his arrival, Macartney had

requested permission to visit Beijing from the customs house in
Canton, not through the provincial governor as required by the
Celestial Regulations. The governor, unsettled by this ignorance
of court etiquette, had sent an anxious memorial to the emperor
seeking further instructions:

> Upon their arrival in Canton, the English barbarians asked to be taken
> to the Customs Office to present a request. We immediately granted
> them an audience. Their report states that the King of England . . . has
> dispatched an envoy. The Rites require that barbarians, once granted
> permission to enter a port, present a copy of their sovereign's request,
> along with a list of the articles of tribute. The king of England, however,
> has supplied us with neither of these two documents. We have only the
> letter submitted by the English merchants. Your humble slave dare not
> present such a document to Your Majesty.

The memorial was returned with annotations in vermillion
brushstrokes from the emperor's own hand: "We will transmit instructions to you." The countless cogs of the state's vast bureaucratic
machinery had glided silently into motion. From that moment,
every step of the embassy was monitored and logged, every act
recorded and transmitted to the emperor by special runners who
worked in relays that could cover as much as six hundred *li* in a day.
Edicts from Beijing were dispatched back to the provinces, copied,
given a response, and returned. The emperor added his final mar-
ginal notes in red ink before the runners headed back posthaste to
the provinces. The system had operated for centuries and had been
overhauled by Qianlong's father, the Yongzheng Emperor. In Qianlong's reign, hundreds of documents could be on the road at any
one time, connecting the center through a web of highly trained
mandarin officials across vast distances to the daily affairs of every
far-flung corner of the empire.

The embassy cast off from Macau to the sound of church bells calling the faithful to Mass. It proceeded up the coast and stopped at the

Zhoushan Islands, off the coast of Zhejiang, just south of modern-day Shanghai. It was here that the embassy had its first inkling that protocol was to become a major obstacle to its success.

The mandarin official sent to accompany the embassy to Beijing refused to step on board the ship. Imperial regulations required imperial officials to "descend onto the barbarian vessel," but the ship was too large for the Chinese to construct the customary bamboo walkway *downward* from the quay toward the boat. It was simply inconceivable that the mandarin would contemplate clambering *upward* onto the decks, so he refused to go on board at all. Instead he sent provisions including some twenty steers, more than a hundred sheep and hogs, a hundred ducks, and 160 sacks of flour as the first, emphatic demonstration of the excesses of Chinese hospitality.

Confusion over the gifts brought for the emperor from England was the next difficulty; etiquette required Macartney to understate their value but he couldn't bring himself to describe them as "mere trinkets from our poor country," as the mandarin had suggested. Next he discovered that the Chinese version of the list of gifts was riddled with translation errors. Passing from English to Latin, then to Chinese and finally into official court language, it had been converted into gibberish. Macartney had brought a planetarium to demonstrate Europe's achievements in combining an understanding of the motion of celestial bodies— including the four moons of Jupiter—with the latest in precision engineering. But the Chinese had no idea what it was. *Planetarium* had been translated phonetically and rendered meaningless. After much discussion it was listed as a "geographical and astronomical musical clock." In the end, the Chinese never read the list or even wondered what the articles might be; all that mattered was that the number of individual items was correct and that the list was complete.

These translation difficulties propelled an unlikely character to the fore. Macartney's deputy had brought along his son, a boy named Thomas Staunton, who had picked up some Chinese language from the two priests on the long voyage. The youth, whose "senses were more acute and organs more flexible, proved to be a tolerably good interpreter," so he took over much of the translation.

Once the gifts had been properly categorized, the ships moved farther up the coast toward Tianjin, where the gifts were to be packed into crates, loaded onto junks, and transported to the docks at Dagu. There they would be transferred onto smaller junks and taken inland by canal before finally going ashore for the twelve-mile journey to Beijing. A memorial to the emperor read:

> In all, there are 590 pieces to be transferred from the barbarian ships to the port. The handling operation is proceeding without interruption but is not yet complete. The passengers of the ships will enter the port only after the tribute has been fully unloaded.

"This is excellent and we fully approve," wrote the vermillion brush.

It was at Dagu that the embassy first encountered Chinese delaying tactics. They had been traveling for almost a year and were impatient to see the emperor. But now they were told that a viceroy had suddenly arrived to greet them. Ushered into a large hall in a temple, surrounded by tents with streamers and guarded by horsemen with bows and arrows, they were entertained with elaborate tea ceremonies, inquiries about their health, and explanations of "the emperor's satisfaction with their arrival." Macartney fumed quietly and fidgeted throughout the banquet until the viceroy suddenly announced that the embassy would only be granted an audience in Jehol, the emperor's summer retreat, rather than in Beijing as previously planned. This sudden change in destination presented a major complication; many of the delicate instruments would be damaged on such a long overland journey to Jehol. But before Macartney could respond, the viceroy announced that he would be leaving the next day and planned to return only after six weeks.

Around this time, the central problem of the embassy became clear. For a foreigner to meet the emperor, or even receive an edict from him, he had to perform the *ke-tou*, or *kow-tow*. This "head-bumping ceremony" consisted of first standing upright, then groveling on the floor, banging one's head against the ground three times, standing up, then going back down on all fours, banging the forehead again, and repeating the whole procedure three times so that nine head bumps were performed in all. It never occurred to the Chinese that Macartney might object. As far as they were concerned, the *kow-tow* was simply a formality by which a barbarian submitted to the perfection of the Celestial Empire in order to prepare himself for the benefits of civilization. Anyway, there was no precedent for doing anything else. But Macartney was having none of it; as representative of George III, he only agreed to go down on one knee. He only went down on two knees for the Almighty, so groveling on all fours in front of some Oriental despot was entirely out of the question. So the two sides entered a phase of protracted negotiations. The Chinese addressed the matter obliquely—first by suggesting that the Englishmen might like to change their clothes, since the *kow-tow* would be easier to perform without garters and knee buckles. Macartney made a counterproposal: he would produce a portrait of George III and whatever ceremony he performed in front of the emperor, a mandarin of equivalent rank would perform in front of the portrait of the English king.

Meanwhile, Macartney had been informed that the characters on the banners on boats escorting the embassy had been quietly changed from 禮—envoy bringing gifts—to 貢—envoy paying tribute. But appearances were maintained; the embassy set off from the docks to the rousing sounds of a military band, while the Chinese responded with earsplitting hammering on copper gongs. After seven days on the canal, deafened by cicadas and tormented by mosquitos, the embassy alighted at the port and set off overland for Beijing.

On August 21, 1793, a little short of a year after leaving Portsmouth, the embassy passed by the great corner watchtowers of the imperial city. Guards of honor fired salvos from the ramparts while three thousand porters passed through the enormous double gateways carrying nearly six hundred packages, some so large they needed thirty-six men to carry them. They were followed by eighty-five wagons and thirty-nine handcarts filled with wine, beer, and other European produce. Eight pieces of artillery brought up the rear. Inside, the visitors were confronted by a human anthill. Brides went to their future husbands with squalling music and gongs; mourners dressed in white wailed over the departed. Wheelbarrows groaned under stacks of watermelons next to pots of live eels while, under the swooping eaves of the great gateways to the Imperial City, long lines of dromedaries brought coal from Tartary.

The embassy settled into the quarters near the Old Summer Palace, the Garden of Perfect Brightness, and awaited instructions to proceed to Jehol for the audience with the emperor. The accommodation was adequate, although one member of the expedition couldn't help noticing the smell of "putrefying garlic and over-used blankets."

By this time, Macartney had begun to realize that China had the most ritualized society on earth. Ceremonial rites formed one of the key foundations of Confucianism, and Confucianism underpinned the Chinese sense of identity. The Celestial bureaucracy consisted of six tribunals, equivalent to ministries, and the Tribunal of Rites enforced strict observation of court ritual. It also supervised the imperial examination system, which had first been conceived by the Han as a way of selecting and promoting civil servants. Introduced properly by the Sui in the sixth century, the exam system had been perfected four hundred years later under the Song and it had been in use for centuries by the time it was abolished by the Qing in 1905. The tribunal also controlled the movements of envoys and receipt of tribute.

Macartney, however, knew little of this as he haggled about the *kow-tow*. After several rounds of unsuccessful negotiations, he noticed that the old mandarin who had refused to board the ship at Zhoushan had vanished. Apparently he'd been replaced by another official. Macartney was delighted with the change, as he had heard that the new official was a cousin of the emperor and so assumed that he had more power at court. But there were hundreds of "cousins"; all it meant was that he was related to one of the emperor's numerous concubines. In fact, the old mandarin had been a salt tax commissioner and his replacement had at one time been in charge of the Ming Tombs. Both were quite junior and hopelessly out of their depth. Meanwhile, behind the scenes, the vermillion brushstrokes moved across the pages—silently, alone, in secret—directing every move.

Finally, the embassy was allowed to travel to Jehol, where the emperor spent the summer, some hundred miles northeast of Beijing. They traveled through hills and patches of dense farmland, finally passing under the Great Wall and out into a fallow, wilder landscape. In places, the road was so steep that extra horses were needed to pull up the carts. The smooth imperial roadway was off-limits to the British; for eight days the horses limped and stumbled along the rocky pathways.

During an overnight stop, one of the mandarin officials asked to see the "admirable rarities brought for the Emperor," explaining that he'd heard they were carrying fowl that ate coal, an elephant the size of a cat, and a "magic pillow." All this, said the mandarin, was "surely true" because "he had read about it in the newspapers." Macartney noted in his diary a few days later that the interpreter "had amused us" with a newspaper report of similar idiocies, including a "horse the size of a mouse."

By the time that the embassy reached Jehol, many of the saddles had lost stirrups, but the atmosphere was jovial. Perhaps it was the clear mountain air, the almost Alpine scenery, or just the thrill of finally seeing the glazed yellow tiles and vermillion walls of the imperial palaces lying in the valley below. The British marched in a procession through the gates of Jehol to the strains of "God Save the King" from a military band. While the aristocrats may have been smartly dressed, one of the lower members of the party recorded that "the rest of the company exhibited a very awkward appearance: some wore round hats, some cocked hats, and others straw hats: some were in whole boots, some in half boots, and others in shoes with coloured stockings. In second-hand coats and waistcoats, [we] did not enjoy even the appearance of shabby uniformity."

The embassy was to remain in Jehol for nearly two weeks, from September 8 to 21, during which time the British, still refusing to *kow-tow*, felt the atmosphere become hostile. Macartney had presented a copy of George III's letter, but there was no response; a cold silence reigned. There was no word from the mandarins and nothing to do but wait.

On the day appointed for the imperial audience, Macartney was woken up at three in the morning. The emperor was to receive him in a large tent about three miles from their lodgings. No lamps were sent and they stumbled around in the dark, at one point finding themselves "intermingled with a cohort of pigs, asses and dogs, which broke our ranks and put us into irrecoverable confusion." They arrived at four o'clock and were kept waiting for nearly three hours. A huge throng of people had assembled there—Tatar princes, viceroys, governors of cities and districts, mandarins of all types and ranks, soldiers, acrobats, and musicians—several thousand people all waiting for the simultaneous appearance of the emperor and the morning sun. Eventually Emperor Qianlong arrived, proceeded by ministers in yellow robes, and carried on an immense open chair by sixteen men. According to the ambassador, all but the British threw themselves to the ground. Qianlong was dressed in brown silk and wore a velvet cap with a single large pearl. Although he was more than eighty and hard of hearing, the British gained the brief impression of a man much younger in years before he quickly disappeared into the tent. Some time later, Macartney, his deputy, and the boy translator were ushered inside.

It's not clear exactly what happened next, and scholars still argue about it. Macartney insisted that instead of performing the *kow-tow*, he only went down on one knee before the emperor. But the boy noted that as the emperor passed the crowd on the way to the tent, "[we] bowed our heads to the ground." One of the other members noted that "we paid our respect in the usual form of the country, by kneeling nine times to the ground"—all of which sound suspiciously like a *kow-tow*. The boy Staunton records that, inside the tent, they went up to the emperor's platform and "made the same ceremony as before." Whatever really happened, Macartney presented the emperor with the letter and there was a short exchange of pleasantries before the emperor inquired whether anyone in the embassy could speak Mandarin. The boy was brought forward and spoke a few words, to the obvious delight of the emperor, who took a small purse off his belt and gave it to him. Next they were taken to an enormous banquet and returned to their residences before nightfall, having eaten too much and accomplished precisely nothing.

Following the audience, there was no response to George III's letter. Whenever Macartney attempted to raise it with the mandarins, he was parried with a new round of gifts or treated to unwanted entertainments, including on one occasion a four-hour theater performance. At the end of the play, the stage was filled with imitation dolphins, sea monsters, rocks, and sponges before an enormous whale appeared and disgorged several tons of water from its mouth, which drained away through perforations in the floor. As soon as the play was finished, a circus appeared with jugglers on their backs using their feet to throw ceramic urns high into the air with children inside. Next there was an enormous firework display, which concluded "with a volcano or general discharge of suns and stars, squibs, bouncers, crackers, rockets, and grenadoes, which involved the gardens for above an hour after in a cloud of intolerable smoke." Finally Qianlong personally sent yet more food, consisting of "a variety of refreshments, all of which, as coming from him, the etiquette of the court required us to partake of, although we had dined but a short time before."

Several days later, the embassy was again woken well before

dawn and escorted to a pavilion, where they were kept waiting for the usual three hours. This time the emperor never even appeared but instead sat behind an enormous screen. Muffled drums and bells were heard in the distance, before silence fell once more. Suddenly the whole court fell flat on their faces and a concealed orchestra erupted with the wails of strange stringed instruments and the deafening hammering of gongs. An immense red cloth was spread on the ground. At each of its four corners stood a man with a whip and, at the moment that the emperor was supposed to have mounted his throne, the cloth was whipped nine times in sets of three strokes each. Before they knew what was happening, the ceremony was over and everyone left. The embassy went back to the lodgings having no idea of what they had witnessed and it was never mentioned again.

On September 21, still waiting for a response to the letter, the embassy took the same stony route back to Beijing. Just before leaving, the atmosphere darkened after a minor diplomatic incident when one of the men from the Royal Artillery died, "having eaten no less than forty apples at breakfast." The mandarins were indignant; it was against regulations to die in one of the emperor's palaces.

Macartney's final meeting took place in the Forbidden City. Summoned once more without warning and crippled with rheumatism, he hauled himself out of bed and donned the required ceremonial dress, only to be kept waiting yet again for the customary three hours. Almost fainting with fatigue, he was finally asked to *kow-tow* to a letter addressed to George III that had been placed on a yellow chair in the gateway of the Hall of Supreme Harmony. He wasn't allowed to read it for several days. When it was translated, it was heavily edited to avoid offending the king's sensibilities. In fact, it was to be years before a full translation revealed the extent of the embassy's failure. Every one of George III's requests had been refused. Qianlong's letter began:

> We, by the Grace of Heaven, Emperor, instruct the King of England to take note of our charge.

Although your country, O King, lies in the far oceans, yet inclining your heart towards civilization, you have specially sent an envoy respectfully to present a state message, and sailing the seas, he has come to our court to *kow-tow* and present congratulations for the imperial birthday, and to present local products, thereby showing your sincerity. We have perused the text of your state message and the wording expresses your earnestness. From it your sincere humility and obedience can clearly be seen. This is admirable and we fully approve. . . .

After this somewhat unpromising start, the letter went on to deal with the king's main request:

As to what you have requested in your message, O King, namely to be allowed to send one of your subjects to reside in the Celestial Empire to look after your country's trade, this does not conform to the Celestial Empire's ceremonial system, and definitely cannot be done. There are fixed regulations of the Celestial Empire, and presumably you know them O King. Now, however, you want to send one of your subjects to reside at the capital. But he could neither behave like a Western Ocean man who comes to enter our service, nor could he be allowed to go in and out and to have regular correspondence, so it would really serve no purpose. Moreover the territories ruled by the Celestial Kingdom are vast and there are definite regulations for all the envoys of vassal states. If like you, they all beg to send someone to reside at the capital, how could we grant their request in every case? It would be absolutely impossible. How can we go so far as to change the regulations of the Celestial Empire, which are over a hundred years old, at the request of one man—of you, O King?

The emperor finished with an exclamation of withering condescension that dismissed all ideas of opening China to trade:

The Celestial Empire, ruling all within the four seas, simply concentrates on carrying out the affairs of government . . . we have never valued ingenious articles nor do we have the slightest need for your country's manufactures. . . . Hence, we have commanded your tribute envoys safely to return home. You, O King, should simply act in conformity with our wishes by strengthening your loyalty and swearing perpetual obedience so as to ensure that your country may share the blessings of peace.

This is a special edict.

Mystified and empty-handed, Macartney was escorted from Beijing at the start of the long journey south to Canton via Hangzhou, where he stopped off at West Lake to view the Pagoda of Thundering Wind. Prior to his arrival in Hangzhou, while in the highlands of Shandong, he was presented with what was recorded in the Imperial Archives as a piece of curd from the emperor. With their characteristic sycophancy when dealing with the emperor, the mandarins reported back to Qianlong that on receiving the gift:

> the tributary envoy and the others removed their hats and bent their knee. Joy could be read on their faces. They declared "We have received numerous favours from His Imperial Majesty. Today He has given us cheese. We are touched to the bottom of our hearts. To benefit, during such a long journey, from the precious foodstuffs His Charity has bestowed upon us is, for us, like acquiring treasure."

In reality, Macartney was beside himself. Embarrassed, frustrated, and profoundly confused by the Chinese response to his expedition, he fulminated in his notebook:

> Can they be ignorant that a couple of frigates would be an overmatch for the whole naval force of their empire, that in half a summer they could totally destroy all the navigation of their coasts and reduce the inhabitants of the maritime provinces, who subsist chiefly on fish, to absolute famine?

It was an ominous portent of what was to come. After a few short decades, there was war.

THE FIRST CHINESE RULE

When I first read about Macartney's expedition, it was as if a string of firecrackers had exploded about my head. Despite the passage of more than two hundred years, almost every detail of his visit to China was instantly familiar from our trip to Quzhou: The experience of being kept waiting for hours and then receiving demands for an immediate meeting; never knowing who is really in charge; being abandoned by intermediaries and translators; the swapping of personnel with no explanation; the pointless meetings with local officials for exchanging meaningless pleasantries while the clock ticks away and you're left squirming on a sofa clutching at your airline tickets and almost screaming with impatience. The absolute refusal of Chinese counterparties to be elbowed into a deal; the senseless newspaper reports—these days mostly in the foreign press; the delight of senior officials at a few mumbled words of Mandarin; the obligatory overeating at banquets that you're never allowed to pay for; the exchanging of presents that nobody wants and are too big for hand luggage; the firework displays, the interminable theater performances—now replaced by karaoke—everything was so familiar down to the most insignificant and minutest of details. The crunching on melon pips, the smell of overused blankets—or is it now carpets?—the gales of stale tobacco smoke billowing across the table, the swarms of insects . . . All these individually inconsequential elements of a foreigner's encounter with China seemed suddenly to coalesce into a broader picture so staggeringly familiar that I felt compelled to ask myself the simple but exasperating question: Is there one *single* thing about the experience of visiting China that has changed in the last two centuries?

Why is it that the Chinese way of doing things seems so robust and resistant to change? Why is it, as Voltaire observed, that "in four thousand years neither their laws, nor their morals nor the language spoken by their men of letters has changed"? In the century following Macartney's expedition, China sank into utter chaos. Central authority was shattered. But China managed somehow to stagger into the twentieth century still clinging to its ancient idea of order, with an emperor wobbling precariously on top of a highly literate civil service chosen by exams and struggling to administer a vast mass of semiliterate farmers. How is it that, after another century of limitless turmoil and crisis, China is emerging almost casually from the catastrophe of war, famine, and a decade of self-destruction with many of its basic characteristics intact? A less resilient civilization wouldn't have stood a chance.

Perhaps that's the key to understanding China: to view it not as just another country, but as a civilization. For the people of modern-day China might be loosely compared to the population of America, Canada, Russia, the whole of Europe and Japan crammed into one landmass with a common recorded history of several thousand years, where everyone knows Latin and is still ruled from Rome.

In China, there are extremes in climate, differences in local customs, economic conditions, living standards, even physical appearances, but the people there, with some notable exceptions at the periphery, share an affinity with a common cultural heritage that developed over thousands of years. They seem to feel what the sinologist Lucien Pye described as a "profound, unquestioned, generally unshakeable identification with historical greatness."

It's not particularly unusual to hear a taxi driver reciting poetry that was written a thousand years ago or to find people singing opera in the parks of Beijing. Officials point to the brushstrokes on paintings that seem to transport one almost physically back in time to watch flocks of cranes soaring above the roofs of Song Dynasty temples or long caravans of camels struggling through the snows of a Ming Dynasty winter. History seems much more alive in China than in the West both in everyday life and in the pronouncements of its modern leaders. In the nineteenth century a governor who was confronted by an imminent flood consulted Tang Dynasty records written a thousand years earlier to see how they'd coped with the problem. I've never felt such a link between the living and their ancestors, except perhaps fleetingly on the banks of the Nile River. But it is impossible to imagine that the Egyptians of today—or the Greeks or Italians—would think that the brilliance of their own history could offer any guide to their present difficulties, and yet that is precisely what most Chinese believe. Their history is not merely a treasure house to be enjoyed at one's leisure; it offers direct strategic and operational reference points for dealing with the challenges of today.

The basic building block of the West is the nation-state, which emerged from the fragmentation of Europe. But for China the foundation is civilization. China never had the experience of the nation-states of Europe—jostling against each other as relative equals. China *was* Europe, if such a thing can be imagined as united and ruled from one capital. Of course, China derives its sense of "self" in part from its interaction with others, but the legacy of its own internal experiences seems particularly resilient—its common values and ways of thinking, its philosophers, familial ties, its ancestor worship, its rituals, medicine, and diet. All of these things far predate China in its current form as a nation-state.

This thing that's most precious to Chinese—the enduring sense of China's own Chineseness—has been under constant threat throughout its long history. Since it was first united in 221 BC, China has been invaded and occupied by foreign powers—the Liao and the Jin in earlier times, then the Mongol conqueror Genghis Khan in the twelfth century, and more recently the Qing, whose ancestors were from Manchuria. But civilizational values can survive the destruction of the nation-state. After each invasion, foreign ideas were absorbed in China but the essential elements of the indigenous culture survived, transmitted through time by a state bureaucracy inculcated with ancient thought through a system of imperial exams. It is the very robustness of its core ideas that gives China a sense of cultural exceptionalism that can make it almost indifferent to events beyond what it considers its own borders. In two thousand years, the Chinese never even had a foreign ministry. When one was set up in 1861, it was housed in the former Department of Iron Coins in a small alleyway—only a few hundred yards east of our old courtyard—especially to emphasize its irrelevance. Throughout history, China has been receptive to new ideas from abroad that proved useful, but it is highly sensitive to direct attempts from the outside to influence its own domestic affairs. As former U.S. secretary of state Madeleine Albright observed, "China is in its own category—too big to ignore, too repressive to embrace, difficult to influence and very, very proud."

The Chinese emperor was not the only sovereign to claim to embody the state. After all, Louis XIV was famous for his remark "*L'état, c'est moi*." Where it differs is that Qianlong, and to a large extent the modern Chinese government, embodies not just the state but also the whole civilization.

Bertrand Russell said that you couldn't understand China until Qianlong's letter to George III had ceased to be absurd. He was right. Seventy years later, when the Tongzhi Emperor wrote to President Lincoln in 1863, he did not start his message with the words "Dear Abraham," but instead—without the slightest hint of irony—began with the words

> We, who have reverently received the commission from Heaven to rule the entire Universe . . .

Maybe these opening lines reveal a worldview that explains why Wang and his companions hadn't seemed too worried about the Treaty of Augsburg or their reputation in the City.

So here we have the First Chinese Rule:

China is a civilization masquerading as a state. Its essential elements have survived the collapse of central authority and conquest by outsiders over periods so long that there is no equivalent in the West. Endowed with centuries of experience, China will not just cast itself in the image of the West, playing a game of catch-up; China has rules of its own. They are more elusive than ours; they come from accepted modes of thought and unspoken assumptions rather than concise written commandments like "thou shalt not steal." But when the team in Mayfair tried to force a solution in Quzhou that fit their Western context with tightly worded contracts, they were trying to square the circle. The spectacular achievements of free-market capitalism sometimes make it impossible for Westerners truly to believe that there may be a different pathway to success. Many view the difference between China and the West simply as one of timing rather than substance; they believe that the Chinese will eventually "see sense" and conform to the Western model. While it will continue to evolve and reform, and globalization will pull us all more closely together, China will stick to its own path to development. In order to deal most effectively with China, foreigners should adapt to the reality that China has its own set of uniquely Chinese rules.

6

李代桃僵

SACRIFICE THE PLUM TREE IN ORDER TO SAVE THE PEACH

Sacrifice one [smaller] thing in order to gain a second [larger] objective.

*—Eleventh Stratagem of the Thirty-six Ruses
of the Southern Qi Dynasty, c. AD 489–537*

It had been another late night and on the morning of the fifth day in Hangzhou, I could hardly tear myself out of bed. I was short several hours of sleep and late coming down. But I was looking forward to the day; I thought we'd found the sticking point between the two sides. Wang had said he needed to put the whole volume of the carbon from both his production lines into the deal, but Winchester didn't have the finance to take it. I reckoned that with a bit of careful handling, we might find a way to bridge the gap.

But when I got downstairs, rather than finding Mina bouncing around in the lobby and harrumphing over her laptop, she looked subdued and anxious. She showed me a message that had arrived overnight from one of Winchester's colleagues in London. My heart sank as I read it. It said that following our phone call, they had reconsidered the situation. They had concluded that the Chinese partner was not behaving in its own best economic interests so there must be other, hidden reasons for them to insist on late changes. The message told us to go back to the Chinese side and "convey in the strongest possible terms, the sense of betrayal we felt when they changed the contract." It went on to say that they couldn't accept that the problems were due to misunderstandings or cultural differences; it was simply a matter of principle that the other side had to stick to the original arrangement. The message finished with written instructions that we were to go back to Wang and categorically insist that he go back to the original contract. If he refused, we were to leave Hangzhou immediately and come straight back to London.

I looked at Mina. "If we go back in there and insist on the original deal, you'll lose the whole thing."

"You reckon?" she asked skeptically.

"Definitely!" I said. "If you try go back to the old deal, they'll just walk away, end of story."

I could see she was hesitating.

"Look, we have to be realistic. Wang's got a valuable deal here with plenty of options. We know there are other buyers out there and Wang's not going to worry about knocking over the odd piece of regimental silverware in Mayfair. If we don't figure out a way to bridge this gap, he'll just sell the carbon to another buyer and that'll be the end of it. Wang is operating in a totally different system. We have to find out why he's so insistent that the second production line must go in. Then we have to figure out how to explain it to Winchester and his colleagues so that it makes sense to them from inside their own system. That way, we can start to rebuild trust between the two sides and cobble together a solution. London doesn't wake up for another six hours. Turn off your laptop and let's see what we can do."

"I can't do that!" she said tersely. "They'll fire me if they find out."

"They're going to fire you anyway if we don't get this deal," I said.

"Great!"

"Look, if there's a problem, just tell 'em the phone lines were all down. It's only a few hours. Come on—let's see what we can do."

When we arrived at the "Holding Talks Room" Chain-smoking Chen was buried behind a newspaper. On the table there was a jar of hot water with some tea leaves floating in it and the familiar dish of dried melon seeds. I'd seen Wang downstairs in a room off the lobby poring over some documents with some colleagues, so I grabbed the chance to talk to Chen. At first he wouldn't be drawn, but eventually he put down the newspaper and the story came out.

It seemed that the second line had been built several years earlier by a joint venture between the chemical factory and some Russian investors. Under Chinese government rules, joint ventures were not eligible to generate carbon credits, so Wang had to exclude it from the first round of discussions. But, Chen said, once the factory management realized the size of the revenues that they might get from carbon reductions, they quickly approached the Russian investors with an offer to buy them out of the joint venture. They figured that even if they had to pay more than the market price for the Russians' share in the production line, the money they'd get from the carbon would more than compensate for that. The deal had recently been completed. Now that the second line was wholly owned, Wang planned to install an incinerator and claim credits.

"Fine," I said when Chen had finished. "That explains why Wang has changed his position from last time, but even if you want to get carbon revenue from the second line, why can't you just sell it to someone else? Then we can go back to the original contract."

Chen explained that the Chinese government approval process was horribly complicated. I had seen from Mina's papers that because the Kyoto Protocol was an agreement between sovereign countries, each side of a carbon project—the buyer and seller—had to get an approval from their respective governments. In the United Kingdom, it was just a matter of applying to the Department of Energy and Climate Change and the approval would be faxed over in a few days. But in China, the process involved laborious meetings with multiple provincial departments before it was sent to Beijing for a further lengthy review. There were more than eight different central government departments and bureaus that had to sign off simultaneously before the project could go ahead. Wang was worried about trying to get two separate approvals through the process at the same time. One of the officials would be bound to ask why both lines couldn't be submitted as one project. If there were two separate applications, he thought, they might be rejected or get stuck somewhere inside the bureaucracy. Or, worse still, one line might be approved and the other one rejected.

But I was still puzzled. "Why would the government ever want to reject a project that brings so much benefit to a Chinese business?" I asked.

Chen told me that the size of these projects had attracted the attention of top-level officials. The huge amount of carbon revenue generated by refrigerant lines in China was large enough to upset the balance in parts of the whole chemicals industry so it had raised some politically sensitive issues. In particular, there were some big state-owned chemical plants up in the old rust belt towns in China's far northeast that competed with Wang's factory across a range of different products. These factories supported tens of thousands of workers, but they didn't make refrigerants. They were complaining that the huge revenues available to Quzhou would put them at a significant disadvantage across a whole range of other competing product lines. The provincial governments responsible for the old factories had been lobbying Beijing to delay its approvals and introduce levies that shared the carbon income across the whole industry. The officials in the Chemicals Ministry were split; some favored the factory in Quzhou but others worried about unemployment if the other factories there were driven out of business. The final decision makers in the National Development and Reform Commission in Beijing had initially told Wang that they would approve the project in Quzhou, but more recently they had been hesitating. Wang and his boss, General Manager Gao, had decided that they had to push through both lines in one project as soon as possible, even if it meant they got less favorable terms; otherwise they risked getting nothing.

"Hmm . . . but I still don't understand why Old Wang didn't tell us about the deal with the Russian investors," I said. "Winchester and his guys in Mayfair think that he's been hiding something and now they're quite difficult to calm down."

"Well, Wang was probably embarrassed," Chen explained. "He didn't know about the negotiations to buy out the Russians until the last minute and he doesn't want it to look like he was kept in the dark. Anyway, we assumed that you knew about all of this," he said. "It was announced at the stock exchange in March. You can see it right here in the *Economic Daily*!"

"Really?!" I said, turning to Mina. "So why didn't Cordelia spot that?"—but she just rolled her eyes and put her head in her hands.

This new information presented a tricky dilemma; it was now clear why Wang was boxed in and needed to include the second line. On the other hand, we could hardly admit to him that ECF couldn't expand the contract because it didn't have the money. The syndicate had been lined up but it was still not formally signed, and anyway it wasn't big enough for both lines. ECF was a new outfit and if Wang had any suspicion that the funding wasn't solid, we'd risk losing the first line as well. There was only one way forward: we had to find a way to convince London to include the second line. I figured that Winchester's discussions with the big Dutch pension funds might provide the route out of the impasse.

When Wang reappeared just before lunch, we went downstairs and hammered out a deal around one of the big circular tables in the dining room on the first floor. As he crunched through a plate of "knife fish"—a local delicacy with strange, slim fillets of bony fish with chopped celery in vinegar—I took Wang through our understanding of the story, trying not to implicate Chen. I told him that we understood that the second line had originally been owned by a joint venture, so Wang had to exclude it earlier on, but that now it was wholly owned by the Chinese side and eligible to generate credits. Two separate approval processes would be troublesome and would increase the risk that the project might be delayed or even refused.

He nodded in agreement throughout so we suggested that we could combine both lines into a single approval document for the government. Although there would be only one buyer for both lines, we could have two separate contracts to buy up the carbon. The first line would go under the existing contract and the second one would be taken up by a new, much larger fund that ECF was currently arranging. By the time the project was approved by the Chinese government, the new fund should all be in place. In the meantime, we would be able to get some letters from a few of the new investors confirming their intention to invest; a couple of huge Dutch pension funds had already been lined up. "Besides," I added, "the best way for you to get comfortable about the deal is for you to come over to London and meet ECF's management. That'll give you a much better feel for the company; I think it would be good for both sides."

Wang disappeared for an hour or so to report to Old Gao and when he came back there was a look of relief on his face. While there'd be no formal guarantees from any of the investors in the second fund, Wang and Old Gao had calculated that the risk that ECF's second fund might not be established was a better bet than trying to get two separate approvals through the government or starting from scratch with another buyer. Besides, the size of the commitment was now so large—at €300 million—that there was only a limited number of buyers in the market. Wang told us that they'd decided to go ahead but there were two conditions: they wanted to see the confirmation letters from the pension funds— and they wanted to come over to London.

Mina spent some time updating the contract and I cobbled to-gether some wording for the pension fund letters together with Wang. It looked as though we'd reached agreement, so I asked him to provide a "chopped" confirmation on the company's red letter-head to convince Winchester that there would be no more changes to the contracts. Getting a chopped document in China was always a key step. There were always complicated procedures for using a company chop, so if Wang could get approval from all the relevant company departments, it would prove that all the key people in the management team had united around the decision and the deal would be much less likely to unravel later on.

Late in the afternoon, we got the letter with the chop and sent a carefully worded report to Winchester setting out what we had found. There was no reaction for several hours, but eventually he called Mina on the speakerphone in the pantry. It was a difficult conversation; Winchester's people couldn't understand why getting government approval was so risky when it was in China's economic interest just to accept the cash. I had a tough time explaining that the Chinese government was caught in a never-ending balancing act between different domestic interests and that it wasn't just a question of simple economics. The team in Mayfair had the typical notion of foreigners that the Chinese government could do whatever it liked, so explaining Wang's position was a laborious process. But since the original financing was preserved and they ended up with a much larger deal without any formal commitments, Winchester was inclined to go ahead and we finished the call by asking him to try to get the confirmation letters from the pension funds.

That evening, Wang organized a dinner on a little island by the edge of the lake in Hangzhou; it was a beautiful evening and the moon was high in the sky as the sun set over the opposite bank. Old Gao, the manager of the factory, finally appeared and seemed happy that a deal had been struck; we took some celebratory photographs standing on the ornamental rocks at the water's edge and, just before nine, I headed for the airport to catch the flight home. By the time the plane was on the runway, I was in a deep sleep.

I had got onto the plane feeling elated, but I arrived at home in England to find a mood of black despair. One of the horses was ill and the children were all worried. Max, my eldest stepson, had been training a huge old mare, a lovable but blundering cob that he had been bringing up for show jumping. When he first started, I had wondered whether he would ever manage to stop her charging straight out of the ring and rampaging through the stalls, or smashing the jumps to pieces with her giant hooves at their first attempt to get over them. But he loved the old horse and spent hours out in the field putting her over the jumps, so I'd kept my thoughts to myself. Now the old mare had lost all her energy and could hardly walk.

I went out to the field and found her in the corner, standing quietly, her legs shaking slightly with the effort of standing and her head drooping toward the ground. She hadn't eaten for days. Her eyes were blank and she had been losing a lot of blood. Lorraine had already taken her to York for tests but they couldn't find anything wrong; the vet had been out to our home several times while I had been in Hangzhou. That evening, the old mare was looking no better so we called the vet once more. The tears flowed freely as the vet led her gently toward the shade of some trees by the edge of the stables. He placed a short metal cylinder on her forehead and struck it with a tiny hammer. With a sudden start, her head flew upward, but it was all over in an instant. For the last time, the old horse lay still among the buttercups and daisies scattered in the grass around her.

The next day, I was called down to London. I knocked on the polished black door and waited for the click, just as I had a week earlier. Given how the trip had gone, I'd expected some minor celebrations, or at least a friendly welcome, but I was kept waiting for nearly thirty minutes. When I was eventually shown into a wood-paneled meeting room at the back of the offices, I found six or seven people, all in dark suits, waiting around a long table. Mina was sitting in the middle, looking deflated. Her boss sat at the end of the table, with Winchester on the opposite side about halfway down. At first I couldn't understand why the atmosphere was so dour; we'd just rescued a landmark deal and doubled its size to more than €300 million.

I was confused, but as the conversation progressed, my hands became clammy. It began to sink in that the only thing they wanted to talk about was why we had ignored their instructions from London to insist on the original deal or break off discussions. Winchester was most persistent and asked how I expected them to conduct operations from headquarters if they'd no information from the field. I tried to explain. Events had moved rapidly. Besides, they'd been asleep; the time difference meant that we couldn't have called them. In the end, the objective had been achieved. I tried to move back to a more positive note; they'd just clinched a deal that would catapult them into a leading position in the carbon markets. But Winchester was having none of it and the conversation became touchy. At first, I fought back. If we'd followed the instructions and done what they'd asked, they'd have lost the deal and that would have been the end of it.

"That's not your concern," he retorted.

"But the whole point going out to Hangzhou was to try to save the deal!" I protested.

"We're not looking for superstars here," he said. "We just need you to follow instructions!"

I was amazed by the turn of the conversation, and shocked; it was so far from what I had expected that I found it difficult to react. At first I just took the beating, but gradually I became more alarmed. After Mina had called me on the quiet coach, everything had happened so quickly. I'd had so little knowledge of carbon that I'd gone out to Hangzhou without an agreement for a success fee. Now I'd come to London to try to sort it out from a much weaker position and it was looking worse by the minute. After the meeting ended, Mina's boss took me up to the attic offices. He told me that they'd agree to an hourly rate for the time I'd spent in Hangzhou but if I expected a bonus for saving the deal, I had to sign an exclusivity agreement that would block me from working with anyone else in the carbon markets for the next eighteen months. "Company policy," he explained drily. Fifteen minutes later, I left the office with blood pounding in my ears.

That evening, I sat brooding on the train on its way north. It had been a horrible couple of days since I had got back to England.

Looking back on it, finding a solution in Hangzhou hadn't been so complicated, but it had all looked pretty dire when we first arrived. With the two sides so far apart and no way of communicating, there was no way that ECF could have completed the syndicate. I had seen from correspondence that the deal was effectively dead but after five days we'd ended up doubling its size and delivering a great result for both sides. It was by far the largest carbon deal in the private sector; only the World Bank had done larger ones. Now I was faced with the choice of walking away with almost nothing to show for saving the deal or tying my hands for eighteen months.

I thought briefly of calling Wang and derailing the deal—but what would be the use of that? I felt badly treated, of course, but it was at least partly my own fault for going out to Hangzhou with no contract; whatever had happened, there was no point in looking back. I had to figure out what to do next. As I stared out toward the sun as it sank behind the hills, the fields flashed by in the gathering gloom. In the distance, I caught the familiar silhouette of a stone church standing out on a little hillock, with a weather vane at the top of the steeple; I'd be home before long.

As I thought through the hours we'd spent in the Holding Talks Room, I began to relax. It had been just over a week since I had received the phone call from Mina. I had learned so much in that time and besides, I remembered one of the Thirty-six Ruses—the old battle plans from China's ancient past—"Sacrifice the Plum Tree in Order to Save the Peach." I had a hunch that if I sacrificed the fee but managed to complete the deal in Quzhou, I might have stumbled across something much more valuable, something that might open up a whole new range of opportunities in China. But for the time being, I put thoughts of future plans to the back of my mind; the first thing to do was to complete the deal in Quzhou.

Over the following week, I called Wang each morning, pacing up and down by a tall yew hedge in Yorkshire, delivering messages from London and gently nudging him forward. There were a few loose ends in the contract to be sorted out and Wang's trip to London still had to be organized, but the letters from the pension funds had gone over and Wang seemed satisfied.

Two weeks later, Wang and Old Gao arrived in England with a large entourage. The trip had been arranged so that the team from Quzhou could meet with the senior people in Mayfair and see one of the trading floors at Deutsche Bank. It was unusually hot in London on the day the Chinese delegation visited—the hottest day in July since 1911—and the Chinese sat quietly sweating under the ornate ceilings and plastered cornices in the ballroom before Winchester blustered in with his team. The translator from Cordelia's office had accompanied the delegation to London, only to find out that none of her credit cards worked, which had caused much embarrassment at the hotel.

When the meeting started, Winchester gave an introduction to the company and its plans for buying up carbon credits and investing in clean energy and environmental projects in developing countries. The meeting passed smoothly except for the occasional mistranslation; each time, Winchester would pause, sensing the confusion, as each of the Chinese managers on the other side of the table peered at the ceiling, blinking and smiling politely while they wondered what on earth he had meant. Toward the end of the meeting, there was a minor commotion when an elderly man in a badly fitting tweed jacket wandered into the room and Winchester and his colleagues leaped up to greet him.

"Who's that?" I whispered sideways to Mina.

"I think it's Lord Oxford or somebody?" she said. "Used to be chief scientific adviser to the cabinet, or something. He's the one that's organized the dinner tonight in the House of Lords."

"Really?!" I said. "Looks more like someone's gardener's just wandered in; you should tell him the allotments are on the other side of Hyde Park."

That evening, Winchester had arranged a reception for the Chinese delegation at the Palace of Westminster. Before dinner, Lord Oxford took us on a long tour of both Houses, along a labyrinth of passageways with thick carpets, strange Gothic doorways, and somber oak paneling, past crowded tearooms and down winding stone staircases. At last we arrived in the chamber of the House of Lords, with its elaborate gilded ceiling and deep red leather benches. We were allowed to sit on the benches during a debate and stopped for a while to listen to the speeches about health-care reforms. Lord Oxford seemed happy explaining various points of interest, the history of the building and how Parliament worked, but I was exhausted by the effort of translating *woolsack*, *black rod*, *white-stick-in-waiting*, and *Lord Chancellor* into Mandarin. Eventually, we crossed a large chamber with stone fireplaces and two immense green tapestries showing scenes from the Battle of Trafalgar and arrived in a smaller room with a throne at one end.

"This is the robing room," said Lord Oxford.

"This is where the queen puts her clothes on," I said, exhausted. Wang nodded.

"And the throne there has a small stool next to it because Queen Victoria was quite short."

I translated and Wang said, "Oh."

"Someone once asked our current queen how heavy the crown is," continued Lord Oxford. I translated.

"And she said, 'About the same weight as a large salmon.'"

Wang just looked at me blankly and asked, "Why did she say that?"—at which point, I gave up.

The trip to London had gone well. The offices in Mayfair were impressive enough and the Chinese successfully sidestepped the Stilton at the dinner in the House of Lords. They visited Deutsche Bank's offices in the City, inquiring politely about the slowly ticking grandfather clocks and the portraits of the Victorian bankers on the walls in the old Morgan Grenfell boardroom and surveying the rows of computer screens that stretched out into the distance on the trading floor.

A couple of weeks later, Winchester and his team went over to China to visit the factory for a signing ceremony of the formal contracts. Two of the traders from Deutsche accompanied us on the trip and I sat next to them on the bus journey through the long, flat valley from Hangzhou inland to Quzhou. Throughout the long journey to the factory, they bantered about "deltas," "structured carbon streams," and "spiking volatility," laughing uproariously at their own jokes about high-velocity arbitrage trading.

Several hours later, we arrived in front of a huge set of factory gates with whiteboards displaying vertical lines of Chinese characters on either side. A sentry standing on a little platform saluted as we went in. I saw immediately that the plant was immense. Columns of pipe-work rose up in the distance; there were chimneys and tanks and towers with gantries where great hoops of rusted tubing sat coiled up in knots or poking out at strange angles. Clouds of white steam billowed from cooling towers; bundles of pipes, with tattered lagging, drooped between old rusting supports that stood at intervals along the roadside. The rainwater in the potholes reflected the sky.

Deep inside, we came to a refrigerant plant. It was a modern site with the workings hidden behind metal cladding and a control room inside that had flowcharts with lights and dials monitoring the flow in the pipes and pressure in the tanks; it was an impressive display. Wang took us across the road to the main offices, where there was a large-scale model of the whole factory site. It was vast and covered an area of about two thousand acres. The old part of the factory, which had been built in Mao's day, was about half a mile from the river on the opposite bank from Quzhou City. The more modern factories had been built behind the old site, farther away from the town and toward the foot of the mountains.

Closer in, along the banks of the river, a huge area had been taken over by the workers' housing. A high perimeter wall sealed off rows of drab seven-story apartment buildings, housing for the families of the eighty thousand people who were supported by the main factory or the other factories that supplied it. Wang pointed out four primary schools, a cinema, and soccer fields; the factory even had its own TV station. As the factory expanded and ate up the land, the peasants who farmed there had been relocated, but I noticed that a little pocket of farmland had survived within the perimeter fence. Wang told me that it belonged to a family who were direct descendants of Confucius. Rather than move them off the land and destroy the ancient buildings, the authorities had agreed that they could stay there and open up the village to visitors.

Wang took us to inspect the workshop at the end of the refrigerant line, where the Japanese engineers had just installed the incinerators; one set, consisting of a large gray machine with pipes and gauges, was already working. It stood on a platform about two feet above the ground. A low hum rose from the furnaces inside. Mina beckoned me over and I stepped up onto the platform to look through a small circular window and stare at the tiny flame, just a thin tongue of fire burning up millions of tons of greenhouse gases and pumping more millions of euros through the world's financial system on a ceaseless search for profit.

After the contract signing, the celebratory dinner that evening was an equally impressive affair involving multiple courses and large doses of alcohol. It took place in one of the factory's large dining rooms, which was hidden deep inside a hotel complex at the end of a long paneled corridor that smelled strongly of Chinese liquor and stale beer. In the center of the room, an enormous circular table big enough to seat twenty people had been decked out with a yellow tablecloth. Behind the table, there was a large carved lacquer screen with an elaborate chandelier overhead. The whole management team had turned up and Old Gao's boss, Chairman Zhang, took the host's position opposite the door.

Once we were all seated, he started off on the toasts. The formal atmosphere quickly broke down and the table was soon piled high with dishes; a whole fish, lightly steamed with coriander and spring onions, bowls of shrimp, pots of pork ribs in glass noodles, razorblade fish and scallops fried in garlic and piles of dark green vegetables and taro baked in coconut milk. There were medicinal tubers called *shanyao* and a few bony parts of animals that made the point that whenever it comes to food, the Chinese never waste a thing. Soon the thick smell of Chinese white liquor filled the air.

Two places away at the table, I could hear the boys from Deutsche still droning on about hedging instruments to Chain-smoking Chen, who had unwisely asked them what they planned to do with the credits once they were issued.

"Well you can lock in a delta back-to-back with a compliance buyer, or collar the price with some options," one of them said. "Hey, I heard Goldman's doing a put," he remarked chirpily to his colleague.

"You can hedge and trade pretty much anything these days," said the other. "Some people even trade weather."

"Weather?" Chen asked.

"Yeah, it's all just a question of de-risking. You can hedge against practically everything these days, even the weather. If you've got some position in the market that's affected by weather, you wrap up some stocks in ice-cream manufacturers and umbrella factories together with a few short positions in suntan lotion and raincoats, and you're covered; simple as that."

Meanwhile, Winchester was just warming up. Chairman Zhang was explaining that China had numerous different types of highly alcoholic drinks, but the most famous was *bai jiu*, or white liquor, which is distilled from sorghum. The tiny glasses used to serve *bai jiu* create a false sense of security and soon Chairman Zhang had proposed several toasts. I could see that Winchester was loosening up. After several more courses and numerous toasts, Zhang began explaining that China had ancient traditions involving distilled alcohol and that great poets and calligraphers of the Tang Dynasty used it to enhance moments of creative inspiration in the company of fellow artists.

"Yes, we have lots of drinking games as well," Winchester blurted out. "We often played 'fizz-buzz' in the mess. You lot ever tried it?"

"I'm not sure that's what they had in mind, actually."

"Oh go on! Just go round the table counting up, one, two, three as you go round," he said, waving vaguely at the row of Chinese faces on the other side.

"Yes, I know what it is," I said, "it's just that I'm not sure it's exactly what they had in mind."

But Winchester wasn't to be deterred.

"Every time it gets to a multiple of three, you have to say 'fizz' instead of the number, and every time there's a multiple of five you have to say 'buzz.' If it's both, like fifteen, you have to say 'fizz-buzz.' Whenever someone gets it wrong, they have to down the glass!" he said beaming broadly at the blank faces around the table.

We only got through a few rounds before Winchester had downed another four glasses. After two more rounds, several of his colleagues were heading the same way while the Chinese wisely held back. But just as he raised his small glass to down another shot, he suddenly sneezed so violently that he crushed it in his hand, breaking off the stem and sending a jet of *bai jiu* up the back of his nose and out across the table. Once the mist had cleared, he blinked the tears from his eyes, peered at the fragments of glass among the half-finished plates, leaned forward to pick up one of the small damp towels on the table, blew his nose loudly, and continued.

After several more rounds, there had been more sneezes and several more glasses had disappeared. The dinner had to be brought to a hasty conclusion after Winchester stumbled toward the door and crashed full length across a row of chairs in the hallway. The evening's entertainments ended in the early hours after a protracted session in a karaoke bar where the Chinese version of "Why, why, why, Delilah?" resonated in great undulating waves through the corridors of the hotel. The Chinese had—sensibly—disappeared several hours earlier.

The following day, as we made our way back to Hangzhou on a bus, Winchester sat up at the front near to the exit. It was extremely hot and the air-conditioning inside the bus didn't work properly. Winchester had snatched only a few hours' sleep and I could see he was struggling.

It has always struck me as the greatest irony that the Chinese language has no direct translation for *hangover*. The equivalent expression—"the wine rose to my head"—completely fails to do justice to the full, epic horror of a Chinese hangover as it unfolds, like a tragedy, in several distinct acts. I knew from bitter experience that *bai jiu*, properly administered by a skillful Chinese host, can consign a foreigner to twenty-four hours of hell. It starts after about three hours of fitful sleep with cold, juddering sweats, revolting oily burps, and painful stabbing behind the eyes before a dull and slightly frightening ache begins to grip what one assumes is probably the liver. A sour smell, like onions mixed with diesel, oozes from every pore. Daylight arrives to find the victim stumbling out of bed with what feels like a mouthful of salted anchovies and a strange sliding sensation, as if the brain has somehow become detached from the inside of the skull and is swirling around inside like weed-clogged pond water or egg whites. There's only one strategy: sit it out and try not to vomit in public.

Throughout all the years of *bai jiu*–fueled banquets, I'd never seen anyone look so hungover as Winchester; a trace of the stiff formality had returned, but above the set grin and pasty jowls, there was a telltale band of cold sweat glistening just under the hairline and a look of fixed concentration that hinted at some titanic struggle under way in his intestines. As the bus lurched about on the Chinese roads and veered around the hairpin turns on the way up the dusty mountain road, his head bobbed gently against the seat. I could only imagine the spinning sensation and waves of nausea that must have engulfed him and I watched him with some apprehension each time the bus ran over a bump.

Wang had taken a lengthy detour on the journey back to Hangzhou to visit a Buddhist temple and see some famous statues dating from the Song Dynasty. It was the last thing that any of us wanted to do after the previous night's celebrations, but we tramped obediently up a hill in the blazing sunshine toward the temple. Hawkers lined the steps and noisily pressed us with bags of walnuts, sour plums, and dried hawberries; crowds of tourists jostled about on the narrow stone steps as we struggled up past the thickets of thorn-bushes on the hillside.

At the top, behind an ocher wall, there were several pavilions in a grove of gnarled pine trees scattered about with large stone orna-ments. Inside, after our eyes adjusted to the gloom, we gradually made out the shapes of several hundred carved figures covered in a thick layer of dust. Long rows of statues—of monks and holy men—known as *arhats* sat among the beams of sunlight that came down in thick streams from the high windows and caught the tiny specks of dust and decay that danced about in the air. It was cooler inside; the *arhat*s sat on top of raised platforms in various states of ecstasy or deep contemplation. The one nearest the door was enormously fat, with flowing robes and reed sandals, and had huge, fleshy earlobes, tears of laughter pouring down his face, and an empty begging bowl in his hands. Farther on, looming through the shadows, the statues became more and more bizarre; there were images of monks with enormous purple eyebrows and green lips with expressions of un-controllable rage or dreamlike tranquility; some had scores of arms or several heads; one had a purple face and a painfully swollen stom-ach with eels escaping from its navel. Others had strange pavilions growing out of the tops of their heads. At the back, a seated statue had a normal human appearance, except for one enormously long arm reaching twenty feet up into the ceiling. Winchester tramped manfully around the statues with his tongue glued to the roof of his mouth, smiling wanly at first and sweating quietly but looking more and more uncomfortable at the tortured state of the *arhat*s. One glance at the monk with the purple face and the eels wriggling out of his belly button was too much for Winchester; he just groaned and blundered out toward the doorway clutching at his stomach.

An hour or so farther into the journey, the bus stopped so that we could we buy some watermelons by the side of the road. Nearby, a wide, brown river flowed lazily under a bridge. There were a few minutes to spare, so Mina and I wandered over to the bank of the river. On the opposite side there was an open quarry with cement works jammed in between strips of land that were still being farmed. The bushes in a nearby orchard were covered in a sprinkling of white dust from the lime kilns. I stared down into the swirling waters and turned to Mina.

"You know, I reckon we could probably find some other carbon projects in China, don't you think?"

She nodded.

"I think this could be a really interesting business if we got it right and raised some money. What do you reckon?"

Another nod.

"China needs all these new environmental technologies so it could lead on to something else; you never know."

"Right."

"We shouldn't be doing this for anyone else. We should try to start our own business."

"Too right," she said. "I'm up for it!"

We agreed that when we got back to Beijing, we would start to pull together a business plan and send it out to investors.

7

話説天下大事，
分久必合 合久必分

THE SECOND CHINESE RULE:

The Long-Divided Shall Unite;
The Long-United Shall Divide

—Opening lines from Romance of the Three Kingdoms,
one of China's greatest historical novels, Luo Guanzhong, AD 1321

When the English traders ignored Qianlong's letter to George III, the stage was set for a clash between civilizations that reverberated for the next hundred and fifty years. In the decades after Macartney's visit, a thriving community of foreign merchants established thirteen *hong*s—or live-in warehouses—in a stockade along the riverbank outside the gates of the southern Chinese city of Canton.

When I first traveled up the Pearl River from Hong Kong to Canton on the slow boat to China, the scenes along the river hadn't changed much since the missionaries described them in their journals of the 1830s. The flat cargo tugs were still so loaded up with bricks that the gunwales were barely above the waterline; government patrol boats bobbed about and even the noisy ferry that crossed from the jutting pier at Jackass Point over to Honan Island still ran. Migrant farmers from deep within the countryside had replaced the local *ku-li* laborers that the preachers saw soliciting for work, but when I visited the famous Qingping markets—now closed—cats and dogs, owls and pangolins, terrapins, scorpions, and cobras were still for sale. More than a century before, a missionary had seen a man pushing through the crowded market carrying on his shoulder "something like a slab of oak, and was surprised to notice, by the hoof that formed part of it, that it was the hindquarter of a horse." Healers pressed heated bamboo cups on men's naked backs to draw out bad humors; tinkers drilled tiny holes into broken pots and fixed them with fine wire and glue. At sunset, a group of noisy carpenters gathered under tarpaulins slung across the alleyways and called to a missionary to join them. "The wines were circulating briskly," he noted, and the local firewater caused a "degree of inebriation more ferocious than that occasioned by any other spirit." No wonder the preachers complained that the congregation was "somewhat muted of a Sunday."

From their *hong*s along the riverbank, the foreign merchants traded tea, silks, medicines, and watches. They entertained in grand dining rooms and took siestas on the verandas overlooking the river. But there were shadier activities as well. One missionary described how he had visited the "residence of the embassador of the King of Siam. Having made my way up Physic Street . . . to the corner of Shoe Street" he found "the whole establishment in ruins. One of the overseers conducted me to the apartment of the chief embassador whom we found smoking opium and so stupefied as to be almost incapable of conversation."

Opium gnawed at the heart of China; edicts in vermillion ink showered down upon the provincial officials but still the opium flowed. Packed in cases of forty balls each, steadily it came, in ever increasing volumes from the British colonies in India, wrapped in thick coverings of poppy leaves. Around the stockade in Canton, tensions grew between the foreign merchants and the mandarin officials. There were signs of gathering war.

In 1836, a candidate for the imperial examinations arrived in Canton from a small village some fifty miles north. It lay in a belt of forested highland where marauding bandits slipped easily between different counties to escape the five imperial magistrates sent to administer the region. Hong Huoxiu came from a modest farming background but he had passed the county-level Confucian examinations and now found himself among the thousand scholars assembling around the great exam compound in Canton, hopeful of passing up to the next level. As he mingled with the crowd in Dragon Hiding Street, a foreigner handed him a book of block-printed Bible tracts translated into Chinese. He failed the exams, but he kept the book.

After this disappointment, Hong returned to the village. Even though he had failed the prefectural exams, he was still considered a scholar. He taught at the local school among the peasant farmers, whose lives had for generations followed the rhythm of the seasons. After each Spring Festival, the locals held ceremonies at Qing Ming, when they swept their ancestors' graves. A month later, on Dragon Boat Day, they offered horn-shaped cakes of sweetened rice first to their forefathers and then to each other. After the summer solstice, the festival of the Herdboy and the Weaving Maid was followed by that of the Fire God. For three days people prayed for his protection, for fire was the worst of all enemies. Lamps blazed in the streets and occasionally caught fire, sending the crowds running. Later in the year, people hung strings of oranges around the doorways or carved peachwood charms for the Grain Spirits before the year ended with a visit from the Kitchen God, who had to be fed if his favors were to be granted.

Immediately after Spring Festival of 1837, Hong took the exams once more but again he failed to pass. Exhausted and humiliated, he fell ill and had to be taken back to the village in a sedan chair. Once he was home, Hong's sickness deepened and his family gathered around his bed convinced that he was dying. For days he raved in bed, drifting in and out of consciousness, sometimes lying limply in a stupor, other times rising to sweats of violence, waving his arms as if in combat or chanting wildly the same verses over and over again. His family muttered that he must have gone mad; they quietly bolted the doors, for the magistrates held relatives responsible for the crimes of a madman.

Eventually Hong emerged from the stupor and told his anxious relatives that he had seen a vision of a great crowd gathered around his bed, with men playing music and children in yellow robes. He had ascended up to Heaven and, passing through the gates of a great city, he had met his "father" seated on a golden throne. Hong's "father" gave him a sword and a shining, golden seal to fight a demon that had corrupted the world of men. Up and down the thirty-three levels of Heaven, Hong fought the demon with his elder brother standing behind him, dazzling the devil with blazing light from the golden seal. But at the moment of victory, Hong's "father" forgave the demon. Instructing Hong to change his given name, he recited moral texts before sending Hong back to Earth and the arms of his family.

The illness eventually passed. Hong gradually recovered his strength and took up teaching again; his wife gave birth to a daughter and life returned to normalcy. But Hong insisted on changing his name as his "father" had instructed. His family eventually got used to it.

Hong Xiuquan, as he by then called himself, taught in the obscure inland village as war gathered around him. In 1839, a crisis erupted when imperial officials seized 20,283 cases of opium from the foreign merchants in Canton, mixed it with lime, and flushed it into the river. Crowds of angry Chinese swept through the merchants' *hong*s, smashing mirrors and pulling down weather vanes, chandeliers, and clocks. London was roused. A great ironclad steamboat—the *Nemesis*—arrived in Canton with a naval task force and destroyed more than seventy junks, bombarding the shoreline with shells. British soldiers marched across paddies of ripening rice; gates were broken, food stolen, graves violated, women molested. The villagers around Canton assembled into ragged militia, whose numbers swelled to thousands.

When battle was joined, black rain fell from the skies; paths turned to swamps, and muskets became wet and useless. The Chinese used strange weapons like giant shepherds' crooks attached to long bamboo poles to hook soldiers out of the opposing lines. Eventually, a truce was declared. In an uneasy standoff throughout the sweltering summer, the Qing officials negotiated a settlement that saved the city. But the locals were resentful of the appeasement. In the exam halls, carved ink stones flew through the air, hurled by indignant scholars at the presiding mandarins whom they had come to despise and fear. Bemused, mortified, frightened, the officials protested that they had saved the city, only to find that their sedan chairs had been trashed by a mob outside.

It was in this gathering chaos that Hong, after two more failed attempts at passing the Confucian exams, at last started to read the block-printed Bible that he had been handed several years earlier as he waited outside the exam hall.

As he read the translations of the holy verses, fragments of the ancient writings resonated with the turmoil he saw around him. In Isaiah 1:7, when he read "your country is desolate, your cities burned with fire, your land—strangers devour it in your presence and it is desolate as overthrown by strangers," he envisioned the balls of fire and shattered bodies falling back to the ground after the rockets from the ironclad paddle steamer hit the gunpowder stores in Canton. He felt in the verses the suffering of the soldiers who clung to the stern chains of burning boats until forced to release their grip by the intense heat and sink below the surface. He sensed in the lines the pain of the young soldiers scorched by gunpowder as they fumbled with newly issued flintlocks.

As he read on, he found mysterious and marvelous stories of a man and a woman who lived in a garden at the origin of time, where there was no excessive heat or cold, no want of food, no flood or drought, no sickness or death, but where a serpent demon had offered the woman strange fruit that brought knowledge of evil things and how the man and the woman had been banished. He read that *Ye-huo-hua*—Jehovah—had placed the spirit of his own son into the body of a woman untouched by man and that great armies from God had appeared at the birth crying "Glory to God and on the earth—*Taiping*—Great Peace!" He read of how the child had been studious and hardworking and that, at the age of thirty, he had cast aside his former life and begun to preach openly. The words of Jesus were like nothing Hong had ever read before. He saw that Jesus told his followers to rejoice, not grieve over misfortune:

> blessed are the meek, for they shall inherit the earth; blessed are they which are persecuted for righteousness sake, for theirs will be the— *Tianguo*—the Kingdom of Heaven.

As Hong read the Bible, he began to discern complex explanations for the visions he had seen during his delirium. The great man with the yellow beard—his father—was God. The demon whom he fought through the thirty-three levels of Heaven was the same as the serpent demon that gave the fruit to the woman. His elder brother, who held the golden seal that dazzled the demon-devil, was Jesus himself. By extension, he was Jesus's younger brother. As he read the holy verses, Hong came to believe that he was nothing other than the second son of God.

Hong started to preach. Words poured out of him. He began to write holy tracts. He read the Bible for hours every day. When his anxious family sent a watchman to spy on Hong's activities, he converted him. He began to throw out the Confucian tablets from the local schools, as Jesus had thrown out the money changers from the Temple. At first the local worthies humored him—he was, after all, a scholar—but eventually he lost his job. He took to wandering, traveling south with three companions, emulating the restless journeying of the prophet and his disciples, marching, preaching, baptizing in a long arc around the city of Canton. After tramping for thirty-four days, the travelers split up and one of Hong's companions went far inland to set up a base on Thistle Mountain.

Far away from the wealth and cultured society of the cities, the people of Thistle Mountain survived on the edge of subsistence. Hong's promise of salvation had a particular resonance with those vulnerable people and Hong's disciples easily converted the miners who worked the silver lodes, the charcoal burners and fuel gatherers, the bean curd salesmen and rice flour grinders who lived around the mountain. His new "God Worshipping Society" grew steadily; villagers felt protected in numbers from robbers and bandits who roamed the area. Lawlessness grew as the British tightened their grip on the seas around Hong Kong and drove the pirates inland. River bandits fought with pirates over opium and gunpowder; in a nearby county, a gang killed the Qing magistrate, seized the chops, and ran the county for several months before anyone tried to arrest them.

When Hong joined his companions on Thistle Mountain, his writings became increasingly psychedelic and bizarre. He claimed to have witnessed Confucius arguing with God before being captured and flogged by angels. He began to destroy more idols, pulling down the statues of the local deities in the temples, tearing out their beards, stamping on their hats, and festooning the debris with triumphant poems on long rolls of paper. For the first time, he left notices proclaiming himself the "Taiping Heavenly King, Ruler of the Great Way." Hong proclaimed a new kingdom the Taiping Tianguo, or Heavenly Kingdom of Great Peace.

Over the following months, as the influence of the Taiping spread to the plains below, they moved from their mountain hideaway to a local prefectural township. Hong continued to travel and preach, but it had become so dangerous that he traveled only at night, in tightly knit groups using covered lanterns.

In February 1850, bandits attacked a local village and stole a buffalo used for plowing. The villagers retrieved the animal but the bandits returned the next day only to be beaten off by the Taiping forces camped there. In their hasty retreat, they left cane shields, boxes of gunpowder, and a stash of weapons. The people of the village were so grateful that they donated a large amount of grain to the Taiping, who used it to purchase more gunpowder and weapons, organizing themselves into an army controlled with signal flags, or "banners." Hong bought yellow robes and the Taiping began to manufacture rudimentary weapons at night, which they hid in ponds nearby.

The first open clash between the Taiping rebels and the Qing government occurred during a bandit suppression campaign. The Qing army had tried to capture a village by blockading the narrow mountain path that approached it with hundreds of sharpened bamboo stakes driven at an angle into the surrounding slopes. The Taiping forces attacked the Qing army from the rear, routing them and killing a magistrate. When the Qing sent a well-equipped army led by veteran officers to punish the rebels, the Taiping forces, swollen to ten thousand with new recruits and bandit allies, massed in three well-coordinated defensive positions and cut off the advancing battalions from the rear guard, breaking the Qing lines apart. When the commander's horse slipped on a bridge, he was cut to death by the Taiping, together with three hundred troops.

Fearing massive reprisals, the Taiping rebels abandoned their township and marched on the larger walled city of Yongan. There they bewildered the defenders by riding their few horses around the walls after nightfall, rattling large buckets of gravel to exaggerate their numbers and hurling lighted fireworks over the wall that they'd found in a storehouse in the suburbs. The next day, with the city's residents dazed and exhausted by the explosions and smoke, the Taiping sent scaling parties over the walls protected from the defenders by coffins held aloft on the end of long poles and crossing on ladders laid horizontally from the roofs of nearby houses that the defenders had failed to demolish. By the end of the day, eight hundred Qing solders lay dead. The Taiping had captured their first city.

Hong moved into the magistrate's courtyard. The exquisite gardens, the little pavilions, and the streams running under ornamental bridges must have seemed like an earthly paradise after subsistence living on Thistle Mountain. The Taiping seized the printing tablets in the magistrate's offices and began to issue proclamations, promising to restart the local markets, protect people from bandits, open public granaries, and punish anyone mistreating women. They sent parties out into the surrounding countryside to seize grain, cooking oil, salt, and livestock from the wealthy gentry and placed it in the public storehouses in the city. Those who fought bravely in battle were given hereditary privileges of wearing caps and gowns, ceremonial cowls, and horn-encrusted belts. Each of the senior Taiping leaders was given an honorific title; Hong, as Jesus's younger brother and second son of God, was called the Heavenly King; the key Taiping generals became the North, South, East, and West Kings; Hong's son was proclaimed the Young King.

Hong's forces, numbering more than twenty thousand, mounted a careful defense of the city, ringing the walls with outer earthworks and high wooden watchtowers for launching projectiles. They sent boats to patrol the surrounding rivers and canals. Meanwhile, forty-six thousand Qing troops gathered in a huge encampment to the southwest of the city and started on their own encircling earthworks around the Taiping's outer defenses. As the siege began to bite, the Taiping were driven to extract salt by boiling up and filtering the soil from the floors of the old salt depots, making saltpeter from the crushing of old bricks, and separating sulfurous chemicals for gunpowder by the boiling and evaporation of horse manure in alcohol.

Realizing that they could not hold the city, the Taiping fled through the East Gate under cover of darkness in a carefully planned exodus toward the mountains. The retreating soldiers left mines made out of wooden tubes packed with gunpowder and wrapped with flammable hay. Terrified pigs ran through the erratic explosions with pieces of metal and broken pots that the Taiping had tied to them clanging behind in long trails. But despite the diversions, the Qing killed two thousand Taiping that they caught in the rear guard. Enraged by the slaughter, the remaining Taiping army turned in its fury to face the enemy and, in the driving rain that had started to fall, they loaded heaps of rocks into hastily constructed bamboo cages tied to trees on the slopes that surrounded the narrow mountain pathways. As the Qing struggled up the rain-soaked passes, the Taiping cut the ropes holding the cages, crushing and maiming hundreds of soldiers. Then they fell upon their enemy with mines and projectiles, routing them completely and leaving five thousand dead.

Seizing uniforms, carts, and cannons from the dead Qing soldiers and a large supply of gunpowder, the Taiping rebels set off south, joined by a thousand jobless miners, expert at burrowing under walls and skilled in the use of explosives. But when they laid siege to the city of Guilin—which sits by the Li River among osmanthus groves and the peaks of strange cone-shaped mountains—they could not starve it out. Instead, they headed north along the rivers and locks that connect with central China. As they sailed past one of the Qing city-garrisons, a lone sniper idly fired a single shot toward an elaborate boat in the procession. The shot seriously wounded the occupant, Hong's loyal companion, the South King. Enraged, the Taiping armies smashed against the city walls in wave after wave, while the magistrate inside sent anguished pleas for reinforcements, written with his own blood. After ten days, the Taiping breached the gates and fell mercilessly on all those, inside killing everyone they could find.

Tired, relieved after the battle, feeling perhaps a little reckless, the Taiping seized more than two hundred boats and set off from the city, but after only five miles they blundered into a trap. At a fast-flowing bend, a local militia loyal to the Qing had driven iron posts into the riverbed and formed a barricade with tree trunks and logs cut from the steep and thickly wooded banks. As the Taiping became caught up in the barrier, the militia unleashed volleys of cannon shot and fire-tipped arrows, setting the boats on fire while those behind were carried helplessly toward the inferno. The fires spread from boat to boat, trapping the soldiers inside. Those who escaped floundered out toward the opposite bank, leaving ten thousand of their comrades burned or drowned.

The disaster nearly wiped them out, but the Taiping staggered on, capturing another town, recruiting another army, and marching on toward Changsha, the capital of Hunan Province. There they laid siege to the city, using pontoon boats to cross the moats. When the miners dug deep tunnels under the walls in order to pack them with explosives, the Qing defenders sank great wooden tubs into the ground and, using iron listening columns and blind men whose hearing was especially attuned, they located the sounds of picks and chisels each time the tunnels got close to the walls. Smashing the tunnels open from above, the Qing crushed the exhausted miners with great balls of iron or flushed them out with torrents of excrement. Of the ten major tunnels dug by the Taiping miners, only three reached the walls. Although the explosions there badly damaged them, the walls did not break and the Taiping could not take the city.

Abandoning a second siege, they seized thousands of boats and continued north, shaking off the Qing armies by going ashore at one landing point, crossing the highlands toward another river town, seizing new boats, and eventually reaching the Yangtse itself. On approaching Wuhan, the provincial capital of Hubei, instead of first attacking its huge walls and heavily guarded gateways they took the towns on the opposite bank of the river and waited. The governor, in preparation for a siege, burned all the houses outside the city walls so that their roofs could not be used as staging points to mount the walls with ladders. But despite the preparations, the defense crumbled and in the middle of June 1852, the Taiping gained their first great prize by seizing a provincial capital.

Inside, they found stores of immense wealth in the homes of the Qing officials. They commandeered the weapons from the armories and opened the prisons, freeing the inmates and recruiting them into the army. They raised tithes on the wealthy families—jewelry, silver ingots, rice, ducks, and tea—while the emperor in rage and despair showered his baffled and defeated officials with threats of appalling punishment.

Suddenly, unexpectedly, the Taiping left the city in a great armada of a thousand boats, sailing down the Yangtse toward the city of Nanjing. Past the six hundred miles of river garrisons, forts, and ancient watchtowers, the swollen ranks of the Taiping armies rushed in a mighty procession. Hong had set his eyes on the capital of China's richest province, Nanjing—the great "southern capital" of China—home of poets, philosophers, and scholars where the first Ming emperor had founded his dynasty five hundred years before.

The walls of Nanjing rose forty feet from the river flats of the Yangtse and encircled the city in an irregular ring twenty-five miles long. The Taiping laid siege to the city. They harried the defenders with sporadic attacks, they burrowed under the walls, they sapped the defenders' confidence with explosions and firecrackers, they sent agents inside to turn the inhabitants against the Qing. On March 19, 1853, the Taiping breached the walls with a series of massive explosions, one of which killed hundreds of their own men. After battering down the southern gate, they drove the Qing garrison of fifty thousand into the central citadel. When it eventually fell, the smoke rose and the killing continued for two days, until all were hunted down and slaughtered.

The following day, music burst out over the city. Hong Xiuquan, the lowly farmer boy, four times unsuccessful candidate for the prefectural exams, attired in yellow robes, was carried into the city on a great golden palanquin ornamented with five white cranes and borne aloft by sixteen men, while the people of Nanjing prostrated themselves on the ground. Hong had found his earthly paradise; the Taiping had reached their promised land.

In direct opposition to the emperor, Hong established a court with six ministries and fifty departments to oversee the granaries, the weaving workshops, the gunpowder factories, and the manufacture of war vessels and ceremonial robes. The walls of Nanjing were re-fortified, the gateways narrowed. Around the old porcelain pagoda that stood outside the walls, they built watchtowers and laid acres of close-spaced stakes of sharpened bamboo that lacerated shoes and flesh alike. Regulations poured forth from Hong and his ministries for prayers to be said at precise times of the day, for Bible studies, and for the strict separation of the sexes. Land was to be shared equally among the populace; families were required to rear two pigs and five chickens and to grow mulberry bushes in the shelter of their houses for the cultivation of silkworms. Printing presses were set up to publish the holy tracts; four hundred printers transcribed characters and carved printing blocks in the former temple to the Literature God.

Consumed by curiosity, the foreigners based in Shanghai sent investigators to Nanjing. A Frenchman wrote of the severed heads of opium smokers hanging in cages on the walls. He heard the ten cannon shots fired twice a day while the Heavenly King was at his prayers and calculated that there were a million or more within the city walls. When Captain Mellcrish, the British envoy, arrived on a ship called the *Rattler* and presented thirty questions, the Taiping responded with a list of fifty of their own: "What color is God's beard?" they asked, and "How rapidly can he compose verse?" After the Americans visited, they reported back to the secretary of state about the "melancholy spectacle of an enfeebled and tottering imperial government, ignorant, conceited, and impracticable, assailed at all points by a handful of insurgents, whose origin was as a band of robbers."

When Hong's armies finally marched on Beijing in open rebellion, the seventy thousand veteran fighters were pushed farther west than they planned by Qing defenses. Savage blizzards maimed many with frostbite but the armies came within three miles of the northern city of Tianjin, where Macartney had disembarked on his journey to Beijing several decades earlier. There they dug foxholes and ditches, built up giant earthworks, piling up dikes at strategic points, but they had made a fatal error in choosing the location. Using thousands of conscripted farmers, the Qing built long ditches to divert the waters of the Grand Canal toward a dried-up riverbed that ran through the Taiping encampment. After a month of digging, the Taiping camp turned to mud, then to a lake; gunpowder became sodden, muskets rusted and clogged, and, as the soldiers climbed onto makeshift rafts, they were picked off one by one and executed.

Toward the south, the rebellion continued in the strategic towns along the Yangtse and battles swirled across vast areas, lasting months and killing tens of thousands. Meanwhile, a vast Qing encampment gathered around the walls of Nanjing. The East King launched a massive counterattack and, amid savage fighting, the Qing were beaten back; again thousands died. But after the Taiping victory, a dispute broke out among their leaders when the East King, the main architect of the Taiping military victories, plotted to usurp Hong. Yet the Qing government was unable to take advantage even at a time when the Taiping were split by internal crises. Crippled by the cost of suppressing the uprising, the Qing faced other rebellions toward the north, where rebels had cut the Grand Canal, and had to cope with the slow drift toward war with the British over their insistence on opening trading ports. The imperial archives show that they were driven to melting down bells, ritual vessels, and Buddhist statues to make coins.

Somehow the Qing staggered on and mounted a siege of a Taiping city upstream on the Yangtse, starving it out by blockading the wharves used for unloading boats. Sixteen thousand were slaughtered. From this new base, the Qing advanced on Nanjing and captured one of the lookout camps around the porcelain pagoda outside the south gate of the city. There they began to build stockades and earthworks. When the Taiping troops returned to Nanjing, broken after an attempt to take Shanghai, they faced the Qing across the Yangtse River in full flood. The result, as described by a Western mercenary, was a catastrophe:

[U]pon the arrival of the famished and emaciated Taiping troops at the brink of the river, they were saluted with one continuous cannonade . . . with incredible fortitude they maintained their position, and did not flinch backwards in the face of the terrible fire poured into their dense masses at point blank range . . . the horrible thud of the cannon shot crashing continuously among the living skeletons . . . and the slow effort of exhausted survivors to extricate themselves from the mangled bodies of their stricken comrades were scenes awful to contemplate.

When the Qing commander finally succeeded in burrowing tunnels under the walls, a gigantic explosion hurled sixty yards of colossal masonry skyward and the Qing soldiers poured through the opening only to discover that Hong had already been dead for six weeks after succumbing to a sickness. The remaining Taiping soldiers were killed or fled from the burning city; one of the generals' horses collapsed and he was cut down mercilessly. Finally, after wandering for days without food, frightened and alone, Hong's son, the Young King, was robbed of his remaining clothes by one man and forced to carry bamboo by another. He was captured by the Qing and wrote a short confession, in which he asked to be allowed to take the imperial exams. When he was executed shortly afterward, the revolt by the Taiping Heavenly Kingdom finally ended.

The suffering and misery of the ordinary people caught in the crossfire of those fourteen terrible years was recorded by a missionary writing in the newspaper the *North China Herald*. On arriving at a township and meeting the rebel commander, he wrote:

I had often passed along these streets before. A great change had taken place; where there were once crowded thoroughfares, now all is desolation. The houses are in ruins; the streets are filled with filth; human bodies are left to decay in the open places or thrown into pools or cisterns there to rot. Out of more than a million of the native inhabitants of Suchau city, I was told that not more than thirty thousand remain inside the walls. Once I lived in this city and was familiar with its beautiful scenery. But now, oh, how fallen! how wretched! The people . . . now sit in the dust, sorrowing without hope; their wealth, their pride, their glory all gone . . . the bodies and bones of the dead were mingled in indiscriminate confusion with broken and charred fragments of idols . . . it is emphatically a place of skulls. Human bones lie bleaching among cannon balls and other warlike debris.

The next day, a Sunday, as the missionary preached, he noticed in the audience

several on whose faces had been tattooed the words *Taiping Tianguo*. Some had cut out these four words with a knife and inserted quicklime into the wound in order to obliterate the hateful mark [that had been] set upon the faces of deserters.

During the rebellion, he recalled that he had witnessed a ceremony on a raised platform surrounded by flags and spears in which the rebel commander made a speech:

The Celestial Father has sent the Heavenly King to rule over us, and to subdue all the hills and rivers to his dominion. All you country people, should listen reverently to the commands of the King. From the earliest time to the present, when dynasties were changed, the people were made to suffer . . . the previous distress and suffering which you have endured were sent to you by the Will of Heaven. They are now past, to return no more . . . you have eaten the bitter, now you shall enjoy the sweet.

How many times had that promise been heard through the ages from peasant warlords whose eyes were set upon the Dragon Throne?

THE SECOND CHINESE RULE

Although there was no formal census at the time, scholars esti-mate that the death toll from the Taiping Rebellion was more than 20 million. In the final battle for Nanjing, a hundred thousand died in just three days; fires burned inside the city for three months. If these estimates are correct—and some scholars put the figures much higher—the toll of the Taiping Rebellion is comparable to Hitler's war on Russia. But where Hitler unleashed the full force of mechanized tanks and aircraft, the toll in China was inflicted mostly by spears and hatchets, bamboo cages filled with rocks, famine, and tunnels chipped away with picks and chisels and packed with barrels of gunpowder.

The Taiping Rebellion is not unique; these catastrophes of un-imaginable violence have occurred at regular intervals in China's long history. Ever since its first unification in 221 BC, China has alternated between periods of stability, when the arts and soci-ety flourished, and times of chaos, when China sank into famine, plague, rebellion, and war. When the Tang Dynasty ruled in the eighth and ninth centuries AD, China reached a peak of cultural achievement. Many of China's greatest poets, painters, and calligra-phers lived at that time. Buddhism flourished, having been brought from India centuries earlier. The state was capable of fixing grain prices so that the granaries were well stocked. It built sea defenses, canals for transportation and trade, and huge irrigation projects that supported intensive agriculture.

According to a census in AD 761, the Tang capital had almost two million citizens, making it the largest city on earth. But the dynasty collapsed with two major rebellions, each lasting a decade, when China sank back into chaos and war and millions died. Regional warlords fought over what became known as the "Five Dynasties and Ten Kingdoms."

Reunited in 960 at least partially by the Song, China became the first state to issue paper banknotes and to use gunpowder in battle. It invented movable-type printing and the mass production of books. There were leaps in the iron industry, astronomy, and medicine. But the Song were split apart before being overthrown by Genghis Khan when the Mongols founded the Yuan Dynasty in 1279. The Yuan in turn were toppled by rebels a hundred years later, when the Ming founded a new dynasty that was to rule for three centuries, first from Nanjing and later from the Forbidden City.

Founded by a poor peasant from Anhui, the Ming was one of the greatest eras of orderly government and social stability in human history. China reached new heights in the production of porcelain. It planted millions of trees in massive reforestation campaigns; it constructed canals, dikes, and irrigation ditches over vast areas and greatly increased agricultural production through the redistribution of land. It connected and refortified the Great Wall into its present state. But the Ming in turn collapsed into chaos after rebellion and a series of natural disasters—including the most destructive earthquake in history—and ruinous inflation that bankrupted farmers and left them unable to pay taxes. When the gates to the Forbidden City were treacherously opened to an invading rebel army, the last Ming emperor, having looked into the state coffers and found nothing but dusty receipts, hanged himself on a tree on Coal Hill in what is now the park that I had visited so often as a student. The emperor left a note behind that said, "Having no dignity to face my ancestors, I take off my crown and cover my face with hair. Mutilate my body as you wish, but do not harm a single civilian."

These long cadences and rhythms that have beat through China's history for more than two thousand years have framed Chinese ideas about government. The Chinese have watched great achievements in art and literature, science and society, be trampled upon in times of chaos and pushed toward the next abyss. These cycles have imbued the Chinese with a heightened fear of chaos. There's even a particular expression in Chinese for these episodes of periodic collapse—*da luan*. Chinese know that chaos will inevitably return, so the single, overriding objective of the state is to postpone it for as long as possible.

Here we have the Second Rule:

China's historical experience has left its people with an intense dread of instability. China is not so tightly bound together by anything more than a common acceptance of its Chineseness. Officials seek stability above all else and this drives policy in every corner of China's vast bureaucracy. There is no brooding and all-powerful tyrant at the center; China is as loose as a sheet of sand. All but the strongest and most diligent emperors had their edicts routinely thwarted. The tenth Ming emperor wrote in the sixteenth century, "We live deep within the Nine-Walled Palace, and though We stretch Our thoughts over the entire realm, there are places where Our ears and eyes do not reach." Red-topped instructions from the State Council may have replaced the vermillion brushstrokes of the emperor but policy can still be best understood as a ceaseless search for order. The Chinese ruler is engaged in a constant struggle for unity, balancing priorities in different sections of society to maintain overall stability rather than just issuing directives from above. Whether it is in balancing the rapidly growing wealth along the coast with the needs of China's poorer western regions, or reforming state-owned enterprises but at the same time providing jobs and social security, the Chinese ruler must seek harmony; this endless struggle against chaos is visible in almost every government strategy. Public protests occur in China every day and officials risk punishment for failing to cope with unrest. In our specific case, the income from carbon reductions at refrigerant plants in China was big enough to upset the balance in sections of the whole chemicals industry, so officials would not just wave through Wang's application for carbon income—they felt compelled to consider the other factories in the north of China rather than just let Wang take the money. China is engaged in a timeless quest for stability. Almost every action of the government and the individuals within it can be understood and predicted in that light.

8

修學好古　實事求是

LEARN FROM THE PAST;
SEEK TRUTH FROM FACTS

—The Book of Han, *biography of He Jian Xian, c. AD 100*

The evening we arrived back in Beijing from the signing ceremony in Quzhou, the roads around Houhai Lake were covered with a thin sheen of rainwater and the air was thick with damp. Throughout the summer months, usually in the late afternoon, thunderclouds often roll over the mountains that surround the northern edges of Beijing, bringing torrential rains that clear just before dusk, leaving the city scrubbed and pink as the sun sets over the hills in the west. The traffic had been at a standstill for nearly half an hour that evening while a knot of policemen gathered around a pileup a few hundred meters ahead. Seven or eight cars had skidded gracefully into each other on the slippery film of water; as the last car thudded into the back of the queue, it nudged the one in front up and over the central barrier. There it hung, finely balanced, rocking gently back and forth, with exhaust and axles exposed to the view of the pedestrians and bicyclists who had gathered to gawk at the spectacle.

Mina had gotten out of the taxi and marched to the front to direct the traffic herself, but it was already too late; scores of drivers had already abandoned their cars, each giving contradictory advice about how to get the traffic moving again, so she had given up the attempt to restore order and sat, fuming quietly, in the backseat. Fortunately, no one was hurt, but the Beijing government has a rule that cars involved in collisions must remain in place until the police arrive to apportion blame and decide who can claim on insurance. The rule causes yet lengthier delays in a city already plagued by spectacular traffic jams that consume whole mornings and leave drivers weak from nervous exhaustion before they even get to work. I reckoned we were in for a long wait so I pushed down in the front seat, loosened the seat belt, leaned back, and closed my eyes.

After the trip to Quzhou, Mina and I had flown together with Chain-smoking Chen back to Beijing, where he had meetings arranged with the Department of Climate Change. We'd hired a taxi together at the airport and planned to drop him at his hotel before spending a couple of hours in a quiet bar near the Drum Tower, where we could get started on writing up a business plan.

The "No Name Bar" sits on the bank of Houhai Lake next to the Silver Ingot Bridge, a Ming Dynasty arch of white marble that spans a narrow channel feeding into the lake. Rickshaws clog the narrow *hutong*s that sprawl around the banks and during the late summer months, the waters there are scattered with the leaves and fleshy pink petals of lotus flowers poking through the floating greenery. It's a perfect place to think, relax, and watch the fishermen casting their hooks from underneath the shade of the weeping willow trees. But we were still another mile or so from Chain-smoking Chen's hotel and time was getting late. The taxi driver had tried to dodge down a side street to avoid the backup, but it was blocked with delivery vans and bicycles. We were stuck in gridlock and bored. I dozed off for a moment but woke with a start a few minutes later; my mind soon drifted back toward planning a new business.

I knew that we'd come late to the market, but with the right financial backer, I thought, we could probably catch up. We needed a credible investor, one known and respected in China. I went through the more obvious sources of capital—banks, trading houses, brokers, and so on—but then suddenly a thought sprang to mind. "Chen," I said, "you ever heard of Goldman Sachs?"

"I think so," he said. "Isn't it one of those big American banks?"

Madame Taxi Driver nodded vaguely in assent as she took a leisurely drag on a "Red Pagoda" cigarette, while Mina fidgeted around in the back.

"How about Banque Paribas?" I said. There was a sniff from the back, but no response.

"Or Credit Suisse?" I continued. Chain-smoking Chen thought he might have heard of them but Madame Taxi Driver shook her head, flicked some ash out of the window, and spat.

"How about Merrill?"

"Nope."

"UBS?"

"Never heard of it."

"Morgan Stanley?"

Madame Taxi Driver perked up when she heard the name Morgan.

"It's a steel company in America," she said, taking a big slurp of tea from the jam jar wedged by the hand brake and wiping her mouth with an old towel.

It wasn't a bad guess; as well as giving his name to the bank, Morgan had bought up most of the steel industry in the States during the early 1900s and built United States Steel.

"How about HSBC?" I said. "Or Standard Chartered?"

"Maybe," she said.

"How about Barcap?"

"No."

"Macbank?"

"Who?"

"SocGen?"

"Nar."

"Citigroup?"

A sigh from the back. After a few moments, I said, "How about Bill Gates, then?"

"Gates? Of course I heard spoken of him!" said Madame Taxi
Driver. "He is Microsoft's head. He last month at Beijing University
made a speech!"

The Bill & Melinda Gates Foundation is the largest charitable organization in the world, with almost $70 billion available to im-
prove health care, widen access to education, and tackle the causes
of poverty. Bill Gates is an iconic figure in China—almost a household name in the big cities—and his face appears regularly on news-
stands and on the covers of magazines. I remembered saturation
news coverage a year earlier when Hu Jintao, then president of
China, stopped off in Seattle for dinner at Gates's house on his way
to the White House. I wasn't surprised that Madame Taxi Driver
had picked out his name from the list of faceless banks. In China,
individuals are often more recognizable than the organizations they
work for and Gates is an icon for the millions of people dreaming of
riches in provincial towns throughout China. Admired as a maver-
ick who bombed out of college, he had bucked the system and built
one of the most successful businesses on the planet. And, of course,
he is also very, very rich.

Gates and his wife, Melinda, started the foundation after they
read an article about millions of children dying each year in poorer
countries from diseases that had been eliminated long ago in the
West. The article mentioned one disease they had never heard of
caused by rotavirus, which was killing five hundred thousand children every year. At the time they thought, "That's got to be a typo.
If a single disease was killing that many kids, we'd have heard about
it, because it would have been front-page news." But it wasn't a typo;
and the article forced them toward the conclusion that we live in
a world where some lives seem worth saving while others are not.
Spurred into action, they established the foundation with a gift of
several tens of billions of dollars to try to do something about it. A
few years later, Warren Buffett topped it up with another $30 bil-
lion.

The foundation makes grants of hundreds of millions each year in medical research, education, and in projects for the eradication of disease and poverty in the poorest parts of the world. With such huge amounts of money, the foundation sometimes finds itself criticized in the press for being too powerful, but I found that to be like "looking for bones in an egg," as the Chinese would say, or deliberately trying to find fault. To me there is something optimistic and inspiring about the way the foundation had been put together. The benefactors have insisted that all their billions must be spent within fifty years of the end of their lives, showing not only an urgency but confidence that something meaningful can be achieved in that time frame. They've also inspired other wealthy donors to help realize what the foundation calls "the great human promise that all lives have equal value."

The organization operates in two completely separate parts. The foundation employs hundreds of people who select the projects for charitable giving, while the other, called the trust, works independently at a separate location investing the remaining billions. The job of the trust is to protect and grow the value of these funds and maximize the amounts available for future charitable giving. Several years earlier, I had visited the trust when they were thinking about backing an investment program in China.

On that first trip back in 2004, I had no idea what to expect. I remember feeling slightly intimidated as I arrived in Seattle to meet the people managing a fund of such awesome power and size, but my apprehension quickly gave way to curiosity as I arrived at some well-kept lakeside offices and couldn't find my way in. There were no signs to say who might be inside. Eventually I found an elevator, went upstairs, and came out into a corridor with a line of unmarked doors along one side. After a few minutes of wandering up and down looking for a receptionist, I pressed a buzzer next to one of the doors and waited. With a click it opened onto a large open-plan office with a spectacular view across the lake. On the other side of a strip of blue water, giant redwoods stood behind a narrow shingle beach with their furrowed, rust-colored trunks towering more than a hundred feet above the shoreline. Nearer there was a small harbor with brightly painted wooden jetties; the waves lapped gently against a cluster of sailboats bobbing about in the breeze.

Sunlight streamed through the windows onto about eighteen people sunk deep in concentration in front of computer screens. Thick carpets deadened all sound, but as I took in the sight of these people immersed in their work, it was easy to imagine a low hum, the sound of their brains working as they tracked the billions of dollars through luminous graphs and charts that flashed on the screens in front of them.

On that first trip I met with a small group of people led by a man named Jerry, who'd been an economics professor before moving into business. His team had seemed more interested in getting a feel for what it was really like living and working in China than in discussing any particular project. They had asked questions about China's geography and the state of its environment, the conditions for ordinary people in the towns and countryside, how the government planned to deepen reform in the financial sector, and whether the benefits of China's economic boom had really trickled down to street level. The meeting must have gone well; a few weeks later, they invited me back.

Jerry had originally trained in economics and statistics at a college in California, continuing through postgrad and teaching as a professor in Los Angeles before moving into business. Several years later, he found himself at the head of one of the biggest savings and loans businesses in California, leading it out of near bankruptcy after a financial crisis hit the industry in the late eighties. Jerry had refocused on the core business of careful lending and pulled the business back from the edge. Several years later, he had been coaxed out of retirement to join the Gates Foundation trust, which was run by one of his former students. Mild mannered and meticulously polite, Jerry had a sort of folksy charm, a slightly aw-shucks approach to problems. He'd probe complicated issues with simple, well-aimed questions and he would never be pushed into a conclusion; he took the time to think. He'd show up at meetings with a large mug of Starbucks in one hand and a blueberry muffin in the other, wearing a checked cotton twill shirt with an open neck. Sometimes I thought he'd fit more easily into a scene with a flickering fire, piles of leather books, and the singey smell of toasted tea cakes with a group of attentive children gathered around his feet rather than an office that managed $70 billion worth of assets.

At the second meeting, Jerry had invited a group of professors along from a local college; over the following months, we exchanged ideas about setting up an investment fund in China, but in the end it didn't come off. After these first contacts, we had kept vaguely in touch, so when I came across the carbon markets several years later, I immediately thought of Jerry. It was the kind of esoteric, cerebral investment that might produce a good return for someone prepared to put in the time to think it through properly.

Mina and I had sketched out a brief business plan in the No Name Bar, so I wrote it up and sent it over to Jerry in Seattle. Trying to raise money for a new business is always a long shot so I hadn't expected much of a response. But after I got back from a trip to central China a week later, I found a message in my inbox as I downloaded my email using a rickety pay-as-you-go computer at the airport. The message mentioned that the team in Seattle had looked briefly at the carbon markets a year earlier when a colleague had been assessing a power company for investment. They said that they thought some sort of cap-and-trade carbon system was here to stay and there was a short list of questions. The message ended by asking, "Can you give us a feel for your ideal timing in this matter? Though we are not encumbered by committees or paperwork, we will need some time to reply thoughtfully." It was an encouraging start.

Over the coming weeks, the pace of the exchanges picked up and the questions became more detailed. We had several conference calls and, after a couple of months, Jerry called to say that we were making real progress; he asked me to propose a draft agreement for establishing a fund of a hundred million euros.

With such rapid progress toward turning the ideas that Mina and I had sketched out in the No Name Bar into a reality, I took a moment to draw a breath. Before we finally went forward, I wanted to take a better look at the fundamentals; deep down, I felt unsure about the science of climate change. If I was planning to risk some-one else's money, I had to be sure in my own mind that we were not going to be investing in a scientific hallucination.

As I started reading up on climate change, I quickly discovered that most of the discussion in the press isn't about the science at all; it's about politics. On one side, we get reports about activists blockad-ing power stations and protesting against globalization, while on the other, the skeptics try to claim that climate change is just an enormous swindle by left-wing academics. Neither side seems espe-cially interested in the science. For people like Senator James Inhofe of Oklahoma, who called man-made global warming "the greatest hoax ever perpetrated on the American people," "green" is just the new Red.

So I started reading up in academic journals, going back to the original papers. I'm no climate expert, but I read physics at univer-sity so I'm not put off by technical language or numbers.

It's fair to say that—on average—mountain glaciers are shrink-ing, and we've all seen the footage of polar ice sheets collapsing into the sea. In Siberia, the permafrost is melting. Insects are migrating northward. In Finland, a river where records have been kept for centuries now melts earlier in the springtime than when the records began. But the question is whether these changes are part of natural cycles or whether they result from human activity.

There are plenty of facts we can "learn from the past" that show temperature changes that could not have been caused by humans. Song Dynasty ledgers show citrus orchards and ramie fields grow-ing much farther north than today; there are studies of sediments in lakes, different layers of snow in ice sheets, and the buildup of deposits in stalagmites. In a high mountain pass in the Alps, nearly four hundred items have been excavated from as far back as Neo-lithic times—shoes, clothes, pots, and hunting equipment—and the dating of those objects shows that they had all originated in separate, narrow bands of time. Archeologists think that the pass had been open as a trade route when the glaciers had melted, but then froze over again and became impassable. These cycles of freezing over and remelting lasted for six thousand years, so they could not have been caused by humans.

One theory about natural climate change links it to solar activity. Sunspots were first recorded in the Book of Han in AD 28, when Chinese astronomers observed them through the dust storms of Central Asia. The idea that climate could be linked to sunspots is more than two hundred years old; a German-born astronomer first proposed a connection between sunspots and grain prices in 1801. But there are arguments for human influence on climate as well.

The level of CO_2 in the atmosphere started increasing in the Industrial Revolution and, since the 1950s, it has been measured directly. The tendency of the atmosphere to trap heat was first shown experimentally in the late 1850s and linked to CO_2 in 1938, so none of these ideas are new. Since then, scientists have investigated links between CO_2 levels in the atmosphere and the temperature of the earth by drilling deep ice cores in the Antarctic Plateau, where the ice sheet is nearly three miles thick. The expanse of windswept ice there is the most lifeless place on earth, without plants or animals, where the sun sets in March and rises again the following September. As snow fell throughout the ages, the flakes packed down into layers of ice, trapping tiny bubbles of air and forming a long file of atmospheric records. The lockstep correlation of CO_2 levels and atmospheric temperature found in the ice cores over four hundred thousands years is unmistakable, but a correlation doesn't mean a cause. The correlation does not prove that high CO_2 *causes* high temperatures; it could be the other way around, or they could both depend on something else.

It was the research papers on "abrupt climate change" that convinced me there was a problem. The paper described the earth's climate as a finely balanced system where even small changes in factors influencing it can lead to large-scale disturbances. Small changes become magnified into large-scale trends by feedbacks in the climate system; for example, the polar ice caps act like giant white reflectors, sending the sun's energy back into space. As they melt, more energy gets absorbed by the darker exposed surface, which melts more ice and in turn absorbs more heat. Vast deposits of methane lie trapped under the oceans and the thin layer of permafrost that covers the Siberian plateau. The endless expanse of peat bogs there are turning into a mash of fermenting organic matter and stagnant ponds. Oil rigs sink, gas pipelines bend and twist, and as they melt, the peat bogs release enormous quantities of methane into the air, which traps more heat energy and accelerates the process.

The arguments are bound to continue, but I reckon that since we derive all our energy in some way or other from the huge thermo-nuclear fireball in the sky, it seems simplistic to think that the earth's climate wouldn't be affected by what goes on inside the sun. On the other hand, if you spend a couple of centuries digging up millions of years' worth of carbon deposits and then burning them into the sky, it is naïve to think that nothing will change. And just because there has been natural climate change in the past, that doesn't mean that man won't affect it in the future; the question is in the degree.

Policy depends on risk; if the idea of abrupt climate change is right, then we are living in an unstable, finely balanced climate system with huge reserves of natural carbon balanced on top of pin-heads. In the long run, governments aren't just going to ignore that. But in the short term it is impractical to close down coal-fired power stations and tell everybody to stop using cars. The world needs to wean itself off fossil fuels, and deep down everybody knows that; the question is how it might be done. Alternative energy sources are being developed in the rich economies, but at the same time, huge new infrastructures are being built in the developing world with cheap, old-fashioned high-carbon technology.

In the coming decades, the populations of the low- and middle-income countries will rise from five billion to roughly nine, while the population in the developed world will be roughly static. The

developing world has already begun to pass through a similar process of industrialization as the one Europe and America did a hundred and fifty years ago. The vast new infrastructures being built in
South America, the Middle East, and Asia will be in use for at least a
century; so if the rich world could find some way to help developing
countries put in low-carbon infrastructures now, it could end up
avoiding a far larger amount of carbon emissions than could ever be
achieved in their own economies at home.

I knew that the UN Clean Development Mechanism wasn't perfect, but it did seem to provide some hope of getting rich nations
to contribute to the cost of the developing world choosing more
sustainable options. We decided to go ahead

The reading took me most of the summer. In October, I got a call
from Jerry to say that they had agreed to our proposed term sheet.
Mina had been chomping at the bit for months and had identified
several promising targets in China. She wanted to go ahead and sign
up the Chinese counterparties right away and worry about the details later, but I was more cautious; the new business would take time
to establish and I didn't want to make promises we couldn't keep. At
the end of the year, we went to Seattle and the deal started to coalesce. As the new business started to become a reality, we started
to think about putting together an office in Beijing, so I made a call
to an old colleague.

"Michael," I said, "can I tempt you into one last adventure in
China?"

I'd first worked with Michael twenty years earlier, when our paths
crossed in Australia; later he'd spent time at one of London's biggest
investment houses. After I'd teamed up with the American banker
in the mid-nineties, I'd persuaded Michael to join us as we waded
into the chaotic world of Chinese investment. For nearly ten years,
we had worked our way through all the problems with our Chinese
partners, recovering a lot of value from the mess once we'd figured
out what to do. A year or so after I had left to do "distressed invest-

ing," Michael joined an HR consultancy. I figured that he might be bored there; he was far more methodical than I was, more suited to detailed planning. He was objective and shrewd, less emotional than me, but what he really enjoyed most was building a business from scratch. He also had an offbeat, deadpan sense of humor that could defuse the odd moment of tension, so I knew he'd be good to have around. "If you sign up to this," I told him, "your role is to take all these half-assed ideas Mina and I have about carbon and transform them into a business." He signed up and ran the operations for the next five years.

Mina brought on board a friend who had been working in an environmental consultancy in Beijing. Cissy had studied Chinese at a university in England and had a feel for China. She was comfortable down at street level and as happy in a coking plant or a rolling mill as in one of Beijing's most expensive nightclubs. She'd traveled widely through the country; she was bright, charismatic, and knew instinctively how to win over the grittiest Chinese cadre with her easy banter and self-deprecating charm. When Cissy joined up, she had all the enthusiasm of a young and talented saleswoman fresh out of college and determined to nail her first deal. But she soon grew into a wider role; her natural buoyancy was good for morale and, while she had no formal background in science or engineering, I was impressed with how quickly she learned to handle the more technical side of the business.

The third key member of the team was a Chinese national whose hometown was Harbin, up in the frozen north; Frank had worked in the Chinese Foreign Ministry for ten years before moving into business. When we first met him, he was working in a factory in the south, where he had to deal with a large, poorly educated workforce miles away from home. He was frustrated and it didn't strike me that he was in the right place. Frank was considered, thoughtful, cautious, suited to the careful deliberations needed at the Foreign Ministry. Slightly cerebral, he was a perfect person to navigate the differences between foreigners and Chinese and find a point of balance; in such a new and unfamiliar field, I knew that problems were inevitable. Frank signed up and for the next five years, he and Cissy formed the core of the team out in the field, her more forceful and instinctive, impulsive nature balanced by Frank's careful, cautious Chinese style.

The following February, I got an email from Jerry in Seattle saying that they'd received final approval to commit €50 million to our new business. I sent an email back saying, "Forgive my brass neck, but could you make it a hundred?" A couple of hours later, they agreed. After another three weeks, we signed the formal documents and found ourselves with €100 million to deploy in China. We were euphoric, of course, but deep down, I was torn. We were about to embark on a groundbreaking new venture in China but I felt a gnawing anxiety. I knew that whatever the future might hold, this business was going to take me away from my family and back into China's chaotic churn.

9

苔花如米小　也學牡丹開

THE FLOWERS ON A LIVERWORT MAY BE AS SMALL AS A GRAIN OF RICE, BUT THEY STILL WANT TO BLOSSOM LIKE A PEONY

—Line of Qing Dynasty poetry, Yuan Mei (1716–1797)

Just as we signed the formal contracts in 2007, the news broke that China had become the world's largest carbon emitter. We threw ourselves into a burst of activity. Mina started by calling all of her old contacts from her days at the World Bank. She had a stack of name cards from local Chinese entrepreneurs who had entered the carbon markets early on. Some of them had teamed up with local science institutes in the provinces and seemed willing to work with us. I knew that there were hundreds of coal mines, power plants, and iron foundries across China that used antiquated equipment. With €100 million under management, we were confident of finding Chinese partners that needed help with improving energy efficiency and reducing their carbon footprints.

Mina flew off to Hubei and spent several days in a steelworks looking at heat exchangers before heading to Canton to visit a solar park. Cissy traveled south to see a group of wind farms and then north into the deserts of Gansu to visit a water treatment plant attached to a paper mill. Frank came back feeling hungover from a trip to a coal mine that planned to capture methane from the mineshafts and use it to drive generators, while Michael went off to Wuhan to look at blueprints for generators powered by animal waste. We found municipal heating projects in Inner Mongolia, and farther south, in Jiangxi, there was a plant converting cement kilns to use chemical waste instead of limestone. In remote country villages, local officials were building boilers that used rice husks instead of coal and installing fermenters that produced gas from pig waste for cooking stoves. All of these projects needed financing.

The UN will only issue carbon credits after a lengthy vetting process. Each project needs to apply for registration at the UN with a document in a standard format showing the calculation of expected CO_2 emission reductions and proving that the project could never have been financed without the extra income that it would get from selling credits. All the details in the document had to be checked and certified by an independent expert called a "validator" before the project could be submitted to the UN. This "validation" process was strict and we had to be sure that all the data was properly backed up. Obtaining the validator's certificate was a key step in the UN registration process.

As we conducted our own checking of potential projects, questions piled up. Several project developers had engaged local science institutes to help them prepare the technical information for the validator's audit, but these local research groups had no experience of applying for carbon credits and found it difficult to prepare documents in a format that the foreign validators wanted to see. We became caught up in arguments with the technical institutes over small presentational issues but there were more serious problems as well. Sometimes the factories hadn't kept complete records, but rather than tell us that, they just cobbled together new documents, where the figures often didn't agree to the original government approvals. Other projects turned out to be completely impractical; we found a plant in Shijiazhuang that tried to burn municipal waste to generate electricity, but the rubbish collected in the cities of northern China in the winter was often so damp that it wouldn't burn. A steel mill in Shanxi tried to capture the heat from the top of the blast furnace to drive a boiler, but they could only get it running in hot weather. Other projects were profitable in their own right and could be financed using ordinary bank loans, so they didn't meet the UN's requirements for claiming extra income from credits. Copies of Chinese approval documents had to be submitted to the UN, but often key certificates were missing or the dates were out of order, with construction starting months in advance of the approval certificates from the authorities. As the weeks passed, each of the projects started to fall apart in our hands, one by one.

In an effort to stop our wheels spinning, we decided to focus all of our efforts in one technical area to try to build up some expertise. China burns more coal than any other country in the world, and numerous projects across the country involved switching to less carbon-intensive power sources. The main effort was in electricity generation, where there was a shift toward renewables—mainly hydroelectric power and biomass—as well as projects that tried to recover heat that was being wasted in the steel industry and use it to generate power and reduce the need for coal-fired electricity. I hoped that this new focus on the power industry might finally help us get traction.

Soon I was visiting some hydroelectric plants in the central province of Hubei. We had been talking to a local businessman down there called Hou; several years earlier, Hou had been a rising star in the Guangxi provincial government, until his boss, the vice governor, made national headlines by being executed. At a dramatic trial, his mistress cut a last-minute deal with the prosecution, switched sides, and testified against him, blowing the cover off a tale that involved bags of expensive jewelry, millions stashed away in secret foreign bank accounts, and elaborate parties in backstreet massage parlors, where scantily clad women leapt in and out of hot tubs together with Party secretaries. He was convicted of extorting money from local businesses, appealed, lost, and was executed in the space of a few weeks, and that was the end of that. Although there was never any suggestion that Hou himself had been involved in any wrongdoing, he was damned by association. Forced to abandon any ambition of becoming a senior official, Hou set up his own business and began developing emission reduction projects in Hubei.

Hou had been unusually persistent, turning up in the office every few weeks, chatting away for a couple of hours and pressing us to visit his projects. He told us that he was working with a hydroelectric company up in the mountains in northern Hubei. The company needed financing and the managers wanted to develop carbon income to support their application for bank loans to build five new hydroelectric plants. Hou had been appointed as their agent. The projects were located in the Wudang Mountains, on the edge of the plateau that rolls north from the banks of the Yangtse; hundreds of rivers and streams cascade through the craggy mountainsides on their journey south, so the region is ideal for hydroelectric power.

The city of Wudang is famous throughout China for martial arts and the temples attract students from all over the world. Stone bridges span the green canals that run between the temple courtyards, and, on the surrounding hills, the floors of ancient pine forests are carpeted with strange medicinal plants. A Taoist monk famous for his enormous hat settled in Wudang after watching a crane fighting with a snake. Greatly impressed by the snake's defensive movements, he founded the temple and spent the rest of his life developing the soft martial art form of *tai chi*.

When Hou came to Beijing to explain his projects, I'd told him very clearly that we didn't want to get involved in the construction of new dams. Although hydropower is cleaner and much less carbon intensive than coal-fired electricity, the reservoirs caused by dams often force local farmers off their land, ruin the natural habitat for animals and birds, and become clogged with vegetation. We asked him to look for "run-of-river" projects, which use long tunnels through mountains rather than dams to create the pressure to drive the turbines. Run-of-river hydro projects not only avoid the problems caused by flooding, but they also have a better safety record.

Dam building in China has been transformed in recent decades, but I couldn't forget reading about a dam failure in a township called Banqiao in central China. Several large dams were built in the valleys there in the early fifties; the main dam wall was more than three hundred feet high and nearly a mile long, but when cracks appeared around the sluice gates a few years later, they were just patched up. It was in the middle of the Great Leap Forward and the whole country was distracted by a campaign to make steel.

In August 1975, a violent storm sent rain lashing down around Banqiao for sixteen hours; two days later, the storms returned. When the unit of the People's Liberation Army guarding the dam tried to release the flow, they found that the sluice gates in the dam wall had silted up. When they sent a flood warning to the local government, there was no response, so they sent up flares, which were misinterpreted. The water was rising rapidly, so the unit requested permission to relieve the pressure by breaking one end of the dam wall by an air strike; however, communications had been cut when the torrential rains brought down telegraph wires.

Just after midnight, a smaller dam farther up the valley broke open and water surged down into the Banqiao reservoir. There is a story that an old woman in one of the work brigades was desperately shoveling gravel and sand to shore up the earthworks. As she saw the main dam wall break open, she shouted above the roar of the water, "*Chu jiaozi!*"—The river dragon has come!—before she was swept away by the torrent. A large section of the dam wall collapsed and a flood wave cascaded down the valley, breaking another sixty-two smaller dams downstream.

A wall of water up to thirty feet high and several miles wide surged down the valley at thirty miles per hour, wiping out everything in its way. The village of Daowencheng was obliterated, killing the nine thousand inhabitants at a stroke. Farther down the valley, at Wencheng, half of the thirty-six thousand people there were killed. More than a billion tons of water poured down the valley and, by morning, everything inside a strip thirty miles long and ten miles wide was destroyed; seven county seats had disappeared under the lakes that formed in the valleys. Tens of thousands of people were washed for miles into downstream provinces. Over the following days, the air force bombed the remaining dams with air strikes to release the water into controlled areas; nine days later there were still more than a million people trapped without food.

Having explained the problems with flooding and silting and re-counting the story of Banqiao—which Hou knew as well as I did—I figured that he'd be able to understand why we wanted to avoid dam-building projects and focus only on run-of-river hydro instead.

When I flew down to Wuhan a few days later to visit the hydro company, Hou was nowhere to be seen. A driver had come to the airport to collect me; after we'd been driving for an hour, I was hungry and expecting to arrive shortly, so I asked how much longer it would take to get to the meeting. I was slightly irritated when he told me that it was a nine-hour drive. We had already been looking for projects for many months and time was at a premium. Jerry and his team at the trust were patient, but I knew that they couldn't wait indefinitely for us to find deals, and the pressure had started to build. The driver told me that his instructions were to take me directly to the project company, which was located high up in the hills. Hou would meet us there, he said.

We didn't arrive until shortly after midnight but Hou took me straight into a meeting room, presented me with a bowl of fruit, and invited the managers to start out on a description of the projects. They had plans to build a series of hydroelectric power projects in the valleys around the township, but they seemed a bit evasive when I probed for details. The next morning, as we drove up through woodlands to the first site, the sun shone from a cloudless sky. As the car came round a bend in the road, we arrived at the bottom of an enormous concrete wall about fifty feet high and clambered up to the top along a set of metal steps at one end. Behind the barrage, there was a lake extending about half a mile upstream surrounded by softly rolling slopes covered with trees and flowering shrubs. I turned to Hou and said, "I thought we said we wouldn't do dams, Mr. Hou." Then, after a short pause, I said, "This is a dam, isn't it?"

"Only a small one," he replied after a while.

I looked out over the lake. It was a beautiful spring morning. Birds flitted between the azaleas along the banks; fish moved lazily in the shallows. After a few moments staring up into the sky, I sighed and turned to Mr. Hou and said, "I think it's time to go home now."

Hou was a cheerful man and took this latest setback in stride, chattering away in the car for the nine hours it took to get back to Wuhan with all the good-natured optimism of the Chinese entrepreneur. It was not the first time I'd traveled halfway across China only to find a proposition that was impractical for foreign investment. Perhaps it's just the consequence of a natural Chinese optimism where they'll try anything just to see if it works, but for sure this characteristic ends up wasting a vast amount of time.

After the disappointments with hydropower, we turned our attention to steel, where there were big opportunities to capture wasted heat energy and use it to generate electricity. The Chinese steel industry had expanded massively in the space of the previous few years, and, despite the efforts of the central government to rein in new investment and concentrate steelmaking at a few larger and more efficient production bases, new ironworks had sprouted up across the country. Many were small and inefficient and used cheaper, outdated technology that wasted enormous amounts of heat energy; even in the larger factories, the scramble to keep up with production targets was so intense that many of the older blast furnaces and coking ovens were still used and just vented the hot gases out into the atmosphere. But by putting in heat exchangers, energy from the hot gas could be used to make steam and drive turbines for the local grid to reduce reliance on coal-burning plants. That way, heat recovery projects raise efficiency, prevent waste, save money, and reduce emissions from coal burning all at the same time, so it seemed like a promising area.

We visited foundries all over China, touring the blown-out hulks of state-owned ironworks up in the frozen north and venturing deep into the mountains on the eastern peninsula of Shandong. There, one of China's biggest steelworks lies wreathed in the yellow smoke that sputters from coking ovens tucked up in the surrounding valleys. Farther inland, in Shanxi, Mina, Cissy, and I spent a morning at the largest stainless steel plant in the world. Giant arc furnaces sent great gouts of molten metal into the air as intense electrical pulses crackled through cables and groaned through crucibles of boiling iron; giant ladles poured red-hot liquid into molds and presses, flattening it out like pastry in mile-long workshops with machines that span huge rollers weighing more than thirty tons each.

Encouraged by the results, Frank and I went back to Shanxi a couple of weeks later to visit a privately owned iron foundry in the western part of the province. It lay in a small rural county called Zeping, about fifty miles from the nearest commercial center. The day we arrived, a light snow had fallen across the fields. Most of the farmers were sheltering from the cold in traditional two-story courtyards close by the edge of the road; wherever the farmers were still working, I noticed more horses than tractors.

When we arrived in Zeping County, we found a dilapidated building in the main square with a tatty signboard in English saying "Welcome to the Gratification Hotel." Just beyond, there was a single line of shabby restaurants and a few wooden carts drawn by mules and loaded with tired-looking vegetables. A group of farmworkers gathered around an old oil drum stuffed with hot coals, enjoying the warmth and cooking sweet potatoes on the top. At the far end of the street, pressed up against a mountainside, stood an enormous iron foundry.

Two blast furnaces loomed in the distance, great blackened towers shaped like battlements at the top with pipes slanting down at odd angles from the sides. Gases blasted from the pipes, and deep inside the coking plant, an oven glowered fiery and red. Slag heaps and mounds of coal slumped in great piles by the side of the road; a rusting locomotive strained at the head of a line of wagons hauling ore and coal from mines deep within the mountains. Cooling towers belched clouds into the skies; black plumes poured from the chimneys. Clinker churned in vast rollers and conveyor belts carried raw iron toward the fires, while gangs of black-faced workers toiled in the heat and the flames.

I had heard that the steelworks employed more than ten thousand people. It had only started pouring iron in the early nineties, but during the boom of the past few years, production capacity had gone from two million tons a year to five. So when I heard the factory was run by a young woman in her mid-twenties, I was naturally curious to meet her.

We found her in an office with a notice outside saying "Factory Director" and with two serious-faced guards standing on either side of the door. She took us on a factory tour, stepping gingerly through the workshops in a pair of flat-heeled shoes with shiny buckles and clutching a pink and purple scarf around her shoulders. She showed a perfect grasp of the business; demand for steel was strong but she was worried about coal prices, which were rising after underground explosions the previous month had killed some miners and the national government began closing down local mining companies. Access to water was a permanent headache. Electricity was scarce so they planned to reduce reliance on the grid by recovering heat from the blast furnaces and using it to generate their own. At the end of the tour, she took us to an exhibition center beside an ornamental lake surrounded by willows. Inside, a series of photographs and mementos captured the key milestones in the factory's history; I searched for clues as to how this young woman had ended up running an ironworks in remotest, rural Shanxi.

Gradually, I worked out that in the late eighties a local state-owned coking plant in Zeping County had gone bust. A man called Li, who had dropped out of middle school to start a soap factory, bought up the old trucks when the assets were auctioned off. The new haulage business prospered, and a few years later Li borrowed enough money from the local railway bureau to restart the old coking plant and expand into steelmaking. Over the next decade, he built the steelworks into the largest privately owned business in Shanxi, becoming one of China's thirty richest men. The photo gallery recounted his early life, the hardship of the Cultural Revolution, and how he had married his sweetheart from the local village. A son was born in 1981 and a daughter—now running the factory—a year or so later. The town prospered and each year Li made donations to improve the local schools and repair the roads to the outlying districts.

Then one day, a man walked into Li's office and shot him through the head. Li's daughter was studying at the London School of Economics when she got the call from China breaking the news. She was not much more than twenty when the family called her back to Shanxi to run the factory with its blast furnaces and piles of coke and its ten thousand souls. By the time I met her, she had been in the job for four years.

After I got back to Beijing, I found from old newspaper reports that Li had known his assassin. The two men were old schoolmates, but their lives had followed very different paths. Li had become respected and powerful while Feng had struggled to turn around an old paper factory that was just outside Li's factory gates. When Feng's business got into difficulties, he asked Li to buy the land but the two men couldn't agree on price. Feng became desperate as his debts mounted. Faced with imminent ruin, Feng arrived one morning in Li's office and when Li refused once more, he shot him with a homemade gun before turning it on himself. As Li's assistants rushed into the office, they found both men dead and an apple still rolling on the floor.

The memorial service arranged for Li some days afterward was almost like a state funeral; bands marched down the dusty streets, somber strains from horns mixing with the clash of cymbals. White funeral wreaths lined the road outside the factory for nearly half a mile and thousands stood by to pay their last respects. The defunct paper mill still stands just outside the factory gates, the last memorial to Feng's troubled life. In another place, Feng might have found someone else to buy his land. But as one of the locals put it, "This is Zeping County. There was only one buyer in town."

The factory was trying to install steam-driven bellows to replace the enormous electrical fans that blasted hot air through the burning coke. The new system used hot gases escaping from the top of the furnace to produce steam and reduce the amount of power needed from local coal-burning power stations. Cissy spent hours trying to figure out how the project could meet the UN requirements, but more and more problems emerged. The waste heat gases from the seven blast furnaces were all connected by huge flues running across the factory site. The UN wanted us to prove that using one set of bellows didn't reduce the availability of hot gases for the other furnaces. The factory had hired a local science institute, but after weeks of trying to get figures on "gas balances," Cissy was tearing her hair out. She found out that the factory hadn't bothered installing meters, so the science institute had just made up what they thought would be believable figures. In winter Cissy found that the gas had cooled so much by the time it reached the bellows, the pressure had to be supplemented with a new set of electrical fans. But using more electricity destroyed the whole point of the project. The task of fitting the project into the UN's neat equations became completely overwhelming so we reluctantly abandoned it.

During this time, I had to report to the Foundation Trust every two weeks. The time difference between Beijing and Seattle meant that the calls took place very early in the morning; I used to watch the red disk of the sun appear over the rim of haze on the horizon as I dialed the number. Sometimes the air was so thick that nearby buildings were almost invisible, but occasionally, after the rains, the air was clear and the jagged silhouettes of distant mountains stood out sharply against the brightening skies. Jerry was always interested in what we were doing and supportive; he knew that investing safely in China wasn't easy. But he had a business to run and I couldn't stretch his patience beyond a certain point. Faced by

mounting complexity on the technical side, we were making painfully slow progress in closing our first deal. I began to feel more and
more anxious.

Having exhausted the opportunities in hydropower and waste heat
recovery, we started to look at biomass. A few weeks earlier, a lawyer
had walked into the office with a bundle of papers about a project
up in the Ordos Desert, which lies in the great hook of the Yellow
River a few hundred miles west of Beijing. In ancient times, wild
camels roved across the desert and nomadic tribes launched raids
into China, prompting the first Qin emperor to build the first sections of the Great Wall in the second century BC. Until recently,
two deserts lay there separated by a band of fertile ground, but after
the Great Leap Forward campaign for industrialization in the fifties
and intensive grazing in the following decades, the deserts merged
to form the Ordos Desert in the early nineties. It is a wild and dusty
landscape, where rainfall is slight. Only a few hardy plants such as
thistles and Chinese licorice survive in the rocks and dunes. In late
winter and early spring, winds howl across the steppes and send
clouds of fine sand high up into the air, causing an unnatural half-
light and wrapping Beijing in the swirls of strange, pale fogs as the
skies become brown and all color turns to sepia.

Michael visited the project and came back feeling upbeat. Out in
the desert, miles from anywhere, a local entrepreneur called Zhao
had rented several hundred square kilometers of sandy scrubland
and planted *sha-liu*, or white saxaul, a rugged type of bush that tol-
erates drought and poor soil, with long, fibrous roots that bind sand
together and woody branches that burn with a strong heat. Nearby,
he was building a 30-megawatt power station with boilers specially
designed to burn the bushes. After the tour, Michael told me that
there'd been a birthday party in the yard of a local restaurant; the air
had been thick with the smell of *bai-jiu* white liquor. Trestle tables
were stacked with plates of cake and piles of mutton ribs. A throng
of rowdy guests, red-faced and smelling strongly of *bai-jiu*, danced

about in the street to the sound of an electric organ that looked like a cross between a glockenspiel and an ironing board.

We knew that desertification and soil erosion is a huge problem in northern China. It sounded as if the project might produce carbon-neutral energy and roll back the desert at the same time, so a couple of weeks later, Frank and I went for a visit.

The town of Ordos rises up out of a flat and barren landscape. In the watery sunlight of the morning, I looked out of a hotel window over a vista of new buildings stretching out toward the desert. The Ordos Plateau is rich in mineral resources; it has the largest coalfields in China and plenty of natural gas. The local government, hopeful that Ordos may become China's Texas, has built a new city on a grand scale. Wide highways pass by enormous billboards advertising ornate villas in walled compounds separated by some distance from the apartment blocks built for the workers. In the center of town, a statue of rearing horses stands next to a huge new library built of stone and glass. Ordos has the highest per capita income of any city in China—but that's because nobody lives there. The city is almost empty. An occasional cyclist struggles against the wind as it sends paper bags and detritus from the desert down empty streets, past traffic policemen with no cars in sight.

We drove more than a hundred miles into the desert. Close to the city, grasslands pitted with shallow ravines rolled out to the horizon and traces of the early morning mist lingered in the gullies. Farther out, a band of fine, rolling sands undulated toward the east, but mostly the desert is flat and drab, dotted with patches of dried-up thornbushes. Every so often we passed by a low house with traces of smoke at the chimney. Horses with hard wooden saddles were tethered outside in the cold. Occasionally the road disappeared and the car lurched about as we took long diversions through the rocks and gullies in the scrubland; a fine dust seemed to cover every surface.

After several hours we arrived at a small village, just a row of

dilapidated buildings in the dust. There was a government compound with an iron gate at the front, a post office, one or two shops
and restaurants, and some dormitories for the workers. High above,
clouds drifted by, torn by the winds like sheep's wool caught on
thorns. The farmers lived in scattered settlements outside the main
village, scratching out a living with hardy goats that could live on
thistles. In the brief summer, there were a few vegetables, but even
then the diet consisted mainly of meat.

We found Mr. Zhao's office at the back of a walled compound,
behind a rusting metal gate. Heaps of gravel and piles of cast-iron
pipe joints littered the ground outside. Stacks of broken machine
parts had been thrown against the front wall of the long narrow
office building; the entrance was blocked by heaps of torn cement
bags with powder falling out. Bits of rusting scaffolding were scattered about among pieces of broken glass. Inside, Mr. Zhao was
holding a meeting with his staff, so we waited in an adjoining room.
I stared at the site map on the table. I couldn't work out the scale for
certain but it seemed that Zhao's project covered an enormous area.

After a few moments, Zhao came into the room, walking with
some difficulty, his right leg shorter than the left, and he lowered
himself heavily into a chair. Sitting upright, throwing his blue cap
onto the table and pulling the site map toward him, he lit a cigarette
and started out on his introduction.

Zhao was in his late fifties. He had spent his whole life on the
Loess Plateau of Shanxi, having been born in the coal-mining district of Linfen, once named the most polluted city on the planet. In
the late eighties, as China's residence permit system started to break
down, Zhao moved from the countryside to the provincial capital of
Taiyuan and started a small retail business trading electrical goods
that he had bought in the wholesale markets on the coast. His tiny
business prospered and he invested in property, taking loans from
friends and business associates. Over a decade, he'd made a fortune
from riding the property boom; now, he told me, it was time to put
something back into society.

A few years later, some minor officials in Ordos had approached him with a plan to use bushes to try to stabilize the edges of the desert. Zhao hadn't been interested, but later he came across the idea of producing clean energy from biomass and started to research the idea more seriously. After a few experiments, he rented a large area in the desert, setting up collection stations every few miles and employing local people to plant and harvest the *sha-liu* bushes. Zhao invested much of his own money building the power plant. It was almost complete when I first visited, fitted out with a new boiler from the Hangzhou Boiler Works and a generator turbine from Harbin. There was an air of excitement about the place; this was China's first large-scale project for burning biomass in the desert. Zhao knew that the project was risky; other boilers had failed after a few months because burning wood leaves an oily residue that can block up the air intakes. But Zhao was optimistic. He knew that the project wouldn't be viable with just one power plant, but he had an inspiring vision of a string of power plants right across the southern border of the desert, burning *sha-liu*, producing energy with close to zero emissions and reclaiming farmland as he went.

I was excited by Zhao's ideas; I thought it was exactly the type of project that should be encouraged by carbon trading. But as much as we tried, we couldn't find a way to fit it into the complex rules at the UN. The standard rules required the biomass in generators to be "waste matter"; the fact that Zhao had deliberately grown it meant that the project didn't qualify. We could apply for a new set of rules, but that would take eighteen months at least. Once again we found no option but to abandon the project. It was dispiriting to be thwarted by bureaucratic rules when the project was so worthwhile.

About this time, the UN rules started to change. Random amendments seemed to emerge each time the Executive Board of the UN's Clean Development Mechanism met in Bonn, Germany. The complexity of the UN regulations, the switchback pace of changes and amendments to the requirements, and the difficulties in understanding the situation on the ground in China began to seem insurmountable. Each time we found a project that we felt was worth supporting and was desperate for financing, we just couldn't seem to fit it into the UN straitjacket. After several more months, we were still spinning our wheels. I had told Jerry that we should get the whole hundred million allocated to deals by the end of the first year. With no feasible project in sight, the pressure to put the funds to work became intense. We decided to call everyone together for a meeting to go through each of the projects and see where we were.

By this time, we had hired a couple of technical experts to help Cissy and Frank unravel the projects. Qualified people were difficult to find because the carbon market was so new and there were very few people with experience. But we were lucky to find two Chinese who had been working in the industry. Yang was a Shanghainese who had worked at one of the validators. His job there had been to certify that projects complied with the guidelines, so I knew that he understood the UN rules. Meng was from Shanxi and had experience working in heavy industry there; it was a good team and I was confident in their technical abilities. We all got together to go through the projects one by one.

We organized a meeting outside the office to avoid the distractions of daily business. The team met early one summer morning at a small restaurant called the Vineyard, tucked along a narrow *hutong* a few hundred yards from the Confucius Temple.

Michael handed out a schedule with all the projects, and after loading up on coffees, we started working through the list. Cissy had given code names for each of the projects using the name of a flower. I recognized most of them—"Delphinium" was a water treatment project in Gansu, "Peony" was a waste heat recovery project at a cement plant in Jiangsu, "Lupin" was a project at one of the steelworks—but some of them were less familiar. As we progressed through the flowers, dissecting each project, the picture became more and more grim.

As we went through the technical side of each of the projects, they seemed to fall to pieces. Data for the waste heat recovery projects in the steelworks was impossible to collect since the local managers there had no monitoring systems; then Yang told us that hardly any waste heat projects had passed the UN hurdles. Even if we managed to get the data, it would take months to get through the review process and it could end up costing a fortune. Frank had been working on Delphinium, the water treatment plant in Gansu, where he faced similar problems. In the south, we'd just sent technical consultants to inspect a landfill site and they told us that the calculations for the number of credits were far too optimistic.

In Jiangsu, Meng had been discussing the Peony project, for waste heat recovery at two cement plants. Meng had seen a copy of some planning documents that showed the project developers had expected to generate heaps of cash from the equipment, so the project could never be eligible for carbon credits; it was profitable in its own right. When he pointed this out to the project owner, they gave him another set of projections the next day that showed heavy losses. But these had obviously been cobbled together overnight just to get around the rules; the tables in the main document didn't tie in with the appendices and the narrative was riddled with inconsistencies. It was an obvious fake, so we dropped the project immediately.

The next project—"Aquilegia"—was in a coal mine. The plan was to install pipes to suck out methane gas from deep within the mineshafts and put it through an engine to drive a generator. That way the project would avoid greenhouse gas emissions from the mineshafts and reduce the need for coal-fired power on the local grid. But I was especially worried about the possibility of fatal accidents. China has a terrible safety record in coal mines. If the machines are properly run, there should be no problems, but I knew that the long pipes—which looked alarmingly like fuse-tapers—had to pass down a mineshaft full of potentially explosive gas and were connected to an engine full of sparkplugs. It looked just like a gigantic firecracker and reminded me of the Taiping miners packed into tunnels with barrels of gunpowder and lighted lanterns. Mina thought I was being overly cautious and the conversation grew touchy but the reality was that coal mines all over China explode every year and thousands of miners die. I was adamant that we weren't going to do anything that risked adding to that statistic.

As we summarized the project list toward the end of the day, things were looking pretty desperate. By late afternoon, we had ticked off the projects one by one and concluded that they were all completely impractical. There was only one more left at the bottom of the list: "Snapdragon."

"Go on, surprise us all," I said to Cissy. "Last one! What's Snapdragon, then?"

"Er . . . it's in Shandong," she said, glancing nervously at Mina.

"So what does it do?" I asked.

Mina interjected. "It's a biofuels project," she said.

"So how does that work then?" I asked. "I thought biofuels ate up crops and so on. Should we be doing this?"

Mina explained that the project wasn't related to producing biofuels from crops but that a local science institute in Shandong had come up with an idea to collect used cooking oil from restaurants all around the province and blend it with diesel for use in trucks and buses. It was meant to reduce the amount of fuel needed for transportation and save on emissions. But this had nothing to do with power generation and sounded very far-fetched to me.

"Well, the sponsor thinks it'll work," she said, "and he's put his money where his mouth is. His company's invested ten million bucks in a plant down in Rizhao. Have a look at the photos."

She flashed up a series of photos on the projector. The first was a large shed with a couple of battered trucks outside. The next showed a scrapyard heaped with wire coils, bags of cement and piles of wooden poles leaned against a big tank that seemed to be refueling a broken-down tractor. Next came a photo of some metal containers in a large empty workshop with a few taps and pipes at the bottom; it looked like a dormitory kitchen. Finally, there was a picture of a large woman at the top of a stepladder, peering suspiciously into a large vat. She was wearing white overalls, had a paper cap over her head, and was using a big wooden ladle to stir an ugly mixture of oily liquids.

"How can this possibly work?" I asked, exasperated. "There's no way anyone invested ten million bucks in that filthy old shed.

There's just a few old saucepans and a fat dinner lady stuck halfway up a ladder!"

"No, really, it's backed by one of the local science institutes."

"Science institutes!" I said. "You know that they're hopeless at these types of projects! Which one is it anyway?"

There was silence.

"Which institute is backing the project?" I repeated impatiently.

Another pause.

"Er . . . it's the Shandong Peanut Institute," said Cissy, concentrating on the curtains.

"Peanut Institute?!" I said.

"Yeah," Mina piped in. "They investigate peanuts; you know, maybe breed them or something, try to find genetic varieties that have better disease resistance and so on."

"Peanut Institute!" I said despairingly.

There was a long pause.

"Okay, so let me get this straight," I said. "We got a hundred million euros from the richest man in the world. But the whole business has boiled down to a Chinese woman wearing a big paper hat stuck halfway up a stepladder in an old shed in Shandong. And she's got a big wooden spoon for scooping grease out of old frying pans and shoving it into trucks for a science institute that's studying peanuts. Is that right? It'll look bloody marvelous in the foundation's annual report, won't it!? Shall we send them the photos?"

There was an uncomfortable silence and a few coughs. Frank stared intently at his shoes. I closed the meeting; it was time to order some beer.

Later, as we sat at the bar and reflected gloomily on the day, Mina tried to raise our flagging spirits.

"Look, we know there are lots of good projects across China," she said. "Wind farms? How about the oil industry? We haven't looked at those yet. It's just a question of finding the right access point. I've done this a hundred times before and it's always difficult to start with, even at the World Bank."

"Right," said Michael. "We just need to press on and not get too discouraged."

"But we've been looking for nearly three months," I said.

"I know, but there's still one person we haven't talked to yet," he said.

"Oh yeah? Who's that then?" I asked.

Mina had guessed. "Cordelia?" she said cautiously, wrinkling her nose.

"Well, there doesn't seem to be much else out there," Michael said.

I sighed into my beer. "Have things really got as bad as that?"

10

兵者 國之大事 死生之地
存亡之道 不可不察也

THE THIRD CHINESE RULE:

The Art of War Is of Vital
Importance for the State; It Is a
Matter of Life and Death; the
Road to Safety or Ruin That Should
on No Account Be Neglected.

—*Opening lines of Sunzi's* The Art of War, *c. sixth century BC*

The Taiping Rebellion dealt such a blow to Qing finances that the dynasty never recovered. As the emperor flailed his impotent officials with edicts from the Forbidden City, the foreigners pressed inland regardless. British traders marched up the Yangtse. In the south, the French took the mountains of Yunnan and the Germans occupied the northern peninsula of Shandong, where Confucius is buried. In 1894, Japanese forces obliterated China's navy in a short, bloody war and China began to fragment. It seemed as if the empire faced the equivalent of the most grotesque of all imperial punishments—the *ling chi*, or "death by slow slicing and dismemberment."

As turmoil swirled along the coast, deep within the countryside the lives of millions of peasant farmers still beat to the timeless rhythms of Chinese rural existence. In 1893, three decades after Hong Xiuquan died, along with his dreams of a Heavenly Kingdom, Mao Zedong was born in a country village hidden among the rolling hills of the southern province of Hunan. Eighty-three years later, as he lay dying near the Forbidden City in an ornamental pavilion called the "Library of Chrysanthemum Fragrance," Mao had taken his place among the handful of peasant emperors who, during China's long cycles of history, rose up from the rubble of a collapsing dynasty and—by brute force and willpower—founded the next.

Throughout his long life, Mao never lost the earthy habits of his Chinese peasant ancestry; his teeth were almost black since he never bothered to brush them and he once famously startled a foreign journalist by absentmindedly pulling down his trousers "to search for some uninvited guests." Even when he was Chairman of the People's Republic, a guard used to follow him out of his quarters into the grounds with a shovel until Zhou Enlai, the prime minister, ordered a squat-down latrine to be built next to Mao's bedroom. But whatever his personal habits may have been, in his final years Mao's authority was absolute; he had dominated China for three decades and when he died in 1976, a power as lethal, unrestrained, and arbitrary as that of the emperors in the olden times died with him, perhaps forever.

The pale ocher mud-daubed walls of Mao's sprawling family home still stand next to a lotus pond in the little village of Shaoshan. It sits in a narrow valley with terraced rice fields and pine woods, and nowadays there's a busy restaurant on the other side of the pond. Inside, a huge black-and-white photograph of a girl perched on the Chairman's knee covers the back wall. By the time I visited the village, the girl was well into her eighties, but she was still milking her association with the Chairman for all it was worth.

Mao's father was a small landowner and held mortgages on some fields around Shaoshan. He supplemented his income by buying rice from the poor villagers and selling it in the county markets, some two days away by oxcart along a rutted dirt track. Mao had a quarrelsome relationship with his father and fought with him as a teenager, but he seems to have been fond of his mother and admired her roundabout way of dealing with family conflicts. He recalled years later that she "advocated indirect attack and criticized any display of emotion or attempts at open rebellion. She said it was not the Chinese way."

From early childhood, Mao developed a love of books. He went to school at eight and learned to recite the Chinese classics. But it was to the great chronicles of Chinese history that Mao would return again and again throughout his long life. As a child, Mao read late into the night, hiding the light from his father, absorbed in the ancient battles between villains and heroes in China's famous historical novels, *Romance of the Three Kingdoms*, *Journey to the West*, and *The Outlaws of the Marsh*.

At thirteen Mao went away to school, and four years later he moved to the provincial capital of Changsha. As he first approached the city by boat, he gazed up at the huge walls rising above the forest of junks on the river. Fifty years earlier, after it had held out against the Taiping siege, Changsha became known as the "City of Iron Gates." The walls were so wide that three carriages could ride abreast along the ramparts. Inside, the alleyways reeked of squalor but behind high, windowless walls, great mandarin officials lived in elaborate courtyards with exquisite gardens set about with pavilions and blackwood furniture. The yellow tiled roofs of the two great Confucius temples rose above the city skyline. In the busy markets the squeals of ungreased axles mixed with the shouts of laborers pulling wheelbarrows up from the riverfront loaded with calico, linen, salt, and medicinal plants such as monkshood and foxglove. Mao had come to study in Changsha, first enrolling in a police academy, then joining a law college, only to move to a soap-making school, before finally retreating to the library for self-study. There he found the huge historical record called the *Zi-zhi-tong-jian*, or *General Mirror for Aid of Government*, which was completed in AD 1084. The 296 volumes of this massive Song Dynasty classic paint the giant panorama of the dynasties' waxing and waning over the prior fourteen centuries. Mao would return to the *General Mirror* over and over again as an old man. Obsessed with his legacy and worn out by age and his years in power, he piled the volumes high around the edges of his huge bed in the Library of Chrysanthemum Fragrance, searching endlessly for hidden meanings, propped up by hard pillows stuffed with rice husks and reading late into the night and through till morning.

In 1912, when Mao was eighteen, the last Qing emperor—a boy of six—was forced to abdicate. Then, after one of the generals of the Northern Army tried to proclaim a new dynasty, several military governors in the southern provinces revolted. Central authority collapsed and for the next few decades, local warlords fought over blocks of territory. During this time of chaos and weakness, the victors in World War I met in Versailles, France, in 1919 to carve up Germany's assets. When the news reached Beijing that they had transferred Germany's concessions on the Shandong peninsula directly to Japan rather than returning them to China, it provoked a national convulsion of rage, frustration, and shame. Three thousand protesters gathered on Tiananmen Square. Suspecting that the corrupt warlord government in Beijing was in cahoots with the foreigners, they marched to the nearby house of a minister and dragged the occupants outside for a bloody mauling in the dust. The minister escaped with a broken ankle as he leaped over a back wall, but his assistant was beaten until he was unrecognizable. Police arrested more than thirty demonstrators and one student died in the melee. As the protestors were marched off to jail, the bystanders cheered them in an expression of contempt for the warlord government. These events—which became known as the May Fourth movement—sparked a nationwide demand for renewal that spread to every corner of China.

After a time in Beijing, where he worked in the university library and first came across Marxism, Mao returned to Changsha. In the heady atmosphere sweeping China after May Fourth, Mao founded a study group to discuss how China could rejuvenate itself and reclaim its sovereignty. He opened an evening school for workers and set up a magazine called the *Xiang River Review*. In the first edition, Mao declared: "The floodgates have opened! The vast and furious tide of new thought is already surging along both banks of the Xiang River. Those who ride with the current will live; those who go against it will die."

Shortly afterward, Changsha was gripped by the story of a young woman forced into an arranged marriage with a much older man. Mao heard that the twenty-three-year-old woman had been taken to the ceremony in a sedan chair decked in red, but when she arrived and the family drew back the covers, they found that she had slit her throat with a razor hidden in her foot bindings. He wrote ten articles about the episode, asking, "Why is it that you never see a woman entering a barber's shop or staying in hotels? Why is it that all the public latrines in Changsha are for men and none for women?" Mao concluded that she must have despaired of ever escaping "the three iron nets"—traditional society, Confucian family obligations, and the wealthy new husband waiting in his residence on Orange Garden Street. Mao blamed the "rottenness of the marriage system and the darkness of society where there can be no freedom of voice in love."

The shocking story of the woman's suicide might have been one of the factors that led Mao to reexamine his ideas at that time. He came to see traditional marriage as merely an economic arrangement controlled by the owners of capital, all of whom were men. He realized that to change China meant to change society; to change society meant to change the system; and to change the system, those who owned capital had to be overthrown. He read an article in the *New Youth Magazine* about Marxism, and when Moscow sent agents to help organize the Chinese Communists, Mao was one of a handful of activists who attended the First Party Congress, in July

1921. By the time that Mao reached his late twenties, a revolutionary had been formed.

Mao became involved in organizing strikes; the first, by masons and carpenters, led to a late-night standoff in Changsha when several thousand angry men massed outside the magistrate's compound. In the following months, the barbers, rickshaw pullers, cobblers, typesetters, writing brush makers, and weavers all went on strike. By November, fifteen unions had merged into one, with Mao as general secretary. Then suddenly, in early 1925, Mao seems to have suffered a breakdown.

After helping establish the Chinese Communist Party, Moscow tried to push it into an alliance with China's Nationalists—the Kuomintang, or the KMT. Mao was deeply skeptical because he thought the Nationalists just wanted power rather than to change society. Exhausted by Moscow's bullying and depressed by his lack of progress, Mao became ill and returned to his home village with two crates of books. For several months he saw nobody except his immediate family.

Over the summer, as Mao recovered in Shaoshan, Hunan was struck by drought. By late August, rice had run out. Landlords were hoarding it deliberately to create a shortage, so Mao organized the peasants to force open their granaries. When rumors spread that the last stocks were about to be shipped to the county markets, bands of ragged peasants marched on the landlord's houses with hoes and bamboo carrying-poles, forcing them to sell the rice at normal prices. Similar conflicts broke out in other villages and before the end of the month, twenty peasant associations had been formed throughout the county. In an effort to control the unrest, the Military Governor sent soldiers from Changsha with a simple order: "Arrest Mao Zedong immediately! Execute him on the spot!" Mao slipped silently from Shaoshan village in an enclosed sedan chair, disguised as a doctor, and went underground.

These events helped crystallize Mao's ideas about revolution. He saw that even though peasant uprisings could topple an emperor, in two thousand years they had never succeeded in changing the system. He began to see the vast mass of oppressed Chinese peasantry as the dark heart of the Confucian empire. Revolution would only come when the peasantry overthrew the entire landowning class rather than just toppling the emperor, so in the first two months of 1927, he went on a tour of five counties in Hunan to gather facts firsthand. In a long and fiery report to his comrades, he wrote:

> the present upsurge of the peasant movement is a colossal event. In a very short time, in China's central, southern and northern provinces, several hundred million peasants will rise like a mighty storm, like a hurricane, a force so swift and violent that no power, however great, will be able to hold it back. They will smash all the trammels that bind them and rush forward along the road to liberation. They will sweep all the imperialists, warlords, corrupt officials, local tyrants and evil gentry into their graves. Every revolutionary party and every revolutionary comrade will be put to the test, to be accepted or rejected as they decide.

Mao's report contradicted the Marxist orthodoxy that revolution started with workers in the cities, so the Chinese Communists argued about it for several weeks. At that time, the leader of the Nationalists, Generalissimo Chiang Kai-shek, suddenly launched a surprise attack against the Communists known as the *White Terror*, executing hundreds on the streets of Shanghai. Thousands more went missing and the Reds were almost destroyed. After a failed "Autumn Harvest Uprising" in Hunan, Mao found himself at the head of a small ragtag army of deserters, vagabonds, and armed peasants, pursued by Nationalist forces deep into the countryside. Mao's rabble retreated up into a mountain hideaway called Jinggangshan, where they regrouped behind a huge natural defensive ring of bladelike pinnacles that jutted out of dense bamboo forests, wreathed in mists and edged by waterfalls that fell in thin torrents down the sheer walls of rock.

In this mountain stronghold, Mao started to build a more disciplined army. He was joined by another column of Red soldiers only to be pushed out of the mountains by Nationalist armies and fled to an even more remote area in the border regions between three southern provinces. There Mao proclaimed an independent Soviet governed by a revolutionary council and held a ceremony attended by six hundred delegates in an ancient ancestral hall surrounded by gnarled camphor trees, some of which were a thousand years old.

Even though Japanese forces were pushing into China from the northeast, Chiang Kai-shek still saw the Reds as the biggest threat to his hopes of a Nationalist government in China. At first, instead of uniting with the Communists and fighting against the Japanese invaders, Chiang began a series encirclement campaigns around Mao's Soviet. In the First Encirclement, Mao's forces were outnumbered ten to twenty times. Mao lured the Nationalists deep into Red territory and then sprang sudden concentrated attacks. Heavily outnumbered, Mao rejected the old ideas of positional warfare and promoted the use of flexible, indirect warfare in a simple sixteen-character slogan for his men:

敵進我退， When the enemy advances, I retreat,

敵駐我擾， When the enemy rests, I harass,

敵疲我打， When the enemy is tired, I attack,

敵退我追。 When the enemy withdraws, I pursue.

"The enemy wants to fight a short war," Mao said, "but we just won't do it. We will let him stew and then, when his own problems become acute, we will smite him a mighty blow."

Four months later, the Nationalists began another series of encirclement campaigns, this time with far more troops, but the Red Army used the same tactics of luring the enemy into traps by retreating and suddenly reappearing and tearing their lines apart. It seemed as if Mao was using tactics from Sunzi's ancient military classic *The Art of War*, which was written in the sixth century BC:

能而示之不能，　When able, I feign inability,

用而示之不用，　When active, I seem inactive,

近而示之遠，　When near, I seem far,

遠而示之近。　When far, I seem near.

On the Fifth Encirclement Campaign, with the help of some German military advisers, Chiang changed his tactics and started to build long lines of stone forts like the watchtowers of medieval Europe, deep into Red territory. Consolidating control at the rear by building roads and communications, the Nationalists put up new forts in the vanguard and inched toward the enemy. But their plans were stolen by a spy working for the Reds who copied them into a dictionary and, taking a rock and knocking out four of his own teeth, left the Nationalists' headquarters disguised as a penniless beggar, his face swollen and bloodied and with the plans hidden under a layer of rotten food in his knapsack. When the Reds saw the plans, they realized that they faced overwhelming force and opted for the last of the Thirty-six Ruses: 三十六计，走为上策；"When all else fails, the best policy is to run."

As the Red Army fled toward the west, leaving the Generalissimo with huge wasted investment in his immovable blockhouses, Mao's future was as uncertain as ever. He had nothing but his clothes, two blankets, a cotton sheet, an overcoat, a broken umbrella, and a bundle of books. Nevertheless what started as an unseemly scramble by eighty-six thousand troops was worked into the legend of heroism and endurance known as the Long March. Over the years, the Communists used the story of the Long March to create an aura of indestructability around the Red Army that their enemies could never erase.

They first headed west toward the mountain ranges using distracting movements to hide their real objective. When the Reds appeared to be marching on the capital of Yunnan, Chiang Kai-shek retreated on a railway toward Burma, only to find out that it was a diversion carried out by a small detachment while the main column moved west toward Sichuan; in Sunzi's words, "遠而示之近"—"When far, I seem near."

In the following weeks, the Red Army crisscrossed the rivers on the southern borders of Sichuan, climbing northwest through a blaze of oleander, azaleas, and bright Tibetan roses. Farther north, they reached the Dadu River and found it in full flood. Desperate to escape Chiang's approaching armies and trapped by the swollen river, Mao ordered a vanguard to head a hundred miles north and secure the nearest crossing at Luding, where a chain bridge spanned the river. After a forced march along paths "twisted like sheep's guts and as slippery as oil" and with the river tumbling across rocks a hundred feet below, they reached Luding to find a single span of thirteen iron chains with open sides and a floor of irregular planks, many of which were missing. According to Communist folklore, the Reds—crablike and with Mausers strapped to their backs—crept through a hail of bullets along the chains at the edges of the bridge, swinging high over the surging waters. When they reached the far side, they disabled the machine-gun station with a well-aimed grenade and the main column crossed the river, breaking free and narrowly escaping the Nationalist armies.

Mao's men stumbled across the Great Snowy Mountains through hailstorms and fierce winds before descending onto marshy grasslands under a sky so vast and empty that it seemed to suck the life out of the remaining fifteen thousand men. Underfoot, a green cover hid a black, viscous swamp that sucked in anyone who broke through the crust, so the marchers drove cattle or horses before them to find the least dangerous way. They emerged from the swamps onto the dusty Loess Plateau of central China, where the pale yellow soil, as fine as powdered sugar, has been worn into twisted shapes by the wind and washed away by rains to form deep grooves in the plateau, where peasants carved cave dwellings out of the soft, dry earth.

There, deep in the powdery heartland of China, Mao was to spend the next twelve years of his life consolidating his grip on the Communist Party and thinking. He lived for a while in a cave near to the city of Yan'an and resumed study; the few surviving photographs from that era show Mao, calligraphy brush in hand, poring over books or writing at his desk with the round cave windows behind. He read for days on end and had long pockets specially sewn into his jacket so that he could stuff them full of books.

Mao wrote long essays on politics, society, and warfare. Where Chiang Kai-shek had used German advisers, Mao took many of his ideas on military strategy from the commanders of ancient China, who believed that victory came from hiding one's true objectives, gathering information about the enemy's intentions, and creating confusion in the enemy camp by spreading false rumors with spies. Mao had used these ideas effectively during the Encirclement Campaigns, when one of the Generalissimo's brigade commanders had complained, "Everywhere we grope around in the dark, while the Red Army walks in broad daylight." But above all, Mao knew that success relied on waiting for favorable conditions. In one of his essays, he recounted the story of a battle in AD 222 in which a general allowed the enemy to penetrate deep inside the kingdom but "avoided battle for seven months until the enemy was at his wits' end and his troops were exhausted and demoralized. He then crushed his adversary by taking advantage of a favorable wind and setting fire to his tents." As well as timing, Mao knew that "the so-called theory that weapons decide everything is one-sided. Weapons are an important factor in war, but not the decisive factor; it is people, not things, that are decisive."

After the Japanese surrender in 1945, China sank into full-scale civil war before the Red Army finally triumphed over the Nationalists.

When Mao proclaimed the founding of the People's Republic in October 1949 from the gates of the Forbidden City, he was faced with
the task of administering not just a base area in central China, but
in a country three times the size of Europe that contained nearly a
quarter of humanity. But throughout his twenty-six-year rule, Mao
never really adapted to running a peacetime economy. For him,
time had no meaning. He would sleep at irregular hours, waking,
perhaps, in the late afternoon, or calling meetings without notice
in the dead of night, where he would announce a sudden switch of
direction that would leave his colleagues bewildered and demoralized. Mao's ethereal nature and his deep immersion in the Chinese
classics gave him an otherworldly, whimsical style of thinking and
speaking. He often quoted from Chinese literature or history in a
way that even his own people couldn't follow. The first time that
Mao met Stalin in the Kremlin, the Soviets' interpreters found him
so confusing that they had to ask repeatedly for clarification. When
Mao gave even vaguer explanations, the conversation petered out
and Stalin was reduced to asking whether China had a meteorological service and whether Mao would like his books to be translated
into Russian.

Mao's commitment to overthrowing the landlord class meant that
the revolution in the countryside was a very brutal affair; the peasants were allowed to mete out justice to former landowners as they
saw fit and many people were killed. In the cities, technical advisers
arrived from Russia, and helped in the haphazard, piecemeal nationalization of industry. Conditions for ordinary people improved
both in the cities and the countryside, but over time, tension crept
into the relationship between the two Communist giants. After
Stalin died, Khrushchev, his successor, denounced the excesses of
Stalin's purges in a secret Kremlin speech. But Mao defended his
former ally, saying that "out of ten fingers, only three of Stalin's
were rotten." Mao felt that however bad Stalin might have been,
it was the height of irresponsibility for Khrushchev to tear down
the leader who had been an icon for millions of Communist believ-

ers throughout the world. So when Mao went to Moscow again in 1957, deep rivalries had set in. At the Congress there, Khrushchev boasted that Russia would overtake the U.S. economy. In that case, Mao retorted, China would overtake Great Britain in fifteen years.

In early 1958, China mobilized a hundred million peasants to dig ditches and irrigate thirty thousand square miles of farmland. It had only taken four months and Mao was buoyed up by the success. He said, "I have witnessed the tremendous power of the masses . . . on this foundation, it is possible to accomplish any task whatsoever!" A few months later, Mao tried to replicate the mass campaign in the economy. Planning was like mahjong, he said: "you just double your stakes."

In a campaign called the Great Leap Forward, the central government set hopelessly ambitious targets for growth. As the movement gathered pace, ministers started competing with each other with increasingly fantastic targets. The Chemicals Ministry announced a program to build a thousand fertilizer plants; the Ministry of Roads planned sixty thousand miles of new highways. When the Steel Ministry proposed increasing output from six to nine million tons, Mao replied "What!? Make it snappy! Let's just double it. What are you hanging about for?! Make it eleven million!"

By the middle of 1958, steelmaking had become an obsession. In Hebei Province, the local government started building seven huge iron foundries; farther south, Hunan drew up plans for a thousand small steel mills. In the countryside, the peasants began building backyard furnaces with earth bricks and abandoned the fields to scavenge for fuel and scrap. Pots, woks, knives, scissors, bicycles, doorknobs, ladles, iron gates, and bedsteads were all hurled into the flames, consuming entire forests in the process. At the height of the campaign, sixty million people were smelting metal; according to one foreign visitor, everywhere she looked there was "a furious, seething, clattering scene of frenzy . . . people carried baskets of ore, they goaded buffalo carts, tipped cauldrons of white-hot metal and unloaded wheel barrows of scrap iron; they stood on rickety ladders and peered into furnaces."

Nurses toiled on hand-driven bellows into the early hours while hospital wards were left unattended; ministers scurried from meetings to shovel scrap metal into the flames. The editors of the *Beijing Review* abandoned their desks to set up a "reverberating puddling furnace" in the backyard; even China's top politicians had furnaces next to their quarters so that they could join in the struggle. Mao used to stand on his rooftop in Beijing, staring at the glow in the night sky from a thousand furnaces in the outlying counties and dreaming of Tiananmen Square covered with belching smokestacks. Millions of tons of steel were thrown into the flames, but the whole gargantuan exercise was completely pointless. The only thing anyone cared about or even reported was the tonnage of metal melted. In order to reach Beijing's targets, useful tools and implements were melted down to make ingots that were then turned back into the same types of tools that had been melted down in the first place.

At this time, Mao also began to reorganize farming into "People's Communes," where thousands of families lived and worked together in single production units. Not only was land brought under collective ownership, but also livestock, tools, and houses. Mass canteens replaced home cooking; tens of thousands of laborers were organized to work on farms that covered huge areas. The government set grain production as the key target, regardless of local conditions. Traditional crops were often abandoned. Tea bushes, mulberry trees, and ancient citrus groves were dug up to make way for fields of wheat.

With all this tumultuous activity and chaotic management, productivity collapsed. By the end of 1958, the first signs emerged that a major disaster was brewing. Many of the top officials in the central government were worried by reports filtering in from the countryside, but Mao seemed exhilarated. His campaign slogans became more and more meaningless as he called for "shock troops" to launch "surprise attacks" on the fields. Nature seemed almost to have become an enemy; Mao drove the campaign forward under the mantra *ren ding sheng tian*, or man must conquer nature. When reports of drought in the provinces were followed by more urgent calls for relief food,

Mao remained dismissive: "Just because for a time there are too few vegetables, too few hair grips and no soap . . . some people will waver in the great storms of history," he said. But as the campaign rumbled on throughout the year, bad weather compounded the problems. The Yellow River burst its banks and typhoons battered the coast. In Henan half a million hectares were stripped bare by a plague of locusts. By 1959, there simply wasn't enough to eat.

Over the next three years, millions died in the largest famine in history. Whole communities disappeared   people devoured tree bark, and ground up stones to thicken soup. Bands of starving peasants attacked grain depots and trains. When the unfolding catastrophe finally became clear in Beijing, even Mao was worried. His personal doctor wrote that for a long time, Mao could neither eat nor sleep.

Some estimates put the toll at forty million dead. Vast tracts of land had been laid to waste with irrigation systems left untended and whole forests devoured by the furnaces. Surviving peasants were left angry and confused at the wholesale cutting of trees—trees they had known from childhood for providing shade, hunting grounds, firewood, and chestnuts—and at the destruction of local temples, where ancient ramparts and rafters had been taken down to fuel the flames. As one old peasant said, "We were just left with a big mess of metal—wood can never burn hot enough to make steel!"

After the calamity of the Great Leap, Mao took a step back from the front line and, with the sour taste of failure in his mouth, he brooded. Throughout the early 1960s, as China's leadership struggled to cope with the disaster, the daily affairs of government were taken over by Mao's dour but more practical deputy, Liu Shaoqi, who became China's head of state.

Liu like Mao was born in Hunan and had trained in Moscow before returning to China in the 1920s to organize strikes. He had been on the Long March and, although he had strong backing within the Party, he lacked Mao's charisma. Liu was somewhat bookish, persevering and stoic by temperament, a man who had ascended step by step rather than through bold leaps.

As he set about repairing the economy, Liu was aided by China's long-serving prime minister, Zhou Enlai. Zhou was charismatic and intelligent, but he was also careful never to challenge Mao. Together, Mao, Liu, and Zhou had become the three dominant personalities in Chinese politics. Zhou was more cautious than Liu and kept his thoughts to himself. He once said of Mao, "With a single brushstroke, all your past achievements will be canceled out should you fail the final test of loyalty." Conversely, Liu had dared to criticize the Great Leap openly. It was to prove a fatal error.

As the government rolled back the failed policy of collectivization, Liu tried to improve management in the countryside and root out corrupt cadres. But Mao remained much more concerned with ideological backsliding, which he feared would lead to a restoration of capitalism in the countryside and undo his life's work of liberating the peasantry from two thousand years of servitude. He became obsessed with "revisionism," the watering down of Communist principles that Khrushchev had pursued in Russia.

When Khrushchev was ousted in 1964, Mao heard that a drunken Soviet defense minister had told a visiting Chinese delegation, "We got rid of Khrushchev, you should get rid of Mao." Mao had always worried about being denounced after his death but now he felt the danger of being unseated during his lifetime. Gradually the lines began to form for a final battle that Mao was to describe later as a matter of life and death. Outnumbered in the leadership group, Mao could not attack openly, but instead he would fall back on all the skills of psychological combat that he had learned from Sunzi's *The Art of War* and all his experience of "indirect attack" so favored by his mother. Where Clausewitz had said that "war was the ultimate form of politics," Mao was to reverse that dictum by bringing the ancient Chinese skills of warfare into politics.

The Great Proletarian Cultural Revolution—Mao's convulsive battle to lock communism into China's destiny by a fundamental change in its culture—all started with a display of petulance at his

seventy-first birthday party. Holding up his Party card and a copy
of the Constitution, he made a cantankerous speech complaining
that no one ever listened to him but that he had a right to be heard.
Since Mao could not move openly against the leaders in charge
of cultural affairs, he first softened them up by engineering a row
about an obscure play by a Beijing academic. Rather than doing it
directly, Mao sent his wife to Shanghai to enlist the help of some
intellectuals there.

Madame Mao was twenty years younger than the Chairman,
having been born in 1914, in a dusty lane in Shandong full of dogs
and gossipy neighbors. Her father was a carpenter who owned a
wheelwright's shop, some farmland, and a small inn; almost nothing
is known of her mother and even her name has been forgotten. In
her teens, the future Madame Mao ran away from home, drifting
for a while before becoming an actress in Shanghai and appearing
in plays and films. In 1937, as the Japanese advanced toward the
city, she fled to Yan'an, where she joined the Communists, working
as a drama instructor on propaganda plays. She was poised, beautiful, ambitious, and quickly caught the Chairman's attention. But
the other Communist leaders were scandalized by the relationship
because Mao was already married and his new lover had a checkered
past on the stage and screen. Nevertheless, they married a year later
on the condition that Madame Mao would not be involved in politics for thirty years.

The relationship soured after the Communist victory and the
Chairman and his wife led increasingly separate lives. She began
to harbor a deep sense of unfairness at being kept on the sidelines;
the natural grudges against those who had barred her from politics
were fed through the years by loneliness and long periods of painful
illness. Without peers or companions to occupy her mind, she grew
bored and willful. Later, she was to say famously, "Sex is engaging in the first rounds, but what sustains interest in the long run is
power." By the early 1960s she had neither.

Mao turned to her again at this time of crisis. When he decided
to launch his attack against Liu through a Cultural Revolution, pol-

itics became theater and theater became politics. Madame Mao was the ideal instrument to use in his attack on traditional culture; in return, she gained a platform to take power and, as was in her character, revenge as well.

At Mao's behest, after several months of secret planning, she engineered a long article in one of China's main papers attacking the Beijing playwright for "bourgeois revisionism." Falling directly into the trap, the leaders of the cultural committee in Beijing defended the play. Spurred on by Mao, the Shanghai clique intensified their attack and, after weeks of bitter infighting, the leader of the Beijing cultural committee was forced to resign. Round one had gone to the Chairman. Mao then started to manipulate a mass movement at China's schools and universities that would end up toppling his rival, Liu Shaoqi, China's head of state.

Throughout the first half of 1966, the atmosphere at Beijing University had been tense. A left-leaning Party secretary in the Philosophy Department was about to lose her job because of a vendetta against the university president for being a rightist. In the early afternoon of May 25, she put up a poster on the campus accusing the university authorities of being "a bunch of Khrushchev-type revisionist elements." Chaos ensued. Within hours, hundreds of revolutionary "big character posters" were pasted up on walls, "striking"—as one of them said—"at the black gang of the university authorities like artillery shells." Zhou Enlai sent officials to try to calm the situation, but a rival faction of left-wing radicals in the central government scurried over to support the protesters. When Mao heard the news at his villa in Hangzhou, he immediately sensed an opportunity to turn the student protests against his enemies and he wrote across a copy of the poster, "It is very important that this text be broadcast in its entirety. Now the smashing of the reactionary stronghold that is Beijing University can begin." Liu Shaoqi, who had no advance warning of the broadcast, was startled to hear it on the radio that evening at eight thirty. Mao summed up the situation some months later: "I really caused a huge uproar by having that Beijing University poster broadcast!"

In the following weeks, China's universities stopped functioning. Tsinghua University was festooned with more than sixty thousand posters accusing teachers of holding bourgeois views or supporting revisionism. In the middle of June, students seized professors, threw ink in their faces, and paraded them through the campus with wastepaper baskets on their heads and posters stuck to their backs. By the middle of July, classes had been suspended throughout the whole of China. More than a hundred million students from primary to university level were told to stop attending lessons and to engage in "class struggle" instead. But no one knew what it meant. Mao was nowhere to be seen; he deliberately held back and kept others in the dark about his true intentions while waiting for the situation to develop in his favor. Factional struggles broke out all across China. Behind every factory wall, every university gateway, and in every office, power struggles raged, notionally about politics but more often about long-standing personal grudges.

Suddenly, the seventy-two-year-old Chairman burst out into the open. With a triumphant demonstration of vigor that was splashed all over the national press, he joined five thousand participants on the annual cross-Yangtse swimming competition, spending more than an hour in the water and telling a woman next to him, "The Yangtse is deep and the current is swift. This can help you train your body and strengthen your will power."

Two days later he returned to Beijing and hauled in the top leaders. Dressed in a pair of worn-out old pajamas, he roundly criticized Liu for trying to restore order in the universities by suppressing the masses. "Who suppresses the students?" he asked angrily at a Politburo meeting shortly afterward. "The Northern Warlords did!" In an artful use of the stratagem "Kill with Borrowed Knife"—the third of the Thirty-six Ruses, which relies on using the strength of others to overcome an enemy—Mao had scarcely needed to be involved himself. Turning the full fury of the students against Liu, he stepped aside as the two opposing forces fought it out between themselves.

Mao then called a Central Committee meeting in Beijing and wrote his own big-character poster urging the students to "Bombard the Headquarters"—effectively to attack the Party center—and had it pasted on the door. He arranged for one of the army generals to make a speech urging the delegates to "turn the world upside down, be noisy and boisterous, blow tempests and make big waves, cause major disturbances and lots of trouble so that for the next six months not only the bourgeoisie but even the proletariat will be unable to sleep." The committee was bullied into agreeing to sixteen points that declared a Cultural Revolution that "will touch people to their very souls. It must change the mental outlook of the whole of society and transform education, literature, and art and everything not in line with the socialist economic base." Liu Shaoqi was demoted from second position to ninth in the Party hierarchy.

In the atmosphere of repressed violence, twelve people were badly beaten at a rally on August 13. The news spread like wildfire and that night a red terror rolled out across the city. The worst violence occurred at middle schools rather than universities but Mao refused to intervene. "Beijing is too civilized!" he exclaimed. "I would say there is no great disorder . . . and the number of hooligans is very small." Students started arriving in the capital from faraway provinces. Mao began to hold rallies on Tiananmen Square; on August 18 a million students gathered there. When Mao appeared on the Gateway of Heavenly Peace with a red armband, students were ecstatic and started forming Red Guard Brigades. The capital was swamped with millions of young students who were received by Mao in vast rallies. Violence accelerated across the city.

In two weeks in western Beijing more than a hundred teachers and education officials were beaten to death with belts and buckles, sticks and staves. Tens of thousands of homes were destroyed; seven million library books were burned and the two-thousand-year-old temple at Confucius's birthplace was ransacked. Mao had encouraged boys and girls to assault, batter, and kill older citizens with no means to defend themselves. They began to hold huge rallies where they denounced "capitalist-roaders" on the flimsiest evidence, often with more than a hundred thousand people baying at the terrified victims. Madame Mao had not started the violence, but she fanned the flames more vigorously than anyone else; people were terrified of her. "For Madame Mao," said one observer, one would "roll on the ground eating horse-shit and call it a gorgeous cake!" At the end of the year, at his seventy-third birthday celebrations, Mao toasted the "all-round unfolding civil war" in China.

Red Guards started to organize into rebel groups and seize control of ministries and local governments. Rival groups began fighting. In Shanghai, twenty thousand "Scarlet Guards" attacked a hundred thousand "Red Guards" in front of the Shanghai Party headquarters. After four hours of chaotic fighting, all of the municipal government officials were dismissed and the Red Guard faction declared that Shanghai had become a commune. Railways were blocked and production ground to a halt. In Beijing, one group of Red Guards took over the municipal government and occupied the fifth floor of the offices while another occupied the third, each group claiming authority over the city. In Wuhan, fifty-four rival groups of Red Guards were engaged in pitched battles. The Provincial Party Committee there collapsed and workers and students banded together to form a "Wuhan Revolutionary Rebel General Headquarters." Red Guards started to take over provincial committees, municipal governments, and factories all over China. Munitions factories were broken open. What started out as rival Red Guard factions fighting with cudgels and knives ended up as machine-gun and artillery battles. Prime Minister Zhou flew to Wuhan to try to stop the fighting; Mao arrived on his special train, but the top officials sent earlier from Beijing to sort out the mess had been beaten senseless. Hundreds were killed; industry was so disrupted that there were shortages of household goods. Clashes broke out all over China; there were riots in the Zhengzhou Cigarette Factory and the Kaifeng Chemical Works. Tens of thousands went insane or killed themselves. A choking pall of fear mixed in with the blackened smoke that rose from the cities; corpses floated down the Pearl River past Hong Kong and out into the sea.

Wherever he went, Mao had a terrible, incendiary influence. "Why can't we arm the workers or the students?" he asked. "I say arm them!" There were pitched battles in Hangzhou where rebels "liberated" more than a million rounds of ammunition. In Wenzhou, two battalions of the People's Liberation Army mistakenly opened fire on each other. In Chongqing thousands fought with weapons looted from an army depot; the docksides were razed to the ground with tanks and artillery. At Canton airport, a terrified Japanese pilot took off without any of his passengers. In the Shanghai Diesel Engine Works, eighteen died and nearly a thousand were hospitalized. Finally, after months of being paraded in front of jeering mobs, Liu Shaoqi, China's head of state, died alone on the floor of a prison cell in the city of Kaifeng. Mao had comprehensively annihilated his enemies. Elevated to the status of a deity and utterly dominant over every aspect of life in China, in 1969 Mao finally started to rein in the Red Guards.

THE THIRD CHINESE RULE

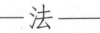

法

Out of the thousands who devoted their lives to the Chinese revolution, only Mao was able to claim his place among the handful of peasant emperors who throughout history rose out of chaos and built a new dynasty. China's twentieth-century revolutionaries devoted their whole lives to the cause of overturning the old society, yet out of all the key leaders who navigated the Chinese people through this colossal upheaval, ironically it was Mao who was most steeped in Chinese traditional culture.

Once, in the fifties, long before the Cultural Revolution, Mao,

Liu, and Zhou were planning the nationalization of Chinese industry. They likened it to feeding chilies to a cat, because they knew that business owners would do everything to resist it. Following the analogy, Liu Shaoqi said he'd approach the problem like shoving a hot pepper down the cat's throat with a chopstick. Zhou Enlai said he'd starve the cat and wrap the chili in meat. If the cat was hungry enough, Zhou argued, it would probably eat the chili. But Mao said he'd rub the chili into the cat's ass and when it started to burn, the cat would lick it off of its own accord and be grateful. Of the three methods—force, deceit, or manipulation—Mao's was the most effective.

Western methods of dealing with conflict rely mainly on the use of overwhelming firepower at a decisive moment in a direct physical attack; blast open the gates and "bomb the enemy back to the Stone Age" with devastatingly superior weapons. Local businesses get swamped with so much money from multinationals that they can't compete; special interest groups quash the more moderate middle ground. China's concepts of conflict are the polar opposite; they rely not on overwhelming firepower but on silence, stealth, surprise, manipulation, and deceit.

So here we have the Third Chinese Rule:

> *Chinese methods for dealing with conflict and competition are indirect. The traditional Chinese method is to bide time—for decades if necessary—until external factors are favorable, use spies and counterspies to gather information, disrupt the enemy's alliances, sow discord among his followers, frustrate his strategies, and use the strength of another. These are realities that Westerners need to learn how to deal with. Complaining that it's somehow "unfair" is the equivalent of the Brits grumbling that in the American War of Independence, the Yankees wouldn't wear red coats to make it easier to shoot them. We don't need to agree with any of this, but we do need to understand it. "Melons ripen," Mao said. "Don't pick them before they're ripe. When they're ready, they'll fall off of their own*

accord." The Chinese way is to overcome an opponent by building up a psychological position that is so dominant that the outcome of any conflict becomes a foregone conclusion. The indispensable preliminary to battle is to attack the enemy's mind.

Although we did not know it at the time, we were soon to find out that our understanding of Chinese tactics would be tested to the limits by conflicts that lay on the road ahead. We were soon to discover that, in Sunzi's words, the Chinese art of war is indeed "a matter that should on no account be neglected."

11

姜太公釣渭　願者上鈎

WHEN MASTER JIANG HANGS OUT HIS HOOK, IT'S THE WILLING FISH THAT GETS CAUGHT

—Traditional saying, after an eccentric military strategist who fished by holding a straightened, unbaited hook above the waters of the River Wei in the eleventh century BC, meaning that a gullible victim is most likely to get hurt

The first time I arranged to see Cordelia, I didn't even make it. The traffic that day was terrible. I'd left plenty of time to get to her offices down in southeastern Beijing, but the taxi got snarled up in road works on the third ring road. A gang of workmen were boiling up tar and asphalt to resurface the road and the smoke seeped into the taxi and caught in my throat. I could see the building in the distance above the fumes from the tar barrels, so, after a few minutes of cursing the traffic, I paid the driver, got out, and started walking between the rows of stationary vehicles, clutching at my nostrils. But when I called to say I might be ten minutes late, Cordelia seemed to have forgotten we had an appointment. "Oh, it'd be better if you didn't come today anyway," she said impatiently. "I'm busy. Why don't you try tomorrow? My office can give you a time." Then she put the phone down.

"Great!" I said to myself as I peered through the fumes at the lines of gridlocked traffic and stomped off in search of the subway.

The next day, I confirmed the arrangement with her office for three thirty and set out at two. I'd left nothing to chance that day but the traffic ran smoothly and I arrived an hour early. Cordelia's offices were on the fifteenth floor of one of the towers in a new complex that had been built on the former site of the Beijing Number Five Tool Works. I could still pick out a few of the old abandoned workshops among the lines of poplar trees behind the crumbling factory walls.

The new site was typical of modern Beijing; apartment blocks and office towers stood on a podium with a parking garage underneath. Low-end clothes shops, coffee bars, and ice-cream parlors with names like "Sunmile Pinkish Delicious" and "Gangbao + Lazy" surrounded an area of parched grass. On one corner, there was a food outlet selling chicken necks boiled in aniseed and fermented bean broth; the smell was terrible. The towers looked as though they had been encased in glass and white plastic, which gave the place a sterile, empty feeling. Even though they were only just finished, the buildings looked dusty and worn. I sat on a stone bench under a tree for forty minutes before wandering off to buy some water. I found the office tower and waited downstairs by the elevators. There was a sign in English that read "No gambolling"—the Chinese meant that children shouldn't play in the lifts.

Just before three thirty, I went up to the fifteenth floor, crossed the bare white tiles in an empty hallway, and knocked on some large double doors. As I was shown into a meeting room, I caught a glimpse into the back office. It was cramped and looked hot and airless. There were rows of cubicles crammed with unhealthy-looking techie types with thick glasses, pasty faces, and badly cut fringes, all hunched up over computer screens. The remains of a takeout meal sat among a pile of discarded chopsticks and dirty teacups. Flowcharts with equations and symbols for heat exchangers and turbines were scribbled on whiteboards; yellowing spreadsheets were taped to the walls. Outside the meeting room, next to a fish tank, a chart recorded timelines and milestones for around twenty different carbon projects. It looked as though Cordelia was working on wind farms, landfill gas sites, and waste heat recovery projects all over China. Next to the chart, there was a list of hydroelectric projects in a string of mountain villages in the southern province of Jiangxi.

Inside the meeting room, a polished wooden-topped table stood next to a few display stands with glass ornaments and photographs. They showed rows of people under long banners at signing ceremonies in technical institutes, coal mines, and iron foundries across China. In each photograph, toward the center, I noticed the same woman with a fixed smile, large sunglasses, and sharply tailored box coats. After a minute or two, someone brought in a coffee; it must have been boiling for hours. It was bitter and thick with a strange burnt smell that reminded me of yesterday's asphalt. Blobs of white powder floated about on the grayish surface. I stared at it on the table in front of me and waited.

After half an hour, a young woman popped her head around the door and apologized. "Miss Kong is running a bit late," she said, "but she'll probably arrive sometime later." I sighed, got up, and stared out the window past the other white towers in the office complex. Springtime had brought the first touch of color to the trees far below. Farther north, the ring road was blocked again and a long line of stationary traffic stretched out toward the horizon in the fading sunlight. I gazed out over the city, lost in thought for a long while until there was a sudden commotion outside. A door slammed and some heels clattered across the hallway. Someone dropped some files on the floor and I thought I caught a few flustered explanations before a sharply raised voice began to berate someone with a catalog of complaints. The Shanghainese accent was unmistakable. Someone had messed up some figures and a batch of documents had been sent out to a client with errors in them. After a few more sporadic yells, there was a mumbled apology and an exaggerated sigh before another door slammed and Cordelia sailed into the room.

She snapped her fingers for some green tea, took off her sunglasses, shook out her hair, and settled down on the other side of the table, assessing me coolly for a few moments without any reference to the fact that she was nearly an hour late. After a few minutes of small talk, I started out in Chinese with an introduction to the work we were doing and how we'd gotten started. But she interrupted almost immediately in English.

"Which carbon methodologies do you consider yourself most expert in?" she asked.

"Er, well, we're generalists, really," I replied limply.

"Uh-huh," she said, tossing her head and looking sideways out of the window, mouth pursed. I continued, but she interrupted again.

"And how do you expect the Chinese sellers to believe that you will actually be able to pay for the credits?"

I explained that we had the Gates Foundation Trust as backers, but she sniffed and cut in again.

"And what is your real experience of doing business in China?"

Here I felt on safer ground, but after a few sentences, I could see that her attention had wandered. I felt myself falter and trail off. After a few moments of silence, she folded her arms, breathed in heavily, leaned back, and cocked her head slightly.

"The market is flooded with new people like you," she said. "I really can't see where you have any distinguishing advantage."

I struggled to finish the rest of the pitch. The only time she'd showed any interest was when I'd mentioned our backers, but the conversation petered out as she examined her fingernails intently. I'd expected her to close the meeting, but then, quite suddenly, she looked at me directly for a few moments as if she was having second thoughts. After a pause, she seemed to reach a decision and sighed. With a peevish look, an obvious lack of enthusiasm, and picking at a few imaginary specks of fluff on her skirt, she started out on her own introductions.

I discovered that she'd graduated from Fudan University in Shanghai and had become interested in environmental work while studying in Canada in the late nineties. When she returned to China, she made contact with some of the officials in the Climate Change Department in Beijing. It was several years before the carbon markets had taken off and the officials there were grateful for any attention they could get. Cordelia had put together an informal group of policy makers and experts and started publishing a monthly magazine on climate change, appointing herself naturally—as the editor. As the demand for carbon offsets from China grew, Cordelia set up a business, which she called Kong Capital. It was one of the first movers in the carbon space and quickly built up a reputation as one of the key brokers and technical consultants in the market. Foreign buyers began to beat a path to her door. Before long, she'd signed up two of the Europe's largest power companies as clients and put together some of the first private sector carbon deals in China. Two years on, she was running an office of twenty people and had carved out a niche for herself brokering deals, drafting technical documents, and handling the applications for registration at the UN.

At the end of her introduction, she strummed her fingers impatiently on the table for a few moments before saying that she'd think about whether any of her Chinese clients might be interested in cooperating with us. Then she got up and ended the discussion. The whole appointment had lasted barely fifteen minutes.

As I thought about the meeting in the taxi on the way back, I could understand why Cordelia had seemed so self-possessed. With the explosion in the markets and the dearth of local expertise, she was perfectly positioned between China's big businesses, the government, and the hordes of foreign companies with big checkbooks but precious little experience, all scouring China for carbon deals. Her business was thriving and she made no pretense of needing new clients. Her English was excellent. She seemed to pick her way through each sentence purposefully and without haste, pausing here and there to emphasize each syllable. Throughout the meeting, she had leaned over the table, peering sideways out of the window, only half listening and rattling the thick metal bracelets on her wrist and the big polished stones on her necklace. The diamond-studded sunglasses discarded casually on the table beside her, the bob of glossy hair tucked neatly under the hairband, the bloodred nail polish, and the stiletto heels on her patent leather shoes completed the picture of a businesswoman at the top of her game and she knew it.

So I was amazed a few hours later, just as we were settling into the first beer, when Mina received a call. She glanced down at her phone and looked up sharply. "It's Cordelia!" she said, wrinkling her nose in surprise. "Wonder what she wants!"

Mina stepped out into the hotel lobby and, after a few minutes, came back with the message that Cordelia wanted to meet up that evening to discuss a couple of "fuel-switching" projects down in the Yangtse Delta. "Fuel-switching?" I said, before downing the beer and heading straight out to find a taxi.

Mina had arranged to meet Cordelia for supper in one of the hotels opposite her offices. Over the coming months, I came to dread the buffet there, with its bowls of cold jellyfish in vinegar, boiled peanuts, salted duck eggs, and lotus roots, but we could never persuade her to try anywhere else. That evening, given the short notice, Cordelia brought along her six-year-old daughter, a sweet girl in a short pink dress with thick tights and clumpy shoes who seemed permanently glued to a handheld Nintendo.

Cordelia told us that Huaneng, one of China's "Big Five" power companies, had decided to switch their plans for building two coal-fired plants—one in Shanghai and the other in Nanjing—and replace them with two new gas-fired plants instead. Gas-fired power stations produce lower emissions than the coal-fired equivalent, but they are more expensive to run. The investment was huge—around €300 million for each power station—so when Huaneng did their calculations, they realized that the gas-fired alternative wouldn't be viable unless they could get additional income from claiming carbon credits. Without the carbon income, they said there'd be no option but to go back to the more carbon-intensive coal-fired plans. Huaneng had asked Cordelia to advise them how to apply for credits and prepare the technical documents for the UN. Now she was acting as agent and looking for a buyer for the credits from both plants.

Cordelia's story instantly grabbed our attention. Huaneng was one of the best-known power companies in China, and if we could land them as our first Chinese counterparty, it would be a real coup. After she went through the details, we plugged the figures into a spreadsheet and Mina and I huddled together for a few minutes outside the restaurant to figure out a negotiating tactic. When we went back to the restaurant, Mina pushed down on the price and fees and bargained a change in the other, less critical terms. Cordelia extracted her fee and half an hour later, we'd agreed on the outlines of an "umbrella project" that covered both plants in one deal. We finished up just before midnight, with Cordelia's daughter snoring gently on one of the sofas in the lobby. As Cordelia scooped up her daughter and headed for the door, she turned her head and said, "Oh, one last thing. Huaneng know you're new to this game, so if you're serious about nailing this deal, you'd better find one of the big global banks to guarantee your payments."

The next morning, Mina looked tired. She'd been up most of the night on the phone to New York. We'd been in discussions with several banks about jointly developing carbon projects in China and Credit Suisse had seemed most keen. When Cordelia insisted that we bring along a bank, Mina had called them and offered to share the credits in return for Credit Suisse guaranteeing our payments. They had looked through the numbers and thought they stacked up. Later that morning, Cordelia faxed through the papers and we sent them on to New York. By the following day, we'd signed up a term sheet between all three parties. Huaneng agreed a price for all the credits from both projects; together with Credit Suisse, we would act as joint buyers and, in return for a share of the credits, Credit Suisse would guarantee all the payments. The whole process had taken about thirty-six hours. I could scarcely believe the change in our fortunes. Our "umbrella project" was by far the biggest on the market at the time and aimed to reduce emissions by nearly 65 million tons of CO_2 over the first five years. Huaneng was the largest power company in China. It generated almost as much electricity as Britain, France, and the Netherlands combined. More significantly for us, Huaneng had become the largest single emitter of CO_2 on the planet. With strong backers in Seattle and New York, I felt that if we made a success of the first deal, others might follow. We might end up in partnership with a Chinese counterparty that could have an impact on the growth of carbon emissions that might be significant to the whole world. We had a brief celebration, I sent off a note to Seattle, and, for the first time in weeks, I slept soundly at night. We were finally in business. Cordelia set about preparing the papers for registration at the UN and we turned our attention to other deals.

Throughout the following months, I made of point of visiting Cordelia at least once a week. I used to take the subway over to her offices and, not wishing to test my usual liking for Chinese food beyond breaking point, I took care to avoid the exit with the fermented beans and boiling chicken necks. Cissy became our point person for the Huaneng projects; Cordelia liked her—she was a younger woman with a sharp sense of style and an easy manner that went over well. Cissy started looking at other projects with a couple of Cordelia's project managers and went off to visit some wind farms in Yunnan. She came back with spectacular photographs of the team standing next to some transmission equipment, all dressed up in hard hats and overalls, with the mountains behind covered in dense tropical rain forests rolling out toward the border with Burma. But whenever we asked Cordelia for an update on the projects with Huaneng, she was evasive. Each time we asked her to arrange a direct meeting with Huaneng, they seemed to be out of town. I began to suspect that we were being kept in separate boxes. Cordelia was blandly reassuring. "You don't need to worry," she'd say. "These projects are complicated, but we have the people here who know how to deal with all the technical details."

It was true; by this time, I knew that the carbon side of the business was much more technically demanding than I had originally expected. On top of the specialist knowledge needed for the carbon computations, there were huge problems in trying to explain Chinese business practices to the UN validators. They just wanted to see clear records and precise calculations that satisfied the tight UN rules and had no interest in complex explanations. But the reality in China is that decisions are often made for political rather than economic reasons and documentation is scrappy. Our team became more and more frustrated since we knew that these obstacles could be best surmounted if we could talk directly to Huaneng.

Gradually a sharpness began to creep into the meetings with Cordelia. Each time I went over, she'd keep me waiting for at least half an hour before she clattered in, looking unflustered and oblivious of the time. At first it was just faintly annoying, and I'd sit in the meeting room, staring at the white blobs in the coffee, inhaling the faint whiff of boiling asphalt, and flicking absentmindedly through the magazines in the wire display stand in the corner. But it soon became irritating; we had agreed to pay Cordelia a large fee for her work so I found it irksome that our requests for information were just brushed aside.

The meetings soon developed into a kind of fencing match where I would ask questions and Cordelia would dodge giving straight answers. Often she would call at the last minute to delay meetings or ask me to come over to her apartment instead. It was on the eighth floor of the same tower block as her office, so for days on end she had no need to go outside. I doubted that her daughter had ever climbed a tree or pushed through a hedge in her life. The apartment was stuffed full of enormous pieces of furniture; three huge purple plastic sofas with pink fluffy cushions and lace doilies engulfed the room. There was a flat-screen television big enough for a drive-in movie theater and an enormous fish tank full of bloated tropical fish with weeds floating around inside. Elaborate chandeliers hung on gold-plated chains from the ceilings. The rolling stomach of a Buddha statue poked out from an alcove and there were no books. Once when I arrived there, Cordelia had just finished a foot massage and the woman was packing her things away, but then Cordelia insisted that the woman stay on to give my feet a good pummeling. When I said that I'd come to discuss the carbon projects rather than have a foot massage, she just replied, "Well, have one anyway. It's good for relieving stress!" But it had exactly the opposite effect; I sat for twenty minutes with my feet soaking in a big bucket of paste while Cordelia floated around the apartment deflecting my questions and complaining about foreigners and their pedantic, rules-based approach to Chinese business. Once the massage was over, my feet were bruised and stinging, so she offered me a red-bean-flavored ice cream from the "Sunmile Pinkish Delicious" parlor downstairs to cool down. I knew it would be horrible, but rather than make some futile attempt to refuse it, I took a few licks before shoving it down the sink in the kitchen when she wasn't looking.

The only thing I ever gleaned from the meetings with Cordelia was that she was having trouble convincing the validator that the project complied with the UN rules. He was based in Tokyo and had never been to China; he had been confused by the documents that Cordelia had sent him and it was now obvious that she had lost patience with what she thought were laborious and tedious questions. She told me scornfully that he was a German engineer of the most nitpicking kind. But that didn't explain anything. Validators were supposed to be nitpickers—that was the whole point!

The UN insisted quite rightly that the projects be audited properly and that sponsors should provide enough evidence to convince the validation experts that their projects met all of the requirements of the Kyoto Protocol. I began to suspect that Cordelia was preparing excuses for the slow progress by blaming someone else. It was already six months since we'd signed the term sheet. We were all anxious and irritable—but we were caught. Cordelia had a long-standing relationship with Huaneng that she was guarding jealously and she was the sole authorized contact with the validator. Changing validators halfway through the registration process wasn't an option. As much as we disliked it, we knew we were stuck with Cordelia.

Then suddenly, in the late autumn, there was the first sign of progress. Cordelia had been working on another gas powered plant similar to ours down in Zhengzhou and we heard that it had been certified by the same validator and submitted to the UN. With her time freed up, Cordelia promised that she'd focus on our projects and have them registered early in the New Year. After a year of kicking our heels and waiting for some progress, the atmosphere relaxed a little. A month later, Cordelia called to say that the validator had issued his certificate for the Shanghai power station, the first of the two plants we had signed up under the "umbrella project" with Huaneng. The application for credits from the Shanghai plant had been uploaded onto the UN website and the formal process of registration had begun. It had taken too long, but we were relieved to file the documents. At least there was some progress to report back to Seattle; but in the meantime, there was little to do but wait.

Just before Chinese New Year, we received a request for clarification from the UN technical team. They had sent us two questions: The first was full of equations about "fugitive emissions"—whatever they were—so I sent them straight on to Cordelia. The second question was about something called "prior consideration."

When the developed nations signed the Kyoto Protocol, they agreed to subsidize low-carbon technologies in the developing world but only if they could not be financed any other way. They never agreed to provide windfall profits to projects that could be financed with normal bank loans. The purpose of the UN system was to nudge the development path of emerging economies toward less carbon-intense options, so if the carbon reductions could have been financed anyway, why should the UN hand out valuable credits? But once companies in China became more aware of carbon income, some started applying retrospectively for credits on projects that were viable in the first place. The UN faced a huge problem in trying to decide which projects were properly eligible, so they introduced a test of "prior consideration," whereby project sponsors had to prove that carbon income had been decisive in the planning stage and that without the prospect of the extra income, they would never have gone ahead.

Although there was no exact definition of what the UN wanted to see on prior consideration, we figured that we needed to show somehow that without the carbon income, Huaneng would never have been able to finance the gas-fired plants and this would have forced them to stick with the original plans for cheaper but dirtier coal-fired plants. We asked Cordelia to get Huaneng to dig out their original plans and look for evidence that the management had solved the issue of low returns by factoring in carbon income before they decided to go ahead. I doubted that any decision in China would have been so clear-cut, but a few days later, Cordelia sent over her draft responses to the UN's queries. Cissy replied that she didn't think that the evidence on prior consideration was strong enough, but, true to form, Cordelia ignored her advice and sent the responses off anyway.

I was in England when I saw that our project in Shanghai had been bounced by the UN. There had been a meeting of their Executive Board in Bonn and, late in the evening European time, the minutes were published online. My heart sank as I saw that our project had been sent for a full technical review. When I saw that they wanted more evidence of prior consideration, I sensed choppy waters ahead.

The team in Beijing trawled through the regulations and found that we had ten working days to prepare a full response to the UN's questions and have it certified by the validator. If we failed to meet the deadline, the project would be rejected. If we filed a response, the UN would consider it at their next meeting. Their decision to approve or reject our project would be final; no second hearing, no more explanations, no appeal.

I immediately called Cordelia. I was at a judo competition with my kids at some drafty old Victorian meeting room in a local town hall, and as I stood in a cavernous stairwell dialing up China, the slap of children falling on judo mats echoed up the rickety wooden staircase. I had trouble finding her, but once I got through, it sounded like she was having an early dinner at her favorite "jellyfish buffet" in Beijing. She seemed strangely unfocused, distracted, and kept placing her hand over the receiver, apparently running two conversations at the same time. She told me vaguely that she would probably visit Huaneng the following day to see what they wanted to do. "The UN doesn't seem satisfied by the evidence we sent in," she said, "so we need to look for some more. Just let me handle it. We've got the right technical people who know how to finish the job."

For the next three days, there was no news from Cordelia. Each time I called her, her mobile failed to pick up. The clock was ticking and our confidence was at rock bottom. Given that she had disappeared at the key moment in Wang's project down in Quzhou and that we had only six days left to the deadline, we decided we had to act. At first we thought about contacting Huaneng directly, but the individuals there had no experience of the UN process; the only people we knew directly were relatively junior and might not be able to access the right documents. Multiple requests to the plant for different pieces of information might confuse them and, if we tried to go around Cordelia, we had no idea what she might do. So we decided to start searching independently for evidence that Huaneng had known about carbon income and had considered it before the project started. Hopefully we could use this to prepare a draft response for the UN in case Cordelia failed to deliver.

Mina led the team in Beijing, scouring the Web for scraps of information that we might be able to use in the response. We settled into a rhythm, working around the clock in the two different time zones, with the team in Beijing sending over the results of their work at the end of each day. It would arrive early British time, so I'd spend the day looking through the information, drafting the response, and sending it back with follow-up questions as Beijing woke up the next day.

As the team searched the Internet, there were encouraging signs. They found Chinese press reports about Huaneng attending conferences about carbon trading years earlier—but it was all too circumstantial, so I told the team to keep digging. By the end of the second day, we'd had a breakthrough. Meng, our recent hire, found a report on the World Bank website detailing a landmark technical conference held years earlier in China. The conference had designed the standard carbon methodology for "fuel-switching" projects to use when they applied to the UN. One of the key participants had been Huaneng, so they must have known about carbon income at the time they decided to build the gas-fired plants. We figured that Huaneng could never have just ignored such a large potential income on these two huge, loss-making, flagship projects.

I'd hoped this new evidence might help satisfy the validator, but when I called Cordelia to tell her the good news, she was dismissive. "That's all far too circumstantial," she said. "The UN will never accept that." The conversation rambled on for several minutes until, after a long pause, she said with a sigh, "You have to face the reality that the validator will not sign his report."

"What?!" I said angrily. "Why not?! That means that the project will just die. There's a hundred million hanging on this; all the stuff on the Web shows that Huaneng must have known about carbon income at the time they made the investment."

But she just repeated, "It's more complicated than that. You don't understand China. You have to face the reality that the validator will not sign his report."

"Well, I just don't accept that," I snapped. "We've got solid proof that Huaneng knew that carbon income was available for gas-fired power stations. And now you're telling me that they just 'forgot' about hundreds of millions in carbon income and went ahead with a loss-making project anyway? That's just not plausible!"

"I'm telling you, he's not going to sign his report," she said.

"Well, I just won't accept that," I replied.

We'd finally reached deadlock. Surprisingly, she didn't hang up. I caught the faintest sound of breathing from the other end of the line as both sides seemed lost in thought.

After a few moments, I said, "Where's this guy based anyway? Tokyo, right?"

She said that the validator's office was in some suburb of Tokyo about three hours from Narita.

After a few moments, I told her, "Right, I'm going over there to explain what's happened!"

There was a long sigh. "You can try if you like," she said wearily, "but I'm telling you he's not going to sign that report."

We sent a message to the validator asking for an urgent meeting and the following day the team leader, a Dr. Geiser, agreed to meet on the Thursday in Tokyo. It was cutting it dangerously close; the cutoff for the response to the UN was Friday at 17:00 GMT. Taking account of the time difference, that left us thirty-eight hours between the meeting and the deadline.

I flew to Tokyo, met Mina at the airport, and we took the high-speed train from Narita to the other side of Tokyo. Even after living in Beijing for so long, with its urban population of ten million, I found it difficult to take in the almost limitless sprawl of the Japanese capital. As the train roared through the suburbs, we occasionally broke out again into more open areas with little villages, green hillocks, and winding lanes running through neatly clipped fields. By the wayside, there were carved stone shrines—little *hokurra*, spirit warehouses—placed there to protect travelers on the road.

Mina had brought bound copies of a presentation that the team in Beijing had put together. It was clear and well argued, explaining Huaneng's background, its financial resources, and how the two loss-making projects were large even for China. Given that Huaneng had played a key role in the World Bank's efforts to develop fuel-switching projects, we argued that it was not plausible that Huaneng would have failed to think of applying for carbon income on such a large and difficult project. We rehearsed the presentation several times and by the evening, I was feeling more confident that we might make some progress.

The next day, after a final practice run over bowls of Japanese bean curd, scooped out of wooden tubs in the hotel for breakfast, Mina and I walked the two blocks over to the validator's offices feeling extremely tense. There had been heavy rain during the night but the skies had cleared and all traces of pollution had been washed from the air. We came to a nondescript office building and waited in the reception area. I called Cordelia again and asked her what was going on, but she told me that the plant in Shanghai was having some problems finding the right records. I rolled my eyes and told her to keep looking.

When the validator arrived to greet us, my immediate impression was that of a Bavarian professor, more like a kindly old cobbler out of a Tyrolean children's fairy tale than a "nitpicking" carbon emissions auditor. Once he had shown us into the meeting room, he became a bit distracted and began rummaging through a great pile of disorganized papers in cardboard binders, muttering to himself as we made some introductory remarks. Mina jumped in and started asking all sorts of questions—how long he had been in Tokyo, whether he liked it or not, did he have a family with him—but he just kept on rummaging. When he found the piece of paper he was looking for, he looked up through the wire-rimmed glasses on the end of his nose, smiled, and gave us his full attention.

We talked him through the World Bank study and how Huaneng had been a key participant. We explained the size of the group and how it had funds from the stock exchange in New York. While we were talking, Geiser visibly relaxed. He had spent many years working in Germany and had only moved to Japan two years previously. We could tell by his questions that he wasn't familiar with the Chinese approval process for large capital projects, so we explained how it worked. I guessed that it was the first time he had been able to ask questions about the Chinese system and get answers that he could understand.

When we got to the end of the booklet, he sat back for a few moments fidgeting and then said, "*Ach, ja*, this all makes sense, but we need something more solid from the project itself. Do you think there are any meeting minutes or anything like that?" We told him that Cordelia was in contact with the factory but at the mention of that name, he stiffened. There was a long pause and then he said, "Okay. I understand the story you have explained this morning, but I have a problem here." He pushed the document he'd been searching for in his files across the table, turned his computer around to face us, and pulled up the same document on the screen. "We received this from Cordelia as key evidence for prior consideration on your other project down in Nanjing. And we found some problems with it," he said.

I looked at the letter. It seemed to have been written by Huaneng to Cordelia, appointing her as their technical consultant to develop carbon projects. It was dated March 2005, well before the projects started, and it was signed by the president of the company. It should have been perfect evidence to convince the UN that Huaneng had properly considered carbon income before deciding to pick the gas-fired alternative down in Nanjing. But I looked at it more closely; the letterhead looked strange and oddly informal. The signature looked a bit peculiar as well; the typeface below it was uneven and there was a break in the letters. Geiser moved the cursor over the signature area on the letter and clicked. It came up immediately as a separate colored box. The signature had been cut out of another document and pasted into this one. I frowned, still not understanding what he meant. Then he clicked on "properties" and the details of the document came up; it had been created some two years after the signature date, and the author came up as "Cordelia Kong." Geiser said, "We checked on Huaneng's website and this guy didn't become president until several months after the date of this letter, so he can't have signed it then." I realized that the letter Cordelia had sent him was a forgery.

12

借刀殺人

KILL WITH BORROWED KNIFE

If you are limited in your own strength, use the strength of another.

—Third Stratagem of the Thirty-six Ruses of the southern Qi Dynasty, c. AD 489–537

When Dr. Geiser showed us the fake document that day in Tokyo, everything that had happened in the previous six months suddenly seemed to make sense. We figured that Geiser must have lost trust in any documents coming from China and, feeling hoodwinked and frustrated, he had just put everything on hold. When Cordelia responded with persistent phone calls trying to put pressure on him to sign his certificate, he became so confused and exasperated that he just stopped working altogether. He couldn't read Chinese characters or understand any of the documents, so he had to rely on technical translations. Wherever he looked, he found contradictions and ambiguities. The translations seemed to introduce subtly different meanings and inconsistencies that took hours to sort out.

After several months of struggling to make sense of the mess, he saw the fake letter, threw up his hands, and gave up.

When Cordelia finally realized that Geiser was not going to agree to sign his certificate, she was stuck. She could never confess the real reason for the tie-up so we'd ended up wasting months in a state of limbo. But by then, the clock ticking away on the wall behind Geiser in the meeting room in Tokyo reminded us that there were thirty-four hours left until the UN deadline. If we missed it, our Shanghai project would be rejected and any hope of building a carbon business in China would die with it.

Somewhat clutching at straws, I asked Geiser if there was anything we could do to persuade him to sign his certificate.

He raised his eyebrows and, shaking his head, said, "*Ach*, everyone makes all this so complicated, but it's really not so difficult. All I need for 'prior consideration' is some evidence to show that the carbon income was part of Huaneng's original decision to invest in cleaner technology. They can't have made a six-hundred-million-euro investment without doing some sort of calculations, right?" he said, looking momentarily quizzical. "Go back to the original plans. If there's a record that carbon income was a factor in the decision, that's all I need. It really isn't so complicated."

Geiser explained that there'd been no hint that Huaneng had known anything about the fake letter from Cordelia and that he still trusted the evidence from Huaneng. He agreed to look at anything they sent him, but he insisted that it be sent directly by fax from the plant to his office in Tokyo, and not via Cordelia's office.

We scrambled for the first train back out to Narita. Mina dialed up China and told Cissy and Frank to call the plant in Shanghai and ask them to scour through the old files. "Get them to look for any early records," Mina told him. "Management minutes, consultancy contracts, correspondence with the banks, government approvals, anything that mentioned carbon. Tell them to tear the files apart and see what they can find." Just as we were about to get on the flight to Beijing, Frank called to say that the plant was empty;

no one was answering the phones. The management team was in a training course and he couldn't get hold of them until later that evening. Stress levels were mounting; we had been forced into a race against time to find some hidden documents but had almost no clue where to look. I felt as though we were sleepwalking toward a disaster. As a last resort, I asked Frank to try to find Cordelia and arrange for me to see her later that night as soon as I got back to China. If everything else failed, we'd have to try to make a last-ditch effort to persuade her to coordinate with the plant and dig out the old records.

By the time we arrived back in Beijing, it was almost dark. Only the faintest glow of sunlight hovered above the horizon. As we sped along the expressway toward town, tiny lights appeared like pinpricks high up in the towers that arced around the edge of the city, their silhouettes standing out against the darkening twilight sky. I dropped Mina at the office, braced myself for the ordeal, and went straight down to see Cordelia.

I found her in her apartment sitting on one of the huge purple sofas at a low table surrounded by big bundles of faxed documents. I stared at her aghast as she started going through them one by one, picking them up gingerly with her fingertips, as if her nail polish was not yet dry. She seemed to have assembled a collection of barely legible faxes. There were contracts for water pumping stations and grid connection equipment, a rental agreement for some pile drivers, and quality inspection certificates for the turbines. With one glance, I could see that they were all completely useless. I suddenly felt my head spin and heat rush to my face; these documents had nothing to do with carbon. As if from within a fog, she seemed to be waving handfuls of documents around in an agitated fashion, at once chortling nervously and then complaining bitterly that we'd gone around her and talked directly to the plant.

"Of course we've talked to the plant," I exploded, recovering my train of thought. "Are you insane? We've been waiting for eight whole days and you've done absolutely nothing! We can't just stand by and let you ruin a project that could be worth a hundred million!" I slapped the side of my head despairingly. "Geiser is just sitting there twiddling his thumbs and waiting to see some documents and all you've done is dredge out some drivel about pumping stations and pile drivers."

Looking momentarily taken aback, she stood up from the table, fists clenched and eyes blazing.

"Dribble?!" she said. "Dribble!"

"Look," I said, recoiling and trying a more conciliatory tone, "all you have to do is talk to the plant and get them to dig out their early records."

But she just stuck to her old lines.

"You're much too hot-tempered for all of this," she said, waving a sheaf of papers at me. "Leave it to me. You don't understand China. We've got the experts to—"

"What?!" I yelled. "Hogwash! Those cretins upstairs wouldn't know a carbon credit if someone shoved one up their arses."

"Hogwash?" she said looking puzzled. "Arses? Look, you really need to cool off a bit. It might affect your health."

"Health?!" I replied vacantly.

"Yes, it's bad for you, all this shouting. Why don't you have some of this ice cream? It'll help you to cool down your nerves."

At the sight of a tub of Sunmile Pinkish Delicious red-bean-flavored ice cream being thrust toward me, the storm finally broke. I have a vague recollection of intense heat, a blinding white light, flapping documents, and a sound like the honking of geese before my eyes eventually refocused. I lunged for the door, turning back for one last yell before slamming it with all my strength while Cordelia stared after me with a look of utter amazement.

In the taxi, I sat with my head in my hands. I'd gone over to see Cordelia with vague, fragmentary, lunatic hopes of finally persuading her to look for some management minutes, and I'd left with nothing. But at least the news from the office was better. Just before midnight, Frank told us that the plant had found some early minutes that recorded a discussion of the income they could derive from the

UN system and showed calculations of the effect of carbon income on the project returns. "Frank, that's perfect!" I yelled down the phone. "Get them to send us a copy!"

Frank had finally tracked down the chief accountant, an affable and patient man named Zhang who, together with his assistants, had spent the last couple of hours ransacking the files. They'd also found correspondence with the bank, which included use of carbon income in support of a loan application, but when I got to the office and looked at the documents, I noticed with a shudder that the reply from the bank appeared to be dated February 30. To my relief, Cissy said, "Yeah, we already spotted that. It's thirtieth March, not February." They'd sent us a second copy that showed there had just been a break in the earlier scan of the letter; the middle stroke in the character for for "three" or "三,"—which appears in "March" had somehow been erased in the first scan to read "two" or "二," which meant February. It showed how jumpy we'd become. Mina sent a message to Geiser to tell him that minutes were being sent to him in Tokyo directly from the plant and that he should find them waiting first thing the following morning.

Very early the next day, I went to the airport. The day after was my son Sam's birthday and it seemed as if the problems in China had been solved, so I wanted to get home to see him. Coach class was full, so I flew business that day. Just before the plane pushed back from the gate, Mina called and told me that she had talked to Geiser. He had received all the documents. They were being translated and his assistant had told him that they looked fine. There were phone lines on the plane in business class so I told Mina I'd call in every few hours, just in case there was a problem. Relieved after the tension of the previous few days, I fell into a deep sleep.

After about two hours, I woke with a start. After fumbling around with a credit card for a few minutes, I managed to put a call through to Mina. The line was faint and so it was difficult to hear above the rush of air but she just kept repeating that we needed to talk. She was asking again and again if I could hear her and saying that it was really important that we speak urgently. I called back and this time we managed to get a better connection. Mina was highly agitated; Geiser had called her. Earlier that day, he'd told her that he had been happy with the documents, but shortly afterward another set of documents had arrived by fax from Cordelia's office. They looked similar, except that the pagination was all different. Naturally suspicious of anything he received from China, he was now completely confused and was hesitating once again, not knowing what to believe. Mina told me to call Geiser from the plane to try to explain it to him.

"How can I do that?" I said. "I haven't seen either version of the documents!"

"Well, just explain that there might be two versions of the same minutes," she said.

"What do you mean two sets of minutes?! That makes no sense at all!" I said, exasperated.

"Well, you just gotta man up and call him anyway," she said.

By the time I managed to find Geiser, there were only three hours left to the UN deadline. The line was terrible; I could barely hear his voice against the background noise of the aircraft. He seemed to be explaining that he had been happy with the documents, but then suddenly a second set had been faxed over from Cordelia's office. He couldn't read either of them but they didn't look the same.

"The first one starts out with a Chinese character that looks a bit like a tree with a hat on top of it."

"What?"

"But the second, you see, it starts with one that looks more like a stick."

"A stick?"

"*Ja, ja.* A sort of stick thing."

"What kind of stick, Dr. Geiser? Do you think you could be a bit more specific?" I asked, squirming in the seat. "I'm several miles above Siberia right now and it's a bit difficult to read characters over a phone line."

"Well, maybe it's more like a shovel."

"A shovel?" I said, struggling to contain a scream.

Somehow I managed to get some words out: "Dr. Geiser, we've got about a hundred million hanging on that shovel. Could you possibly fax both of the documents to our office and I'll call you right back when Frank's seen them?"

"*Ja, ja*," he said to himself, "and there's another one here that looks a bit like a ladder. Hmm, interesting . . ."

Twenty minutes later, I called Frank. He was puzzled by the two documents; the wording was identical, but the pagination was different. It seemed like there were two versions of the same document and we couldn't explain why. We put through urgent calls to Cordelia, but of course she was nowhere to be found. He called down to the plant, but our contacts there had no idea where the second document had come from. We were completely stumped.

The plane was only an hour from London. I called Geiser again but there wasn't really much that I could say. I just hoped that with all the evidence from the World Bank report, the letters to the banks, and the minutes we had seen the day before, he would figure that the project was valid for the UN, but we were right down to the deadline and there was no time to find out what had actually happened. He was wavering; I was out of options so I just said that he had to go with his instincts. There was really nothing else I could say.

I was out of contact while the plane prepared for landing but the moment we touched down, I called Mina. She sounded completely exhausted but said in a small voice, "It's okay. Geiser's signed his certificate." It had been uploaded onto the UN website at 16:54. We'd made it with six minutes to spare.

I was in China when, several weeks later, the UN registered the plant in Shanghai as an approved carbon reduction project. It was a big step forward for us. They had agreed to accept it once the validator checked the authenticity of the documents he had been given, so we had a few anxious days while the junior members of the validation team went to Shanghai to inspect the originals. They interviewed the banks, the local government, and the equipment suppliers as well as checking the file records. The trip had gone smoothly; they dug out the first approval documents for the coal-fired plant and the amended plans for replacing coal with gas. Geiser could see that carbon income had been mentioned in the minutes so he had concluded that the UN's requirements for prior consideration had been satisfied and sent off a clean report to the UN.

I went down to Shanghai to visit the plant and celebrate with the team there. I'd never seen a better example of how modern technology can clean up industry. The new power plant was located near to the banks of the Yangtse, next to China's largest steelworks. It was a soulless, windswept area of dilapidated factory buildings. Cheap hotels lined the stretches of elevated highways and concrete canals. The skyline was dominated by the great hulking carcasses of blast furnaces and cooling towers. A column of choking black grime rose up from the steelworks; the stench of burning coke and chemicals caught in one's throat. Everywhere was blackness. The power plant sat just beyond the steelworks behind a mass of wires and ceramic insulators with transformer stations and transmission lines leading off toward the city. Inside, there were two coal-fired power stations built about eight years earlier, with heaps of coal, blackened boilers, and a couple of filthy smokestacks that rose about two hundred feet into the air. Nestling between these two huge structures, there was a small blue building that housed the new gas-fired power station; it had three squat chimneys on top, all painted in blue and white. Hedges and trees lined the yard outside.

The power output of the little gas plant, with its neat buildings, its invisible waste gases rising from the chimneys, together with a thin plume of white steam, is more than a gigawatt—enough for a city of several hundred thousand. It's about the same power output as the two monsters that towered over it on either side, wreathed in black and spluttering out fumes and gases.

We toured the new plant with the local management. There were three large turbines that could be switched on and fully operational within forty minutes. The control room reminded me of the one at Wang's plant down in Quzhou, full of monitors and switches, but the plant wasn't working the day we visited since the supply of natural gas was still intermittent. The government was about to complete the pipeline that covered the three thousand miles between the huge gas fields in Turkmenistan and the Yangtse Delta, with its population of 300 million. Costing billions, the new pipeline was one of the biggest infrastructure projects ever undertaken by modern China, and by the time it was fully operational a year or so later, it carried enough gas for the power needs of eighteen huge cities but with only a fraction of the environmental impact of the much cheaper coal.

Although the Shanghai project was registered and ready to issue credits, we knew the actual number that we could generate would be small in the first year because the gas supply to the power station was still restricted. The pipeline from Turkmenistan had been connected, but the booster stations needed to raise the pressure to usable levels were still being installed. But Nanjing lies farther upstream on the pipeline than Shanghai. We heard that the gas supply there was plentiful and the power plant worked overtime, so our attention switched to the second part of our umbrella project with Huaneng, the gas-fired plant in Nanjing.

As we started trying to figure out how to get the Nanjing plant registered at the UN, we knew that even by Chinese standards we were in a very knotty situation. We were stuck between Huaneng, Credit Suisse, Cordelia, and the validator. Cordelia had never prepared any of our commercial contracts with Huaneng and Credit Suisse, so even though the project had been registered at the UN and was ready to generate carbon credits, no commercial terms had been finalized. The UN regulations didn't allow for changes in the counterparties to a registered carbon project unless each of them signed off, so we knew that we couldn't be booted out of the project even by our much larger counterparties. So Huaneng was locked into us as buyer for the credits at Shanghai, but without any commercial terms; we were stuck with Cordelia because she had all the documents needed to push Nanjing forward to registration; Cordelia had a lock on Huaneng because they had no expertise in carbon and had signed a contract appointing her as sole consultant for both projects; and although the validator wouldn't accept any more documents from Cordelia, they were bound by the their contract with her not to take instructions from anyone else. It was a complete mess.

An uneasy standoff prevailed for several weeks as each party waited nervously for the first move. Then Cordelia suddenly sent us an enormous bill. "Is she nuts!?" I asked Mina when she told me. "Having almost ruined the project, now she sends us an invoice!" When we looked at our agreement with her, we reckoned that no fee was due until both projects under the "umbrella" had been registered at the UN. We sent a message that we wanted to make more progress on the project at Nanjing before we'd settle her bill. Mina and Cissy went to see her to try to reach a deal by which we would take over the registration of the Nanjing project in return for paying her fee, but Cordelia was having none of it. She insisted that we pay her first bill unconditionally and then maybe she'd talk.

Over the following weeks, the gloves came off. It all started when some officials from the local Industrial and Commercial Bureau arrived outside the office with grim faces, demanding to inspect our books and see the visas for the foreign staff. The same day, Frank received a call from the Climate Change Department asking how our projects were progressing; they'd heard there were some problems. I couldn't believe this was a coincidence. It looked as though Cordelia had opened fire with all barrels loaded.

I asked Frank to go over and give the officials at the Climate Change Department an update on the registration of the project—it was, after all, one of the biggest in China—and I drove over myself to see the officials at the local Commercial Bureau. I apologized and told them we'd rectify any mistakes that they'd found. They were businesslike but I got the impression that they tended not to deal with foreigners directly. The only complaint was that our business license hadn't been displayed properly in the office, so I chatted with them over some tea for half an hour and then left. That was the last we heard of them.

The following week, a bundle of legal papers landed on my desk. I lifted the corner gingerly and peered inside. Cordelia had decided to sue us. I could see that we were headed for a lengthy arbitration battle and I was worried. Although it was pretty certain that we would win the arbitration, it would take eighteen months before there was a judgment and we didn't have that time to lose. Mina and Cissy went down to see Cordelia again to try to reach a compromise, but she was adamant: pay the bill first unconditionally and then she might talk about Nanjing. Time was ticking away and there was complete deadlock; we had to try something else.

Frank suggested we should hold a brainstorming session and work through the Thirty-six Ruses, the list of ancient military stratagems that I'd stumbled across in the old dusty bookshops on Tile Factory Street all those years before. Of course, I knew that we shouldn't get too carried away with these ideas and elevate them into some miraculous solution to all our problems. But they can provide a framework to think through different options, rather like a set of prompts or a checklist of tactics that might be considered.

First we tried the Twenty-sixth Ruse—"pointing at the mulberry while cursing the scholar-tree." Frank explained that it relied on scaring an enemy's supporters away from a conflict by making it appear too dangerous to get involved. He thought we should try it on Cordelia's lawyers. Mina went over and showed them a copy of the fake document and we heard a week later that they told Cordelia to drop her arbitration claim shortly afterward. It was our first minor success.

Next we tried the Thirty-third Ruse—"disrupting the enemy's alliances." Cordelia had a cozy relationship with Huaneng and she had been careful to keep us apart. We'd only met Huaneng a few times since we signed the original term sheet. But if we could drive a wedge between them, we might make some progress on the project. Mina and I went over to Huaneng's offices on the west side of Beijing together with Frank. In those days, Huaneng was located opposite the old broadcasting center with its Stalinist wedding-cake architecture and the red star at the top. We waited downstairs in a dingy reception area, but there was no one on the desk. After a few moments, Frank called up to the offices; he told me later that he could hear the sound of raised voices in the background, one of which had a Shanghainese accent.

When we met up with the people there, they seemed suspicious. Although Huaneng was the largest carbon emitter on the planet at the time, it had no specific department in charge of carbon reductions. The people in the commercial division who were dealing with the project had no expertise in carbon, so they were painfully cautious. We had several rounds of meetings to try to persuade them to let us take the lead on the Nanjing project, but they stuck with Cordelia. The strategy of "disrupting the enemy's alliances" had failed. The relationships were too strong to break.

Next we tried the second stratagem—"Besiege Wei to Rescue Zhao." It avoids a head-on battle with a strong adversary, and instead attacks a weaker false target to apply pressure indirectly. The Shanghai project was ready to start generating income, so we told Huaneng that we'd refuse to issue any credits until we had sorted out Nanjing. We hoped that threatening to hold up Shanghai might put pressure on them to move forward on Nanjing, but they just shrugged their shoulders. Huaneng was a state-run business, so nobody had any economic interest in the success of either project. Just like Wang at Quzhou, all they wanted was to avoid making mistakes and getting blamed later on. We were completely stuck. As we flailed around trying to break the knot, it seemed as if we had been dragged into what Sunzi had called the worst possible situation: "a protracted battle on hostile ground."

Around this time, a huge backlog of projects had developed in the UN system. Once carbon trading became better known in China, factories all over the country jumped on the bandwagon in search of extra income. Many of the projects didn't meet the UN rules, and the validators had become submerged under a tidal wave of dubious carbon applications. The UN responded by tightening the rules and rejecting spurious projects. The validators were told to clean up their books and get rid of bad projects. After months of deadlock, Geiser finally lost patience with the Nanjing project and told us he wanted to ditch the assignment. He asked us to meet directly with his assistants based in Hong Kong.

On the way down to meet them, I rehearsed a few arguments to persuade them not to resign from the project. I knew that it was a difficult project; all the other validators were so stretched that they would never take on our Nanjing project, and it was impossible to predict how Cordelia and Huaneng might react if we tried to change the validator. I tried to come up with reasons to be optimistic that we would be able to solve the impasse and move on with the project, but when I arrived at the offices in Kowloon, I found the people there to be much more stubborn than I had expected. They told me that they had been instructed to halt work on all projects where information requests had remained unanswered for more than three months. In our case, it was more than six months since they had received any new documents. They were preparing to withdraw from the project and notify the UN. I knew that no other validator would touch the project, so it would effectively kill it dead.

After about half an hour, there was a break in the meeting; I stared out of the window. It was a suitably depressing and muggy day in Hong Kong. It looked as though storms were approaching. I weighed up the possibilities. We'd been slogging it out with Cordelia for more than six months and there was no resolution in sight. I knew something had to give. Trying to persuade the validator not to resign would just prolong the agony. There was one last option from the Thirty-six Ruses; it was a risky approach but there seemed no option but to try the third ruse—"Kill with borrowed knife," which says that "if you are limited in your own strength and have no means to attack directly, use the strength of another." I figured that the only threat that might persuade Huaneng to get rid of Cordelia would have to come from the validator. Rather than threatening to resign, I asked, how about they instead draft a negative validation report stating that they had concluded that the project clearly broke all the UN's requirements? They agreed to send it to Huaneng and Credit Suisse with a note saying that if they didn't receive the outstanding information within seven days, they would inform the UN that they had concluded that the project was bogus.

When they saw the notice, Huaneng was faced with the prospect of losing the project entirely. By using the indirect methods of dealing with conflict so favored by Mao and his mother, we had presented the management there with an even greater risk than staying with Cordelia. A couple of days later, Cissy went over to Huaneng and after a few hours' meeting, she extracted an official document appointing us as the sole technical adviser to the project. Cordelia was out of the picture. At last we had broken the logjam.

13

摸著石頭過河

THE FOURTH CHINESE RULE:

Cross the River by Feeling for the Stones

—Oft-quoted description of the experimental nature of China's reform process, ironically made first by Chen Yun, one of China's conservatives

When Mao died in 1976, the people of China were grieving, but not so much for the departed helmsman as for the suffering of their country. A few months before the end, Mao had called the Politburo to his bedside and, looking back over his life, said:

> In my life, I have done two things. First I fought Chiang Kai-shek and drove him off to a few small islands; I fought the Japanese for eight years and sent them home. We fought our way to Beijing and at last to the Forbidden City. There are not many people who do not recognize those achievements. . . . The second thing I have done, you all know. It is to launch the Cultural Revolution, which has not many supporters and many who opposed it. But this matter is not yet ended. It is a legacy which must be handed down to the next generation. How should it be handed over? If not in peace, then in turmoil. If this is not handled prop-

erly, there will be a rain of blood and a wind of rotting fish. How will you cope? Heaven only knows!

The man who had no option but to cope with Mao's grim legacy was Deng Xiaoping.

Four feet ten and bullet-headed, Deng smoked, drank, and spat all his life. Toughened by years of war, he had known the extremes of triumph and defeat and endured multiple episodes of disgrace and rehabilitation when he lost and regained power. When he finally emerged as China's paramount leader at the age of seventy-five, no one could have been better prepared. Mencius wrote more than two thousand years ago:

> Heaven, when it is about to place a great responsibility upon someone, first tests his resolution with suffering, wears out his sinews with work, starves his body to skin and bone, exposes him to emptiness and poverty and brings chaos to all that he is. Thus his intentions become resolute and his deficiencies are made good.

Tempered, wiser, and hardened by each successive downfall, Deng finally emerged as China's paramount leader with nearly fifty years' of experience at the center of Chinese politics. In the two decades that followed, hundreds of millions of people in the countryside were lifted out of absolute poverty for the first time in history and China emerged from more than a century of chaos. "In his life," his daughter wrote, "he was overthrown three times and reinstated three times. Each time he drew greater attention and each time he went on to achieve greater success. This is neither myth nor fabrication. It is the true story of Deng Xiaoping."

Deng was born in a small country village in the southwestern province of Sichuan. The climate there is wet and humid and the seasons are distinct. Giant earthworks on the Dujiang River have irrigated thousands of square miles of farmland ever since they were built there in 256 BC. Mulberry bushes, prickly peppercorn plants, and red date trees are scattered on the hillsides; gourds, tea, chives, rice, melons, and potatoes grow in profusion on the fertile basin below. No wonder Sichuan is known as "China's granary."

Deng was born in 1904, some ten years after Mao. His ancestors had moved there from Jiangxi in 1380, the thirteenth year of the first Ming emperor. Deng's father had a plot of farmland where he reared silkworms, and nearby, the limed walls and thick wooden doors of the family's courtyard were protected by geese kept as guard animals rather than for their meat. Deng's childhood had none of the feuding that Mao had endured with his father, and this could explain why he was a steadier person with more inner peace. While Mao was a serial philanderer, Deng—after two brief and unsuccessful marriages—was devoted to his third wife and family and he never suffered the depression that occasionally visited the Chairman.

At fifteen, Deng left home and went to Chongqing to study. This great, seething city, now of thirty million, sat under a layer of heat haze between steep mountainsides carved out by two great rivers—the Jialing and the Yangtse—that meet at the city's eastern tip. It was in Chongqing that Deng became involved in protest. The commissioner of police had stolen public money to buy Japanese goods, which he then brazenly sold in a market outside the police station. Deng joined the students who marched through the streets calling for his arrest.

During World War I, there were labor shortages in France so a work-study program had been set up to help young Chinese travel there. Deng's family provided him with some money and in 1920, he set off on the long journey to Europe. Several months later, dressed formally and with pointed shoes, the young Chinese students arrived in Marseille, "immobile and silent," according to one of their hosts. Deng studied for five months but then ran out of money, so he found a job making paper flowers and then pulling red-hot ingots through a steel mill with long pincers. It was dangerous work; minor misalignments in the rollers sent metal flying in all directions, causing horrible burns and injuries. Deng lived in a Chinese hostel that was so crowded that tents were pitched in the vegetable patch at the back. His time in France had a lasting effect on his life and opened his eyes both to the immense power of European industrialization and the social inequalities that it brought.

While he was in Paris, Deng met Zhou Enlai and joined the Communist Party before traveling to Moscow for training. Returning to China in 1927—just as Chiang Kai-shek launched his surprise *White Terror* attack against the Communists—Deng fled Shanghai and joined Mao in his newly founded Soviet deep in the mountains of Jiangxi. There he became the Party secretary of one of the outlying counties. It was a time of splits and factions within the Party. The central committee wanted to retaliate against Chiang Kai-shek by attacking the cities held by Nationalist forces, whereas Mao believed that the Reds should first build up their strength in the countryside. After long arguments, Mao was stripped of his military command. Deng, as part of the Mao faction, was purged and he lost all his posts. He was ostracized by his closest colleagues; his wife left him and married one of his accusers. But Deng never betrayed Mao. Years later, in the Cultural Revolution, when Mao attacked Deng and dismissed him from all his posts, he never destroyed him. Perhaps this was due to these memories of when Deng's loyalty had been tested all those years earlier in Jiangxi.

Deng was with Mao on the Long March and then in Yan'an. He was always responsible for practical implementation rather than theory. During the years that Mao sat philosophizing in his cave, Deng dealt with the reality of deep poverty in the surrounding countryside, organizing land reform, seizing fields from the landlords, and distributing them among the destitute peasantry.

In 1937, while the Communists were holed up in Yan'an, Japan had invaded China from the northeast. A year later, in a bid to halt their advance, Chiang Kai-shek dynamited the dikes of the Yellow River, causing massive flooding. The river takes its name from the color of the pale powdery soil that it picks up in the upper reaches. As the flow slows down nearer the coast, the fine silt sinks to the bottom. Over the centuries, the banks on either side have been built up to prevent flooding, but the river has continued to silt up, so the dikes have been raised higher and higher. In some places, the bed of the river is thirty feet above the surrounding fields, so the tactic of destroying the dikes to halt an approaching army has been used before. In the late Ming Dynasty, the governor of the city of Kaifeng tried to use the river to destroy a besieging army, only to end up flooding his own city. When Chiang Kai-shek blasted the dikes in the face of the advancing Japanese armies, he only halted them temporarily and ended up destroying thousands of villages in the process, leaving half a million dead and the fields covered with silt where the crops could not grow. The mouth of the Yellow River shifted hundreds of miles to the south. The resulting famine, and Chiang's subsequent failure to protect ordinary Chinese from the brutality of Japanese rule, provided a major boost in popularity for the Communists. So, after the bombs fell on Hiroshima and Nagasaki and the Japanese emperor surrendered, civil war broke out between the two great rivals in China. Eventually, Mao triumphed in 1949 and the Nationalists fled to the island of Taiwan.

After the People's Republic of China was proclaimed in the same year, Deng went back to his home province and established the new government in the southwest. In 1952, he was called back to Beijing and worked first at the Finance Ministry, then as general secretary, ranked sixth in the Party hierarchy. He was recognized widely for his competence and flair and gained a reputation for being decisive.

Deng worked smoothly with Mao for more than twenty years, but after the disaster of the Great Leap Forward, cracks began to appear in their relationship. When Liu Shaoqi took charge after the famine, Deng was responsible for putting the economy back on its feet. Rather than consulting with Mao, Deng just got on with the job. At meetings about Communist theory, he would sit at the back with his hearing aid switched off. Mao complained that he felt like a dead ancestor, "respected but not listened to."

When Mao set out to destroy Liu Shaoqi in the Cultural Revolution, he was determined to reverse the emphasis on practical economics and return to revolutionary class struggle. As Liu's deputy, Deng was inevitably caught up in Mao's onslaught. Labeled "China's Big Number Two Running Dog of Capitalism," Deng was placed under house arrest in the central Party compound in Beijing and his children were sent away. He was attacked relentlessly in newspapers. Threatening posters appeared on the walls of his home and he was subjected to "struggle sessions" where he was insulted by Red Guards and made to kneel on the floor—but unlike many of his colleagues, it appears that Deng was never beaten. Mao protected him from the worst violence; his children were not so lucky. Deng had no news of them for two years, until he heard that, after weeks of relentless threats and violence at the hands of the Red Guards, his son had "fallen" from an upstairs window at Beijing University. No one had dared to treat him at the hospital and he was left permanently paralyzed from the waist down. Deng's wife cried for three days when she heard the news, while Deng withdrew into a great silence, smoking cigarettes one after another late into the night.

In October 1969, Deng, his wife, and stepmother were all sent far away to the south to be reeducated through labor. For the next four years they lived on the top floor of a small house in an infantry school in Jiangxi. Each day, they rose at six thirty for an hour of supervised reading of the works of Chairman Mao. After breakfast, Deng walked to a tractor repair station, where he undertook manual work, much like he had been used to in France. In the afternoon, they did simple household chores. They grew vegetables, raised chickens, split firewood, and washed the floors. Life was spartan, but it was not violent. Deng cut down on his smoking and drinking and their days fell into a fixed routine.

His daughter, who joined them two years later, recalled that despite living in exile and having been shorn of power, Deng never let his emotions run away with him. "He did not become depressed," she wrote; "he never gave up hope." The years in forced seclusion gave him time to think. Like Churchill and Lincoln, Deng used his time in the wilderness to clarify his thoughts about the future.

While Mao had used his time in Yan'an to develop his political and military theories, in Jiangxi Deng paced around the compound thinking about the practical steps needed to rescue China from political turmoil and set it on the road to modernization. Hour after hour, day after day, year after year, he paced along a path around the house, lost deep in thought.

After Liu Shaoqi fell from power, Mao gave the second slot in the hierarchy to one of the top generals, Lin Biao. There were stories that Lin Biao, an obsessive hypochondriac, had sustained a head injury years before in a bizarre accident when he donned a Japanese uniform, only to be mistakenly shot at by one of his own soldiers and fall from his horse. Then, after several years as Mao's deputy, Lin Biao suddenly fled China, fearing that a plot by his son to depose Mao had been uncovered. He scrambled a plane and headed toward Russia with his wife and son but the plane crashed in Mongolia, killing all on board. Mao fell into a deep depression, taking to his bed for several months. China was left rudderless and racked by internal fighting, its economy in chaos. Zhou Enlai, the prime minister, had been diagnosed with terminal cancer, so, with no one else to turn to, Mao at last brought Deng back to Beijing. In 1973, Deng was reinstated as vice premier.

When he returned to work, Deng had no illusions about the depths of China's predicament. Many capable leaders had been dismissed or killed in the Cultural Revolution and there were shortages of basic household goods such as cooking oil and matches. The world had been turned on its head; science institutes and universities were run by peasants and low-ranking soldiers, while scholars toiled in the fields. Workers across the country had put down tools to study the Little Red Book and factories were at a standstill. Deng recalled later that when he was in disgrace in Jiangxi, he had offered for his son to repair the workers' radios, only to discover that nobody had one. He had been shocked that after twenty years of socialism, ordinary people still couldn't afford a radio. So, as soon as he returned to power, Deng set out on a program to bring order to the ruined economy.

Many factories in China were failing to meet targets because they could not get the supplies that they needed. There were almost no highways, so most goods were delivered by train—but the railways were in chaos. Major accidents were common and thousands of railcars were idle. Trains were habitually late because conductors drank on the job and drivers stopped off for lunch. At Xuzhou, a major rail intersection serving the north of China, there had been continuous fighting between Red Guard factions since 1967 and the Rail Bureau had failed to ship its quota for nearly two years. The bureau chief had access to arms and resisted any attempt to impose order. When the Public Security Bureau sent policemen to arrest his subordinates, he just arrested the policemen instead. So when Mao's train was delayed and had to be rerouted around Xuzhou because of the trouble, Deng grabbed the opportunity to tackle the problem.

Summoning key provincial leaders to Beijing to forge a consensus, Deng drew up a plan and had it "chopped" by the Central Committee. Just as had been the case at Wang's chemical factory in Quzhou, a chopped document was critical to show that it wasn't just the idea of one leader who might lose power but a collective decision supported by the whole leadership. Deng's deputy went to Xuzhou with the document, arrested the railway chief, and called mass meetings with thousands of people. Within a month, blockages were cleared and the railways started functioning. Deng extended the success to other railway hubs and from there to the steel and coal industries. His biggest problem in unblocking the economy was that local officials feared that Mao might change his mind and they would be attacked later on for helping Deng. Throughout these years, Deng was under constant fire from the leftists, in particular Mao's wife, who was a major supporter of the Cultural Revolution and still controlled the media and cultural affairs. With Deng embarking on practical reforms to get the economy moving, a tug-of-war developed at the top of Chinese politics between the reformers and the leftists led by Madame Mao.

In January 1976, China's long-suffering prime minister died. The announcement on loudspeakers around Beijing of Zhou Enlai's death provoked an outpouring of grief that might be compared to that in America when Franklin Roosevelt died. While a few old cadres may have thought privately that Zhou had been too willing to work with Mao, most ordinary people felt that he had protected them and curbed even greater excesses in the Cultural Revolution. News of Zhou's funeral spread by word of mouth and despite freezing weather, more than a million people lined the streets for the procession. Two million took wreaths and poems to the Monument to the People's Heroes on Tiananmen Square. Thousands wept silently, reading the posters and shaking their heads, grieving not only for Zhou but for China and for themselves.

After Zhou's death, Madame Mao and Deng squared off in political battle. "In the Party, there are moderates and leftists," she declared during a rally. Drawing her arm around in a majestic gesture, she touched her nose and said, "I—humble I—am the leader of the leftists." The Cultural Revolution had given her a platform for her quest for vindication, self-expression, and revenge. "Man's contribution to human history is nothing more than a drop of sperm," she declared. Her lifelong struggle to escape from being a man's possession had reached its climax as Mao began to fail. As the battle lines were drawn, her aim was to use the living but enfeebled Mao to rule China herself in all but name.

The festival of Qing Ming fell a few months later at the beginning of spring. It's a time to sweep the graves of ancestors and honor the dead. That year, a few days before the festival, white wreaths once more began to appear around the monument on Tiananmen Square. Eulogies for Zhou Enlai were pasted on the balustrades, together with posters attacking Mao's wife and her "Gang of Four." By the time of the festival, in defiance of orders from the Beijing Committee, a million people had visited the square and in places the wreaths were piled twenty feet deep. When the Politburo met to consider the situation, Mao's wife demanded that the wreaths be removed.

Before dawn, two hundred trucks arrived. Workers tossed armfuls of wreaths into the back and hauled them away. After sunrise, the crowds swelled, growing angry as news spread that the wreaths had been removed. Defiant, they assaulted the Great Hall of the People, smashing windows, overturning cars, burning bicycles, and surrounding a small guardhouse where some policemen were trapped inside. Most of the crowds dispersed at dusk before the military moved in to arrest the stragglers.

An official working in the Party archives said that to Mao, this incident was devastating. "At the very site where millions of young Red Guards had shouted 'long-live-long-live' . . . the same multitudes were roaring protest against his rule. . . . He knew the judgment of history would be exceedingly harsh and was overwhelmed by fear and depression."

The Politburo met. Deng was attacked by the leftists and held responsible for the disturbances. Dismissed from office, he fell for the third time, but nothing could disguise the truth. Mao had lost the popular mandate, Zhou had become the people's hero, and Deng, as Zhou's heir, had won the support of ordinary Chinese to become their next leader.

Mao's chosen successor, Chairman Hua Guofeng, took over immediately after Mao's death in September 1976. Hua had spent most of his life as a mid-ranking regional official and his main claim to the top job was a conversation with Mao in which the departed Chairman had allegedly said, "With you in charge, my heart is at ease." When Hua attempted to bolster his position with a propaganda campaign urging people to follow "whatever decisions Mao had made and whatever instructions Chairman Mao had left," it became known derisively as "whateverism." Hua's self-interested idea of blindly following Mao's instructions regardless of the actual situation clashed sharply with Deng's more practical approach. At the end of 1978, the two-year power struggle between the "whatever-ists" and the "practice" faction was resolved at a key Party meeting. Without a single shot being fired, Deng emerged triumphant as paramount leader of the world's most populous nation.

By rejecting Mao's utopian politics in favor of pragmatism, Deng set China on a path to recovery that had eluded the previous ten generations. Henry Kissinger wrote of his surprise at their first meeting: "Deng articulated no grand philosophy. Unlike Mao, he made no claims about the Chinese people's unique destiny." Instead, he talked about the reform of the Metallurgical Ministry and the regularization of railway workers' lunch breaks. The strategy was clear: China would focus on the economic practicalities of development rather than the political heroism of revolution. Dogma was dumped in favor of good management; class struggle and mass campaigns were replaced by humdrum necessities, such as proper accounting records and reliable train timetables.

His first task was to try to heal the wounds of the Cultural Revolution. Deng's predecessor, Chairman Hua, had arrested Madame Mao and the Gang of Four, but the task of finally burying the Cultural Revolution fell to Deng Xiaoping. The fact that Deng's son's had been paralyzed at the hands of Red Guards might have given him a reason to seek revenge, but Deng rejected suggestions of a widespread purge. Instead he tried to lance the ulcer with a televised trial of Madame Mao and her immediate accomplices, collectively known as the Gang of Four. But his plans of an orderly trial quickly went adrift. Madame Mao, her ivory features standing out against an immaculate jet-black trouser suit, groomed to the last degree and without a hair out of place, shouted down the judges and had to be repeatedly bundled out of the courtroom. Alone and defiant, she sat behind a nest of microphones in a barred cage. "Spy!' she shouted during a witnesses testimony. "Revisionist!" Leaning back in her chair, head tilted upward, she would remove her glasses and hold them at an angle in her right hand, facing the judges, and say, "What you are doing is asking a widow to pay her husband's debt.

To you all, I say, I am happy and honored to pay Chairman Mao's debt." At other times, she boxed her own ears, shouting, "I won't listen to this. I have questions to ask of my own!" Her whole defense rested on the case that everything she did was at Mao's bidding and that the court had no right to try the dead Chairman. "I was Mao's dog," she said. "What he said bite, I bit!" Sentenced to death but suspended for two years "to see how she behaves," she was hauled from the courtroom with one last defiant shout: "To rebel is justified! Down with the revisionists led by Deng Xiaoping!" And with that old Cultural Revolution slogan still ringing in everyone's ears, she promptly disappeared from history.

Even though Deng was recognized as China's paramount leader, he was never in control in the same way that Mao had been. But just as in his favorite game of bridge, Deng was ready to play the hand he was dealt. Over time, he became a skillful balancer of the deep rivalries between the reformers and conservatives. Rather than trying to develop some overarching strategy, Deng felt his way forward with ad hoc, piecemeal measures that tried to achieve smooth and orderly transition. Deng pushed bold experiments, broadening them if they worked but quietly abandoning them if they didn't. The only thing that mattered to Deng was results. "Don't argue about things," he said. "Just try it. If it works, let it spread."

Deng had visited the United States for the first time in 1974, when he was vice premier, and he was shocked at what he found. He felt that China had wasted thirty years. "The more we see, the more we realize how backward we are," he said. Several years later, when a top-level study mission went to Europe, the friendliness and openness of their hosts took the Chinese officials totally by surprise. As they toured factories, shops, and science institutes, they were amazed by the high standards of living for workers, whom they had expected to find oppressed by capitalism. They visited ports, rode on trains, and toured airports and chemical factories. They were stunned by the use of computers in a Swiss power plant. Agricultural productivity was higher than they could ever have imagined. When they came back to China they immediately reported to the Politburo. Everyone became so excited that they extended the meeting deep into the night. One member of the team said,

In a little over a month of inspection, our eyes were opened . . . everything we saw and heard startled every one of us. We were enormously stimulated. . . . We thought capitalist countries were backward and decadent. When we left our own country to have a look, we realized things were completely different.

The Politburo concluded that if other countries can import capital and material for export processing, "Why can't we?"

Deng started by tackling state-owned factories. He approved a small trial run in Sichuan, where a few factories were allowed to retain their own profits and make personnel appointments without interference from the local government. The experiment worked so well that even before it became government policy, there were more than a hundred factories operating under the new scheme in Sichuan alone. Soon it was extended to whole cities; as a first step, in a midlevel town in central China, named Shashi, small factories were merged into big ones to reach economies of scale. The pilot scheme worked, so a year later larger towns were included: first Changzhou near the coast, then large industrial cities like Wuhan, Shenyang, and Dalian.

Cautious experimentation was also tried in the countryside, where reform was much more sensitive. The revolution had been founded on the bedrock of land reform, which had liberated peasants from thousands of years of exploitation, so any reintroduction of private ownership into the countryside was a delicate matter. But the truth was that there were still places where the peasants could hardly feed themselves any better than they had done under the landlord class. After the Party secretary of Nine-Dragons village in Sichuan—known locally as "Beggars Village"—secretly allowed the peasants to farm peripheral land and keep the produce themselves rather than turn it over to the commune, productivity leaped three-fold. When Deng visited Sichuan and found reforms under way that had not been reported to Beijing, he just told officials to get on with it. In Anhui Province, destitute peasants at Small Hill Village secretly agreed between themselves to farm plots privately. When the provincial Party secretary asked Deng's advice about how to proceed with such a sensitive new policy, he replied, "You don't need to engage in debates, just go ahead, that's all. Just seek the truth from facts." Between 1978 and 1982, peasant incomes doubled.

The improved efficiency in the fields created a new problem of mass unemployment, and by the mid-eighties, hundreds of millions of peasants were out of work. Once more, the Party improvised by encouraging rural governments to set up cooperative businesses. Because transportation systems were so backward, most villages had their own small workshops for making simple spare parts for tractors or irrigation pumps. When they were allowed to start making other products, they rapidly expanded into new areas like machined parts, herbal medicines, and molded plastics. Within a decade, these "township and village enterprises" employed more than 100 million people. Deng said of these new businesses: "This was not anything that I or any of the other comrades had foreseen; it just came out of the blue."

Deng just stuck to practicalities. On a trip to Guangdong, he was told that thousands of Chinese youths were risking their lives to swim or run to Hong Kong, at the time still a British possession. Instead of suggesting more fencing to stop people leaving, as the officials had expected, he told them to set up exchange centers for fruit and vegetables so that local people could sell produce to Hong Kong. If the standard of living either side of the border was so different, migration was inevitable, he said.

The following Chinese New Year, the governor of Guangdong went to his hometown and heard of the story of "the two Luofang villages." Apparently, hundreds of people had left their hometown of Luofang and fled across the Hong Kong border, where they had set up another village with the same name. Average income in the new Luofang village was more than ten times higher than the old town, so when the governor heard the story, he decided to do something about it.

A Hong Kong shipping magnate wanted a new site for ship breaking, so the governor proposed the idea of a "special economic zone" where foreigners would be allowed to do business. Deng approved of the idea, saying, "During the war, wasn't Yan'an a special zone?!" Four zones were established in minor southern cities, one at the tiny fishing village of Shenzhen, which is now a city of ten million with the busiest container port in the world. As these first zones proved successful, more were opened farther up the coast, but even after five years of operation, Deng still said, "Shenzhen is an experiment. We need more time to see whether it has gone well. We wish it success; if it fails, it will provide some lessons." Shanghai did not become a special economic zone for ten years—the city was too important for experimentation—but in the decades that followed these first experiments, China's exports from these special zones rose to trillions of dollars.

By the mid-eighties, some companies found themselves strapped for cash and started experimenting with selling stocks and bonds to their employees to raise capital. In a northern industrial town of Shenyang, the local government set up a room where people could trade securities. Three months later, Shanghai set up a similar exchange. When the chairman of the New York Stock Exchange visited China in 1986 and asked to see "the Shanghai Stock Exchange," he was taken to a single room of about forty square feet, with a couple of desks stacked with shoe boxes stuffed with strips of paper. Twenty years later, Shanghai's market capitalization was more than $2 trillion. In Shenzhen, the local government just went ahead and started a stock exchange even though Beijing had repeatedly rejected their applications. It already had three hundred trading offices before there was any official permission or regulatory oversight. This lag between practice and policy became known as "get on the bus first, buy the ticket later." Deng had remarked at the time:

> Is the stock market good or bad? Do they entail dangers? Are they peculiar to capitalism? Can socialism make use of them? We allow people to reserve judgment, but we must try these things out. If, after one or two years of experimentation, they prove feasible, we can expand them. Otherwise, we can put a stop to them and be done with it. What is there to be afraid of?

Deng's method of cautious experimentation—that of pushing forward, retreating and consolidating, quietly closing down projects that failed—came unstuck in 1988 when he decided to tackle price reform. Even in the mid-eighties, China still had coupons for rationing household goods such as rice, flour, and cooking oil, and prices were tightly controlled by the central plan. Over the summer of 1988, a debate raged in the Party compounds about relaxing price controls, and when the new policy was announced, there was panic buying in the cities. Inflation took off and there were widespread street protests. The government backed off, but it could not control inflation, which became a source of serious complaint from ordinary people. This policy blunder had come at the worst possible time. As the economy had grown over the previous decade, there were inevitably winners and losers. Stories of widespread corruption, with officials extracting bribes from entrepreneurs in return for favorable policies, fed a mounting sense of injustice and inequality. China's cities were tense.

The following year, in April 1989, one of China's leading reformers, Hu Yaobang, had a heart attack at a Politburo meeting. His shocked colleagues rushed him to the hospital, where, after recovering for a week, he suddenly died. Within a few hours of his death, posters appeared all over Beijing University and the following day students marched to Tiananmen Square. Hu had been popular with students and intellectuals after protests three years earlier against living conditions and restrictions on freedom at the universities. When Hu tried to engage in a dialogue with the students, he had been attacked by the hard-liners and sacked for being too lenient. But it was no wonder the students protested; conditions in student dormitories were notorious. At my old university, I had often seen seven students sharing one small room crammed with bunk beds. Outside, the badly lit corridors were hung with laundry and the cracked floors were covered with spit, old biscuit packets, and rice. Life on campus was full of petty restrictions. And upon graduation, jobs were allocated to students by officials who could use that power to bully them.

At first the police made no attempt to stop the student marches. Over the following weeks, the government mishandled the escalating crisis. Deep divisions in the leadership after the failure of price reforms prevented any unified response. At the end of April, Deng approved a strongly worded editorial designed to intimidate the students into going back to the universities. The editorial backfired badly, emboldening the students and bringing many ordinary citizens out into the streets. There were scuffles around the main Party compound; traffic was disrupted, classes were empty. By May, railway workers were marching in the streets, judges left courtrooms, and journalists refused to report the news. One TV announcer simply said on the air, "There's no news today!"

Although the majority of ordinary people united around the student protests against corruption and inflation, the students themselves were not unified. Some were bold orators who could sway a crowd, but there were no strategists with a long-term unified program. They could only incite people on Tiananmen Square, not control them, and the movement split into factions. After a testy meeting between the prime minister and a group of students who interrupted him repeatedly on national television, the central government declared martial law. But the army could not get through to the square. Hundreds of thousands of civilians took to the streets, stopping the People's Liberation Army in its tracks.

Deng found himself confronted with a mass movement that Mao

would have been proud of, but this time it was against the Party itself. Faced with the prospect of a complete collapse of central authority, the Second Chinese Rule kicked in. Two weeks later, as the world watched in horror, three waves of troops used live bullets to fight their way through a hail of bricks, bottles, and Molotov cocktails, and, in the early hours of June 4, the square was cleared. Many innocent people had been killed. It was a catastrophe that has left a deep and lasting chasm between the Party and the people.

Even at that terrible time of crisis in China, Deng just pressed ahead. Only five days after the tragedy, he said, "We should open up to the outside world instead of closing our doors—open wider than before." But he knew that to have any hope of regaining trust, the Party had to deliver real improvement in the lives of ordinary people. That meant tackling corruption, opening up China to the outside world, and—above all—growing the economy to provide jobs and wider prosperity.

Paradoxically, the collapse of the Soviet bloc coupled with the trauma of Tiananmen seemed to goad Deng into even greater efforts for reform, but the Party was no longer at his bidding; the leftists were in the ascendant. When he warned the Politburo that in order to survive, socialism had to rely equally on markets and planning, he was ignored. Two years later when Deng told senior officials in Shanghai that "reform and opening up is the only path to making the nation wealthy and the people strong," his words were not even reported in the national media.

Finally, at the age of eighty-eight, brittle in body but still sound in mind, in January 1992, Deng set off from Beijing in a special train with his family to spend the Chinese New Year in the south. This iconic journey, which became known as the *nan xun* or "southern inspection tour," evoked memories of the grand expeditions made by the Qing emperors when China was at the height of its power. It took him far away from Beijing, toward the south where market reforms had gone furthest and resistance to austerity was strongest. He stopped off in Wuhan for twenty minutes while the train took on water and supplies, telling the provincial governor on the platform, "Every time you turn on the television you see meetings. We hold countless meetings and our speeches are too long. We should spend more time on practical matters. I suggest you do something about it!" The following day he arrived in Shenzhen, eight years after his last visit, and seemed pleased by what he found. The city had been transformed beyond recognition, with high-rise buildings and heavy traffic everywhere. Deng urged local officials to be bolder in reform. At Zhuhai, he toured high-tech factories and held meetings with the top military officials. Proceeding up the coast, he urged officials everywhere to be open-minded and seize the opportunity to accelerate development.

Deng's "southern inspection tour" came at a pivotal time. The leadership that emerged after Tiananmen was cautious, directionless, and hesitant. China seemed to be drifting. It took two months before the "southern inspection tour" was reported in the national press and it only burst out into the open at the end of March.

I remember the day well. A knot of excited colleagues had gathered at the gates to the office and were discussing the reports, running up and down corridors and shouting; it felt more like reports of a major victory at a baseball game had just broken rather than an eighty-eight-year-old had just gone on a family vacation. But I had failed entirely to grasp the significance at the time. Within months, China was back on track with a new wave of reform and a new way forward; Deng retired finally from all his positions in September of that year, saying, "I have fulfilled my responsibility."

Nearly five years later, a few months before the handover of Hong Kong, Deng died at the age of ninety-three. I remember coming to the office very early that morning. It was cold and damp and a strong wind blew. I hadn't heard the news and Old Lu, a colleague who had arrived before me, just said, "*Deng da ren deng-buliao Xianggang de huifu*"—Big Man Deng wasn't able to wait for the return of Hong Kong. I turned my face to the wind; it was the end of an era.

THE FOURTH CHINESE RULE

When Deng stepped aside in 1992, he had achieved a transformation in China that had eluded its leaders for a hundred and fifty years. He had made China strong again. The changes that took place in Chinese society under Deng were in some respects deeper than any since the Han Dynasty, two thousand years earlier. Yet when he finally emerged at the top toward the end of his long and tumultuous life, he had no overarching dogma or plan. There was no fixed road map, only a goal to aim for. Deng had no time for romantic idealism in which reality had to comply with a theory. Rejecting utterly the Western orthodoxy of economic shock therapy that was applied so disastrously in the Soviet Union, he just stuck to practicalities and muddled through regardless. The results can speak for themselves.

No human being can live without faults and inconsistencies, and Deng's belief that competition in economics leads to efficiency, whereas competition in politics leads to chaos, has left China with an abiding contradiction that has still not been resolved. But as Liu Shaoqi observed, "There is no such thing as a perfect leader in China or anywhere else. If there is one, he is only pretending—like a pig putting scallions up its nose to try to look like an elephant." Deng himself acknowledged this on his famous "southern inspection tour" by saying: "Who dares to claim that he is a hundred percent sure of success and that he is taking no risks? I've never been that sure. Every year, leaders should review what they have done, continue with correct measures, and promptly change those that have proved wrong."

I can see no plausible scenario where China, in the first decades of reform, and having just emerged from the Cultural Revolution, could have achieved prosperity and political freedom as part of the same process. Of course, Deng gave his people no choice on that matter—perhaps there was no choice to be made. When he placed national reconstruction above every other objective in China, individual rights were subordinated to the pursuit of the greater goal. But if we want to understand modern China, we have to try to imagine how we might have faced these deep dilemmas. We need to acknowledge at least the validity of the question, "Can the destitute be free in any meaningful sense?" How is it possible to weigh up the chance of liberating 300 million people from absolute poverty against the use of live bullets on unarmed civilians, when the probable alternative was civil war? These are terrible and perhaps unanswerable questions to pose. In the end, the only people who can try to answer them are the Chinese people themselves when they come to write the history of these times in a more open society. Meanwhile, some words echo down from China's ancient past, when Laozi, the founder of Taoism, wrote in the fourth century BC:

夫樂殺人者, 則不可以得志於天下矣 ...
殺人之眾, 以哀悲泣之。戰勝以喪禮處之。

He who is content in killing people cannot have his way with the Empire . . . when many are killed one should weep in sorrow as victory has become a funeral.

There's no better illustration of the contrast between Western value-based rules and Chinese practice-based truths than an exchange between Deng and some U.S. congressmen in 1979 about China's hopes for the normalization of trade. When one of the senators explained that the Jackson-Vanik Amendment to U.S. federal law required all formerly Communist countries to issue passports and allow complete freedom of emigration before the United States could normalize trade, Deng replied, "Oh, that's easy! How many do you want? Ten million? Fifteen?"

So here we have the Fourth Chinese Rule:

The Chinese have a deep tradition of pragmatic realism rather than fixed, value-based rules; the maxim "seek truth from facts" dates from the Han Dynasty in the first century BC. Centuries earlier, Mencius had rejected excessive theorizing when he wrote "盡信書，則不如無書"*—"better not to have a book at all rather than believe everything that's in it." A thousand years later, the Song Dynasty reformer Zhu Xi wrote that "actual investigation of things is the surest way to get knowledge." This emphasis on practice-based investigation rather than rigid rules makes the Chinese some of the most flexible people on earth. In the 1920s, Marxism was just borrowed from the West to help fix some of China's problems, and later dumped when it was no longer useful. When China outgrew Maoism, the new leaders didn't argue about the theory; they just repackaged it as "socialism with Chinese characteristics"— even though the "characteristics" were all capitalist. Each dogma was merely used as a stepping-stone across the wider river.*

In our carbon business, as we faced the last obstacle to issuing credits from our projects, we were about to find out how much can be achieved using Deng's practice-based approach to problems. We needed to remember that when Deng promoted practice over dogma, instead of proclaiming "ideology is unimportant" and provoking years of pointless arguments about principles, he had been content with the Delphic observation that came to define a generation: "What does it matter if a cat is black or white, so long as it catches mice?"

14

塞翁失馬 焉知禍福

WHO COULD SAY IT
WAS GAIN OR LOSS, WHEN
THE OLD MAN LOST HIS HORSE

—Proverb from the Huai Nan Zi, *a book of*
philosophical fables complied by Liu An in 139 BC

Throughout the previous summer, as we battled away with Cordelia, storm clouds had gathered in the West. A year earlier, when the largest mortgage lender in the United States narrowly avoided bankruptcy, I didn't even notice; it seemed so far from China. Then a couple of Wall Street hedge funds announced billions of losses. A big German bank failed and needed a government bailout. The news broke that the board of one of the biggest global banks had sacked its chairman after he tried to sell it to a competitor without telling the other directors. Not long after, his successor was forced to sell it at a much lower price and thousands lost their jobs. But it was only after I'd seen footage of customers lining up to withdraw their savings in the first British bank run in more than a century that I started to pay some attention.

Even then, I thought we would be insulated from the turmoil. China had trillions in currency reserves and it would never allow any of its large companies to fail. Besides, I could still remember the attack on sterling in the nineties, which showed once and for all that financial power had shifted decisively eastward. When the arbitrageurs turned on the Bank of England in 1992, it took them three hours on the morning of Black Wednesday to blow the pound out of the European currency mechanism. But things had been different five years later, when they turned their attention to Asia. With a wave of massive speculative attacks, first on Thailand's currency, then the Indonesian rupiah, and the Malaysian ringgit, the currency traders on Wall Street trashed those three economies, before turning on Hong Kong.

But when the short sellers took on the former colony, they bit off more than they could chew; backed by their new masters in Beijing, the Hong Kong government declared war on the speculators. When the arbitrageurs tried to break the currency peg by flooding the market with Hong Kong dollars, the government just bought up the surplus. So the arbitrageurs sold again in the market—and the government just bought them up. Caught with billions of unhedged contracts, the speculators only had one way to go. In desperation, they short-sold yet more billions of dollars and Hong Kong stocks, but the government remained firm and still bought. The contest raged for weeks, but the arbitrageurs could not break the peg. When the dust finally settled, they'd lost billions. Hong Kong had resisted the full onslaught of the speculators, whereas it had taken a morning's work to break the Bank of England. I knew then that the world had changed, so I didn't think much of the growing clamor back home. China, I thought, was safe.

Then, in September 2008, Lehman Brothers imploded, sending shock waves through the world's financial system. For a few moments, it looked as if the whole edifice of Western finance would come crashing down. By the end of the month, the Federal Reserve had announced short-term cash facilities of $900 billion to prop up the banks. AIG, the huge American insurance group that had been founded in Shanghai in 1919, was bailed out with loans that eventually topped $180 billion; thousands lost their jobs.

But we just kept our heads down. Huaneng was a huge Chinese company with little exposure to the Western financial markets, so we thought we'd be unaffected and got on with the job. During the summer, we gathered evidence from the plant and prepared the reports needed to register the Nanjing project at the UN. So it was rather out of the blue that in the November following the Lehman collapse, we received a notice from Credit Suisse telling us that they had decided to withdraw as guarantor from both projects. We were left with millions to pay to Huaneng but with no bank guarantee for the payment.

The withdrawal by Credit Suisse had left us high and dry but the difficulties created by their departure were far greater for Huaneng than for us. The Shanghai plant had been registered at the UN and the rules made it impossible for Huaneng to boot us out of the project without our agreement. Also, the team at Huaneng knew so little about the carbon system that the only realistic route for the second plant at Nanjing to be registered by the UN was to let us get on with the task.

I felt confident we'd be able to muddle through somehow, because I knew that it was impractical for Huaneng to try to kick us out. But even though nearly two years had passed since we signed the initial letter of intent, there were still no contracts between us. Cordelia had never presented us with the final versions and there had been no discussions on the commercial terms of the deal for more than a year. Huaneng, it seemed, was asleep. Unwittingly we had ended up in a position where Huaneng was locked into selling millions of euros in carbon offsets to our—comparatively—microscopic company at an uncertain price and with no payment guarantee. When they finally woke up to the reality, it was no wonder the management team at Huaneng was rattled.

The situation became even more complicated a few months later when I went to Seattle to give my annual update on the business. I found Jerry his normal thoughtful self, but the financial crisis had left its mark even on the trust. At the end of the meeting, Jerry asked me if we might be willing to carry on the business without the foundation's support. I didn't understand what he meant at first. He explained that, given the financial crisis, the trust was reducing its exposure to alternative investments. It had a commitment to us of €100 million euros that he didn't think would ever be needed, so he wondered if we would be willing to consider severing the agreement.

At first, I was alarmed by the prospect of being stuck with no financial backing at the other end of a huge contract with one of China's biggest state-owned companies. It felt like being chained to a five-hundred-pound gorilla. "*Qi hu nan xia*," as the Chinese would say—when riding a tiger, it's terrifying to go on but too dangerous to get off. But whatever our predicament might be in China, I could see that it made no sense for Jerry to be unnecessarily on the hook for nearly €100 million when the financial systems were so stretched. Of course, I'd have preferred him to stay in the game, but I felt we owed it to Jerry to agree without grumbling. I told him I'd need a week or so to figure out the options for extricating him from the business.

By the time I got back to China, I'd had time to think and felt a little calmer, but when I told Mina she was flustered.

"Great!" she said. "First we lose the bank guarantee and now we don't even have any money!"

"Who said we don't have any money?" I said. "Jerry's not just going to cut us adrift without a life raft. It could all work out better in the end. We just have to figure out how to deal with Huaneng. Anyway," I said on a brighter note, "if we don't have any shareholders, we get to keep the profits. You ever heard of Sai Weng and his horse?"

She grunted.

"The story goes like this. An old man lived up in the northern borderlands in the Han Dynasty and kept horses that were used for patrolling the frontiers."

"Oh, yeah?" she said.

"Yeah." A pause. "And one day his best horse ran away."

Mina sighed, arched her back, and tapped the table irritably. The story relates that Sai Weng had searched all day for his missing horse but couldn't find it. When he came back home to the village, his neighbors came round to sympathize with his terrible luck. But the Old Man just said, "How do you know it's bad luck? The story's not over yet."

A month later the horse turned up in the village, together with two other wild horses. But when the neighbors came to congratulate Sai Weng on his good fortune, he just said, "How do you know it's good fortune? The story's not over yet."

Sai Weng had a son skilled in breaking horses. The young lad loved the new horses and rode them every day. But once in the forest, the horse was startled by a wild animal and threw the boy to the ground, breaking his leg so badly that he was crippled. The neighbors came to Sai Weng to commiserate, but again the Old Man said, "How do you know this is a disaster? The story is not over yet."

A few months later the tribes beyond the northern borders attacked the kingdom. The emperor ordered all the young men to join an army to defend the territories. Press gangs seized men from the village, but they did not take Sai Weng's son. "You see," he said to his neighbors, "because of his injuries, my son has been saved!"

"Take it a step at a time," I said. "Take it a step at a time. We just have to figure out what to do. It may not be such bad news after all."

The immediate result of the Credit Suisse withdrawal was that the management of Huaneng froze solid. No one would take responsibility for the enormous mess. Caught with no bank guarantee and without even a commercial contract on one of the largest carbon reduction projects in the world, everyone ran for cover. Head office blamed the plant; the plant said they'd never heard of Cordelia until head office insisted that they needed to hire her to close the deal. It was deadlock once more.

Over the coming weeks, we quietly reached agreement with the foundation. I was sorry to see Jerry go. I'd miss his advice but I could see he was doing the right thing. A short contract was drawn up, and once it was signed a month later, we were out there all on our own.

The two teams within Huaneng were both headed by women, one at the head office in the commercial department and one in charge of finance down at the plant in Nanjing.

The characters used for Chinese surnames often have other meanings as well. *Wang*, for example, means "king." *Kong* means "opening." *Gao* means "tall." But there are characters with less obvious meanings. *Chen* can mean "stale." *Zhang* means "bow." *Mao* can mean "hair" or "feather." In our case, the official from head office was called Madame Ma—meaning "horse"—and the head of finance at the plant was called Li—meaning "plum." I never met either of them, but I sensed that both were tough negotiators.

With no response from Huaneng, we tried to divide up the work into two parts. First, we had to get the Nanjing plant registered with the UN so that we could start to produce credits. Second, we needed to figure out the commercial terms for the deal. Old Plum was responsible for keeping the plant records and had the keys to the file store; Old Horse was in charge of the contracts. We focused first on Old Plum; she had the information we needed for registration. Frank went down to the plant and talked with some of the more junior people. It took a few trips, but eventually Frank came back with copies of what we needed and we got to work on the documents.

The information Frank brought back from the plant was riddled with inconsistencies; nothing ever seemed to add up or tie together. Key documents were missing and it took weeks to piece together the story. When we looked at the main feasibility report that was approved by the ministries in Beijing, we saw that the original plans for three sets of generators had subsequently been reduced to two. But the final approval documents had been bungled and included a mismatch in the figures, with the capital cost of three generators but the income from only two—it took months to straighten out the story. Geiser had pages of questions, but eventually he signed his report. After a further six months the project was finally registered. The gas supply at the plant was plentiful and the coastal regions in China were booming. The plant was working overtime so, after almost three years, we were ready to generate credits.

Even after we had registered the second project, there were still no commercial contracts for either of the plants and Old Horse had disappeared from the scene. Carbon income was so new that responsibility for dealing with it fell through the cracks in the Huaneng team. No one would engage. It was a story that was familiar from Wang's chemical factory: the lack of personal incentive and the involvement of the work unit in organizing every aspect of their employees' lives makes managers fearful of taking responsibility for difficult decisions. Managers hide—*duo le*, as they say in Chinese—and for months after the registration, our messages went unanswered. On the rare occasions we could arrange a meeting, Old Horse often turned up late; familiar faces were replaced by new ones and we had to start explaining the carbon system all over again. Frustration on our side was mounting.

Throughout that time, the carbon markets had been nervous as traders watched preparations for a key UN summit in Copenhagen to try to agree on a successor to the Kyoto Protocol. When Mina went over to the conference at the end of 2009, she had come back feeling deflated. She had attended the preparatory sessions for the summit, which involved detailed drafting by delegates from more than 150 nations before heads of government arrived. But the opening discussions had become hopelessly bogged between irreconcilably different viewpoints; Mina told me that one delegation from South America wanted to include a clause upholding "the rights of Mother Earth to continue her vital cycles free from human alteration," while Europeans were haggling away in back rooms about the radiative forcing potential of different fluorocarbon gases. With such fundamental differences in outlook, the work teams from each country were so far apart that it had seemed impossible to bridge the gap. After ten days, when the government leaders began to arrive, there wasn't even a draft of a final text for them to debate over.

Several months later, I met an adviser to one of the small island states that had been in the final negotiations. He told me that there had been about sixty people crammed inside a stuffy conference center, with fifteen heads of government around a table, each with a team arranged behind. President Obama was there, with the leaders of France, Germany, the United Kingdom, Brazil, and India. But the Chinese prime minister didn't even turn up; he remained in a hotel nearby and sent a Foreign Ministry official who had to scurry from the room every few minutes to get instructions. It was a classic Chinese technique called "slicing," which relies on sending low-level officials to negotiate with fully empowered counterparties. That way, the opposition becomes so frustrated that they make concessions to a Chinese negotiator who has no power to make matching offers even if he wants to.

At the end of the conference, a final text was cobbled together and distributed to the wider group, but it wasn't even adopted. There was just a weak statement saying that it had been "noted" by the wider group of nations. The meeting ended without any agreement on carbon reduction targets, and acrimonious squabbling about who was to blame for the failure. With the Kyoto Protocol coming to an end less than three years later and governments deeply divided about what to do about its replacement, the prospects for carbon prices in the medium term were highly uncertain, so we were under pressure to start trading as quickly as possible. Huaneng might have been able to prevaricate but we had no time to lose.

After the failure at Copenhagen, we regrouped and tried to figure out what to do. It was a familiar state of deadlock, but this time with a much larger counterparty. We needed to finalize the commercial terms with Huaneng and start trading, but how could we force them to negotiate when everyone was running for cover?

First, I told the team to go through the list of indirect strategies that Mao might have used. We thought about trying to put pressure on Huaneng by lobbying the Climate Change Department or engaging with the embassy, but Huaneng was just too big for any of that to work. We thought of finding a route to the board of Huaneng to get them to sort out their management, but the situation was too complicated to lobby for a simple solution. Local managers would easily find excuses for the delay. In the end, we decided to follow Deng's example. Rather than argue about principles and try to agree the terms of a contract, we decided to take a more pragmatic course: we just went ahead and started trading credits without a contract and waited to see how Huaneng might react.

In April, we sent off a request for issuance for a small batch of credits. Once the request goes up on the UN website, it's too late to stop the process. After Old Horse got wind of what we were up to, she called me, spluttering with fury. I've never heard a Chinese official so angry. She ranted for fifteen minutes that if there was any loss of state-owned assets, I would be held personally responsible. We'd already sent off another, much larger request for issuance of several million euros' worth of credits, but I just kept quiet about that. By that time, there was no turning back.

As soon as the first carbon credits were issued, we sold them in the markets and transferred a share of the proceeds to Huaneng's bank. Once the cash hit their account, Old Horse could see that the system worked and she relaxed enough that I could tell her about the second issuance. When it was made a few weeks later, several million euros sloshed into our bank account. We left it there and sent a note to Huaneng saying we couldn't transfer anything to them without a properly signed contract. The prospect of a larger payment to the plant finally got their attention and, a few weeks later, the formal contracts were signed.

It had taken three years to raise the capital, find projects, unravel the information, and navigate our way through the UN process. After we finally struck a deal with Huaneng, we traded the credits, made a little money, and proved that the system worked. The two gas-fired power projects were among the largest ever attempted in the power sector and might have acted as a template for others across the developing world. But the financial crisis ground on in the West; in the year following the registration of the Nanjing plant, carbon prices were flat. After the failure of the Copenhagen conference, doubts hit the market and prices became more unstable.

When the Kyoto Protocol expired in 2012 the international community had still failed to come up with any road map for the future. The EU promised to continue with its trading system, but then the Eurozone tipped into recession after the debt crisis. Carbon caps agreed to during the boom years a decade earlier were hopelessly loose for the depressed economy, so carbon prices slumped. When the EU announced a plan to revive the markets by restricting the supply of the credits, all twenty-seven governments of the EU nations met together in Brussels. Twenty-six of them agreed to support the carbon market, and only one refused. Poland relies almost entirely on coal to generate its power, so it blocked the deal.

The commission struggled on for another year trying to broker a compromise, but, just like in Copenhagen, it proved impossible for even a smaller group of nations to reach any lasting commitment to reduce carbon emissions. Local interests proved too strong for governments to take in the wider picture; prices collapsed and the carbon markets were left broken. At the time of this writing, any hopes that the rich nations might use new market mechanisms to help the developing world follow a more sustainable pathway have disappeared into the wind.

The United States has turned to shale gas. Europe went back to the black stuff since the cost of coal has plummeted. The global attempts of the last twenty years to rein in emissions are now in deep disarray. The UN system for carbon trading is dead; it seems that there's almost no forum where a unified approach could even be discussed. Of course, everyone acknowledges that the UN system had problems—it was bureaucratic and failed to understand local conditions—but at least it raised awareness of climate issues in the developing world and produced a large group of specialists who knew how to reduce and verify emissions.

When I think about the failure of the UN's Clean Development Mechanism, I can't help remembering my first visit to Wang in his chemical plant in Zhejiang. Living standards there had improved, but workers' wages were still around eighty dollars a month. For them, the prospect of buying a car seemed light-years away. "A holiday abroad?" I remember Wang saying as we walked through the plant. "You must be joking. It takes all of a worker's wage to fill his stomach, pay college bills for the kid, and foot the medical bills for the old ones." Wang had little money for capital investment; the plant struggled to support the tens of thousands of workers on its payroll. But they all know how we live in the West; images of unimaginable affluence and waste come beaming in from the global networks. "You think we should worry about greenhouse gases?" asked Wang. "We're only just making a living. You lot caused the mess," he says, "so you should sort it out."

I believe that the Clean Development Mechanism, at its core, offered a way to share the costs of a sustainable future more equitably across the globe, but it failed because there is no transnational political structure that can address the global issues that know no frontiers or boundaries.

In the West, we are left watching EU officials haggling in back rooms, horse-trading on everything from banking reform to marketing standards for vegetables, while across the Atlantic, the deadlock in Washington, D.C., can shut down the federal government. Meanwhile, China keeps on going. It's even experimenting with the carbon markets; undeterred by Europe's failure, China opened its first carbon market in Shenzhen last year. In true Deng style, if the pilot plan makes progress, it'll be rolled out to the bigger cities— Beijing, Shanghai—and then the provinces beyond. If it fails, it'll be quietly forgotten. Who knows: with its practice-based truths and a heightened sense of purpose, China may yet be able to find ways of tackling climate change that have proven elusive in more fractured parts of the world.

15

知己知彼　百戰不殆

THE FIFTH AND FINAL RULE:

Know Yourself and Know the Other and You'll Survive a Hundred Battles

—Last sentence of the "Mo Gong Bian," *or* "Attack by Stratagem," *in Sunzi's* The Art of War

After the collapse of carbon prices, the team reluctantly disbanded. Cissy went off to Singapore and joined the start-up scene in environmental investing there, while Frank went to look at green buildings. Mina raised some money to start an NGO promoting water conservation in China. She's still in Beijing using social media and networking to organize campaigns in Chinese schools and universities to teach young people to value water more highly. Michael traveled for a time to England, where his daughter is studying at Oxford. And Cordelia seems to have disappeared in a puff of green vapor; after she was ejected from the Nanjing project, we never heard from her again. Wang is still working at the chemical factory; we exchange the occasional message. Last time I had news, Winchester was working with a renewables investor in London. After the *bai-jiu* incident, I heard he kept clear of China for a while, but he's much too determined an entrepreneur to be deflected by something as trifling as a revolting hangover.

As for me, I'm working on a project to introduce courses on Chinese civilization into Britain's secondary schools. Someone's got to prepare the next generation for what's about to hit them. But I still get my main kicks from dealing with complexity in China, taking on the odd case where foreign investors have found themselves in trouble. I suppose what keeps me at it is the thrill of the duel, the chance to dig deeper and get a bit closer to China's own internal logic.

I knew that I'd learned a lot from the carbon business, but I still hadn't tested these ideas in practice, so when another opportunity came along to apply the Chinese Rules, I grabbed it with both hands. I'd heard that one of London's oldest insurance companies had lent millions of dollars to an apple juice factory in western China and that the loan was seriously in arrears. When the firm's directors asked me to help them recover the money, I gladly accepted the task.

The facts of the case were simple. A Chinese entrepreneur named Mi owned an apple juice plant way out in western China. He was born just after liberation in a village in a remote mountainous region of Shaanxi Province famous for winter peaches. Like most of his generation, he had been sent to work in the fields in one of Mao's rectification campaigns. When he returned in the early eighties, he found a place at a university in the provincial capital of Xi'an, which sits at the eastern terminus of the Old Silk Road. At the center of the city, an ancient bell tower still rises above the fumes and clamor of the traffic swirling around it. Fortified walls with moats and watchtowers march around the city perimeter in an unbroken line eight miles long. Outside, on the powdery plains, antique pagodas and the smoking chimney stacks of a thousand backyard brick kilns reach up to the dusty skies. In the east, long ranks of terra-cotta warriors lie hidden in the crumbling, yellow earth.

In this incongruous setting Mi put together a team of software engineers. It was one of the first in China, and before long, he'd earned enough money to build a factory and start making his own computers. Mi was a risk taker and thrived in China's new market economy. By the time he reached his mid-forties, he was ranked number twelve on *Forbes*'s China rich list, with a fortune of $300 million and a business empire that had diversified into retail, property, and food products underneath a holding company that was listed on the Shanghai stock market. He had all the normal paraphernalia of a successful Chinese businessman: a black Mercedes, a troupe of attentive admirers, and a seat on the People's Congress. From what I could find out about Mi, he was intent on enjoying the results of two decades of hard work and good fortune.

A couple of years earlier, just after the cash arrived from London, Mi had sent a letter to the insurers requesting a change to the loan contract. The original agreements used the new bottling machinery as security, but Mi explained that he couldn't pledge the equipment as collateral due to some vague problems with the local customs house. The lenders in London agreed to change the contracts. Payment dates came and payment dates went, and, by the time I first met Mi, the loan was more than two years in arrears.

As a first attempt to recover the loan, the insurance company had engaged a firm of solicitors in Hong Kong. But when their lawyers faxed over demand notices to Xi'an using the complex "full-form" characters used in Hong Kong, Mi just threw them away. After another six months, the insurers threatened a lawsuit, so Mi made a quick call to the local court, told them to stall proceedings, and then neatly transferred the land and buildings out of the company that owed the money, leaving the lenders holding an unsecured loan against an empty shell. Things really didn't look promising.

As I flew down from Beijing to meet Mi for the first time, I could see the Great Wall snake its way westward along the mountain ridges below. The blades on a line of wind turbines caught the sun as they turned slowly on a valley floor in the distance. On the surrounding slopes, a late spring snow had fallen. The mountains soon smoothed into an undulating plain, with steep-sided ravines carved by the rainwater into the pale powdery soil. Far toward the north, columns of dust rose up into the skies, whipped up by the winds from Mongolia.

We met in Mi's offices around a large circular table with seats for a dozen or so and the customary vase of plastic flowers in the middle. As I waited for Mi to arrive, I took in the long row of photographs on the wall. The first showed Mi poring over a mass of engineering drawings with the provincial Party secretary; next came Mi inspecting a row of fruit-pressing machines with a standing member of the Politburo; then came a picture of Mi in the Great Hall of the People shaking hands with the prime minister of China. Mi obviously had all the connections in all the right places, so I chattered away about nothing in particular and, half an hour later, I left.

Mi was going to be a tough nut to crack. It was a familiar situation; we needed to find a way of persuading a powerful Chinese counterparty to negotiate with us and there were few realistic ways of doing that. I knew that threats of legal action would be useless. I just hoped we might make more headway using Chinese Rules instead.

Rule One: China doesn't play by anyone else's rules. I knew that tackling Mi through Western methods would be hopeless. In order to recover any value based on the loan contracts, we'd need to take out freezing orders over his assets and Mi knew that no local court would do that. But I wondered whether there might be a way to apply pressure from inside the system. Perhaps old friends or colleagues might help us to broker a deal. So I asked the directors in London to withdraw their legal action and call off the lawyers. Surprisingly, they agreed.

Rule Two: Stability is always the key for government officials. Even though Mi was a prominent businessman in Shaanxi, I knew that he couldn't ignore powerful local government officials. We had to come up with a reason for a high-level official to get involved and find someone inside the provincial government who might put pressure on Mi to engage.

Shaanxi Province is located far inland and, over the past twenty years, its economy has lagged far behind the prosperous coastal provinces. Wealth imbalances became a major headache for the central government; more than 150 million workers had risen up in China's deep interior and swirled toward the coastal factory towns in search of a job. This huge population movement began to threaten social stability, always the top concern for officials.

The central government had started pumping billions into the western regions of China to build up the infrastructure and provide employment. The gas pipelines connecting Central Asia to Shanghai, the railways, power plants, highways, and airports built there, were all part of a program called "Open-Up-the-West." It was a major government effort to create jobs and smooth out the imbalances in the economy. At the same time, there had been an overhaul of the regulations aimed at attracting foreign investors into the region. Several high-profile tours had been arranged with press coverage of foreign businessmen touring high-tech zones and industrial parks, promising investment in the west. Given the media attention, I figured that the provincial government in Shaanxi would want to avoid the risk of bad publicity for the "Open-Up-the-West" policy, which might attract unwelcome attention from the central government. If we could handle it in the right way, I figured that we might be able to use the "Open-Up-the-West" policy to put pressure on Mi to negotiate.

Rule Three: Never attack directly. I drafted a short letter and asked the British embassy in Beijing to send it to the provincial governor in Shaanxi. They faxed it over to the governor's office explaining respectfully that there seemed to have been a "misunderstanding" between a large London-based investor with more than $100 billion and an important local business in Xi'an. The letter asked for the governor's advice on how to deal with the situation and suggested trying to solve the problem through friendly negotiations. It ended by asking the governor to support a solution "internally within the Province so as to avoid disturbing the Central Government's strategy to 'Open-Up-the-West.'" This careful wording did not escape the governor's attention; with the intense focus of China's top leaders on social stability in the inland provinces, he immediately sensed that a large foreign investor might go complaining to the central government and cause embarrassment to the province.

A week after the letter was sent to the governor, it landed on the desk of the mayor of Xi'an with handwritten comments in the margin. The mayor added further instructions and sent the letter on to the Trade and Economic Commission. From there, it went to the Municipal Investment Bureau, who sent it on to the Office for Commercial Mediation. When the officials called on Mi, they showed him the handwritten instructions from the governor and he promptly agreed to negotiate.

Rule Four: Stick to practicalities and don't get hung up on side arguments about principles. Mi was the typical Chinese entrepreneur, dodging, botching, ducking, and weaving, muddling his way round rules and obstacles with resolute cheerfulness. At first he delayed with the usual excuses, the standard opening tactic—he told us he should wait for board approval, then that he needed first to finish some tax filings, or that his lawyers were never in town. But rather than accuse him of insincerity or deliberately dragging his feet, a quick call to the mayor's office was usually enough to nudge him forward. When he offered payment-in-kind, we just thanked him and explained that the directors couldn't accept truckloads of apples in the City of London.

Eventually he ran out of options, so we got down to hard bargaining. It took more than a year to reach a settlement, and throughout that time, I visited Xi'an every few weeks to report to local officials or meet with Mi. During the whole process, there was never an unkind word between us. We both knew that the governor was following the case personally and in the end, Mi agreed to repay the loan in installments. It was a balanced solution that Deng might have been proud of—the timing of the installments was slow enough to show that Mi had put up a fight, but fast enough for the foreigners to be sure that they'd get back their money.

This solution could never have been achieved through a court or through a dispute that came out into the open. Mi was respected and well-known throughout the province and he would never have felt any pressure from the local courts; if we'd confronted him openly, ranks of officials would have closed around him, but as soon as he felt some indirect pressure from the provincial government to settle, he made the quick calculation that repaying a few million was a fair price for preserving his high reputation.

I felt that somewhere in the experience with Mi, I might find one more Chinese Rule, something that brought the first four rules together within some overarching frame. Unexpectedly, it was an unscripted remark by Wen Jiabao, one of China's recent prime ministers, that made me think about the Fifth and Final Rule. "China has five thousand years of history and two thousand years of written history," he said on a visit to Britain. "Some leaders come to the table with red faces and crimson ears and negotiate without understanding the history of countries they deal with. I will never be a politician like that."

For ten terrible years, Mao's Dog—the Madame Mao who came to embody the most vindictive aspects of the Cultural Revolution—had fought with Deng's Cat—the cat whose color was irrelevant so long as it caught the mouse. It was a life-and-death struggle for the soul of China and the cat won. Out of this struggle came a new way forward for China, a "way" that relied on pragmatism combined with elements of traditional thought, all mixed in with new methods and technologies brought in from the outside world. Mao's revolutionary radicalism was rejected in favor of practicality; and through that, China has become strong again.

Over the next few decades, China is expected to overtake the United States as the world's largest economy in real terms. Once that happens, China will have regained its pivotal position in the

East and may remain there for a couple of centuries; it will be the world's largest economy, its most populous unified territory, its largest consumer, and its largest polluter. It will be the present-day expression of the world's oldest surviving civilization, and yet the foundations of its history, thought, and traditions are hardly known in the West. As power balances return toward a point of equilibrium, the transition for the West will hopefully be gentler, far less abrupt or traumatic than the one experienced by China two centuries ago. But China has not conformed to a Western model and many in the West remain oblivious to the opportunities and challenges that China's reemergence brings. In short, we are not yet prepared for China.

Over the past century and a half, China has not been so remiss; it had no other choice but to learn about the foreigners. When Lord Macartney arrived in Macau and demanded an audience with the emperor, the mandarins failed utterly to grasp the new global re-alities that the barbarians had brought with them. Trapped in an-cient rituals, narcissistic and complacent, the Qing court dismissed the dangers that the barbarians represented, and then looked on in horror as they charged up the rivers of China in ironclad gunboats, blasting their armies to pieces and corrupting their citizens with opium. After the emperor sent his officials to Canton in 1839, the imperial commissioner, who famously sluiced the 20,283 cases of the Englishmen's opium into the river, wrote a letter to Queen Victoria:

> Our mighty Emperor tranquilizes the central and outside lands and looks upon all with like benevolence. Should there be advantages, he ren-ders them common to all beneath the heavens . . . your barbarian ships strive with each other in coming here to trade because of their eager desire for grasping after gain . . . coveting such vastness of profit they become regardless of the calamities they entail upon men. We have un-derstood that in your said kingdom the prohibitions against the smoking of Opium are of the sternest severity; thus the injurious consequences of the use of the drug must be clearly evident to you all.

Let us suppose that the individuals of another nation were to take Opium to the English country and to sell and to seduce your people to purchase and to smoke it, the Sovereign of your honorable Kingdom would be vastly incensed and with painful anxiety you would completely unterminate it . . . you cherish a heart of benevolence and so you must be unwilling to do to others that which you do not desire to be done to yourselves.

The letter never even reached the addressee. Parliament was called, speeches made. Britain used the destruction of the opium at the docks in Canton as a pretext for war. The comprehensive collapse of Qing forces in the ensuing chaos forced China to sign a series of humiliating Unequal Treaties, ceding control first over Hong Kong, then a string of concessions up the coast. Eventually the barbarians took over a portion of the capital itself. China passed through a period of long and painful introspection; but out of humiliation came renewal.

In a belated effort to arouse the empire from its stupor of genteel backwardness, a handful of scholar-officials petitioned the emperor. "Humiliation stimulates effort," wrote Wei Yuan in an 1843 book called *Treatise on the Sea Powers*. "When a country is humiliated, its spirit will be aroused!" Two decades later, another scholar, Feng Guifan, moved to Shanghai to observe the foreigners more closely. Calling for a Chinese "Self-Strengthening Movement," he set out his ideas about the origin of barbarian superiority in a book called *Dissenting Views from a Hut Near Bin*. In it, he asked the simple question:

Our territory is eight times that of Russia, ten times the size of America, one hundred times bigger than France, and two hundred times that of England. Why is it that they are strong and small, yet we are large and weak?

Western superiority, he argued, relied on more than steam engines, ironclad ships, and firearms; there were deeper themes at work. The West, he insisted, had surpassed China in four critical areas: education ("employing people's talents"), economic development ("profiting from the land"), political legitimacy ("keeping the rulers and people close"), and intellectual inquiry ("calling things by their proper names"). Feng called for China to learn from the West, borrow from the West, but not to rely on the West. In the following century, the quest for understanding continued, and even Mao, whose suspicion of Western capitalism was surpassed by no one, wrote, "Chinese who sought progress would study any book containing new knowledge from the West . . . modern schools sprang up like bamboo shoots after the spring rain; every effort was made to learn from the West."

The product of all this soul-searching is a society led by people who are far better educated about the outside world than Western leaders are about China. When Wen Jiabao, then China's prime minister, came to visit his counterpart in Britain in 2011, he brought with him a book by Adam Smith, the father of modern economics. But he did not bring *The Wealth of Nations*, Smith's most famous work, which praises the free market and the virtuous effects of self-interest. Instead Wen brought with him the much less well known *Theory of Moral Sentiments*—which sets out the limits of the market—and quoted from it at length.

While in England, Wen asked to visit Stratford-upon-Avon, the birthplace of Shakespeare; there he spoke of how literature and culture could be a bridge between nations. While he had read *King Lear* as a boy, he wondered aloud how many Britons knew of the Monkey King of Chinese literature. It was in England that he made the remark about China's long history and how he would not like to negotiate without understanding the history of countries he dealt with. Wen's words echo those of Sunzi from two thousand years ago. In them, he revealed the Fifth Chinese Rule: "Know Yourself and Know the Other and You'll Survive a Hundred Battles."

THE FIFTH CHINESE RULE

A prevailing orthodoxy in the West is that developing countries will eventually cast themselves in the mold of the Western democracies and that free market economics and the ballot box will answer all their troubles. But the mere fact that there has been such a rebalancing of wealth and power from West to East should give us pause for thought. China has broken that orthodoxy. If we look just at economics in China and ignore its history, culture, traditions, and society, we will be like Mao's adversaries in the Encirclement Campaigns who'd said "everywhere we grope in the dark, while the Red Army walks in broad daylight." Without understanding the Chinese path to development, we will never be able to explain or predict; we will be perpetually confused and surprised.

Western academics have written openly about "the end of history," whereby there will be no need for further development of political systems and ideas beyond Enlightenment values. Some Western leaders have viewed the differences between China and the West as being primarily one of timing rather than outlook. In the words of an Oxford intellectual,

> The West needs to stand by its values and institutions at home, and reproduce them internationally to give the rest of the world a genuine opportunity to catch up and recast its domestic organization around Enlightenment principles.

These words remind me of Qianlong's rebuff to George III— "we have never valued ingenious articles nor do we have the slightest need for your country's manufactures"—but applied to the field of ideas. It is difficult to find a greater contrast between this thinking and the words of China's new president in his first speech after taking up office. Turning to foreign journalists, he said,

> Just as China needs to learn more about the world, so does the world need to learn more about China. I hope you will continue your efforts to deepen mutual understanding between China and the world.

The strategy of the United States and Europe for engagement with China for the last three decades—and its inclusion into international organizations such as the G8 and the World Trade Organization—has been based on the assumption that China will become more like the West and adopt its ways of doing things. But what if China follows its own path, as it has over the past two thousand years? What then?

The choice now facing the West as it considers how to deal with the changed world is whether to get caught up in another argument about the *kow-tow* or to follow Napoleon's advice when he heard about Macartney's embassy. "Different nations have different customs," he told his physician. "In Italy, you kiss the pope's toe and yet it is not considered a degradation." If the Englishmen's custom had been to kiss the king's ass rather than his hand, Napoleon asked, would they have requested the emperor of China "to lower his breeches?!"

Do we really have so little to learn from this vast and ancient civilization? In this age of splits and factions, there must be something useful in China's centuries of experience in uniting disparate provinces across an area much larger than Europe. After the near collapse in global banking, maybe we should pause to think about China's reluctance to pull down the barriers to the world of international finance; many in the West would sympathize with China's refusal to yield its sovereignty to the international bankers like the West has done. In these times of aging population, perhaps there may be some inspiration in Chen's attitudes toward family and the elderly in Quzhou—China's constitution places a duty on children to look after their parents. Or, after Iraq and Afghanistan, what might we learn from China's ancient arts of war, where supreme excellence comes from achieving objectives by non-military means?

On the preparation of political leaders for high office, there may be something to learn from China's meritocratic selection system, which endured for two thousand years. Tony Blair wrote, "Prime Minister was my first and only job in government," and that "there is no training that can ever prepare you for the challenge"—yet top Chinese leaders are trained intensively for at least three decades and have governed provinces bigger than European states for years before they even qualify for the final race.

Is there nothing useful to us in China's approach to long-term planning rather than the suicidally short-term decisions that result from rolling news coverage and regular election cycles? Or its traditional diet and medicine, the product of collaboration between hundreds of millions of people and the plant environment over a period of thousands of years?

We don't seem able to change our minds or compromise without being accused of dithering, while the Chinese constantly switch directions and improvise. We can find ourselves bound up in cultural dogma, sometimes left over from a foregone age—the Second Amendment, for example, did not contemplate the domestic use of machine guns. In China, the ability to respond to changing circumstances is taken as a sign of wisdom and power, yet Western politicians turn the opposite into a quality. "You turn if you want to," proclaimed the Iron Lady, Margaret Thatcher. "The lady's not for turning." In U.S. presidential campaigns, candidates are labeled as "flip-floppers" if they think out loud or adapt to a changing scene.

Even, perhaps—and this will make the skeptics choke—China might eventually find something in its ancient philosophies to teach us about our interaction with the environment. Like every country in its stage of rapid growth, China's recent environmental record has been terrible, and no one can ignore it. There are thousands of miles of poisoned rivers, fishless lakes, and choking cities. But perhaps China has recognized the problem at an earlier stage than the West. The Chinese state is building gigawatts of wind power on a scale not attempted anywhere else on earth; the hydropower stations in China's southwest deliver three times the output of the whole of the United Kingdom's national grid. Meanwhile China is planting a billion trees. At a stroke, the Beijing government shut down nearly half of its coal-fired power and replaced it with gas at a cost of five billion. Of course, no one denies that the air in China's cities is horrible; we should criticize the problem, publicize embarrassing data, lobby for better rules, but we shouldn't forget the Great Smog in London, which lasted for four days in December 1952, reduced visibility to six feet, choked cows to death in Smith-field cattle market, and, according to research cited at the end of this book, killed between four and twelve thousand people.

Two wrongs can never make a right; China faces enormous problems and bad things there should be criticized. Everyone knows that lack of democratic accountability from below allows officials to put their own interests above those of ordinary people. Illegal bribes, tax evasion, and theft by officials cost society billions; corruption currently threatens China's very existence, just as it has through the ages. The media exists more to underpin social harmony than to speak the truth or promote accountability; human rights violations and restrictions on freedom of speech are all well-known. But that is even more reason to engage with China and push for better standards as it takes on its new role in the world.

We are all locked together in the emerging global society and China's power is growing as it underpins the world's economy. It is a hard reality that criticism of China by Westerners will only be credible to its leaders if it's based on an honest appreciation of the country's historical context. As well as being critical, we must be open-minded about what the West might learn from China and sympathetic toward its present-day predicament. As Queen Elizabeth II said after her *annus horribilis*: "There can be no doubt that criticism is good for people and institutions . . . but scrutiny can be just as effective if it is made with a touch of gentleness, good humor, and understanding."

The British controlled the seas in the nineteenth century and America controlled the air in the twentieth; the outcome of the next century may be determined by whoever most influences the emerging global "culture," including international standards and norms. That will be a battle of soft power, of economics and other nonmilitary means. The outcome will be affected most by the choices made in the developing world, where the large majority of people live and of which China is the leading champion. As China regains its place in the world, there may be a chance to recover that lost opportunity between Macartney and Qianlong, when, instead of dialogue, there was a fatal clash of pride.

The world will struggle indeed to cope with another six billion people all hoping to live as we do in the West. Without a change in the way rich nations live, we will turn to face the prospect of a final wilderness where the inadequacy of the financiers' equations is laid bare for all to see. Before we reach that crossroads, we might pause to look back into China's distant past in the hopes of finding some inspiration for the long journey ahead.

In the years since I first climbed to the top of the hill behind the Forbidden City, I have often returned to gaze out over the changing city. Last time I went, the same woman was still selling the tickets at the gateway, but it costs three kuai to get in, nearly a hundred times more than I used to pay when I was at the university. I stopped to ask her about the old man. "Is he still here, you know, the old man who practices his calligraphy with the long brush and water on the ground?" I asked. She just shrugged briefly and waved me on in.

"Such big changes in the city!" I said.

"Right," she sighed, pointing her thumb behind her toward the hill. *"Danshi libian haishi neiyang'r!"*—But it's still the same inside here!

I wandered in and climbed the path to the top of the hill through the twisted pines and the aromatic smell of sap in the fading heat of the early evening air. At the summit, the altar had been carved with images of fantastic sea monsters and strange kissing fish. A shining gold Buddha sat upon the top. Tourists from the provinces yelled and jostled and snapped their digital cameras; for a few kuai you can hire yellow robes and pose as an emperor on a crudely erected throne, with the Forbidden City as a backdrop far below. I wandered off down the hill toward the Eastern Gate, where the last Ming emperor had hanged himself on a tree four centuries earlier. The memorial there carved in stone reminded me again of the great upheavals that mark China's long history; the dynasties may rise and fall but the civilization endures. Just next to the site of the tree, where a rock garden now stands, I found the old man with his long brush and small bucket of water, engrossed in the characters at his feet.

I was thrilled to see him, but held back for a while, hidden behind the drooping foliage of a dragon-claw scholar-tree. I watched as, absorbed in the task, he dipped the brush into the bucket and drew his long, flowing brushstrokes in the dust on the paving stones at his feet. I gazed at the characters lying there on the ground. Clearly visible for a few seconds, they hung upon the moment but then faded and disappeared forever as the water evaporated into the warm summer air. He was writing out sections of the Tao—or the "Way"—one of the oldest texts of mankind. It was written as the first rays of sunlight fell upon the banks of the Yellow River at the dawn of the Chinese civilization. The words still resonate across thirty centuries and seem more relevant today than ever before;

知足不辱
知止不殆
可以長久
。

To know what is enough is to
be immune from disgrace,
To know when to stop is to be
preserved from all perils,
Only thus can you endure long.

Observe developments soberly,
Maintain our position,
Meet challenges calmly,
Hide our capabilities,
Bide our time,
Remain free of ambition,
Never claim leadership.

—Deng Xiaoping

BIBLIOGRAPHY

Baum, Richard. *Burying Mao: Chinese Politics in the Age of Deng Xiaoping*. Princeton, NJ: Princeton University Press, 1994.

Bell, Michelle L., Devra L. Davis, and Tony Fletcher. "A Retrospective Assessment of Mortality from the London Smog Episode of 1952." *Environmental Health Perspectives* 112 (2004).

Brook, Timothy. *The Troubled Empire: China in the Yuan and Ming Dynasties*. Cambridge, MA. Belknap Press, 2010.

Coase, Ronald, and Ning Wang. *How China Became Capitalist*. New York: Palgrave Macmillan, 2012.

Deng Mao Mao. *Deng Xiaoping: My Father*. New York: Basic Books, 1995.

Deng Rong. *Deng Xiaoping and the Cultural Revolution*. Beijing: Foreign Languages Press, 2002.

Economy, Elizabeth C. *The River Runs Black: The Environmental Challenge to China's Future*. Ithaca, NY: Cornell University Press, 2004.

Fenby, Jonathan. *The Penguin History of Modern China*. London: Allen Lane, 2008.

Fairbank, John K., and Merle Goldman. *China: A New History*. Cambridge, MA: Belknap Press, 2006.

Hansen, Valerie. *The Open Empire: A History of China Through 1600*. New York: Norton, 2000.

Hsu, Immanuel C. Y. *The Rise of Modern China*. Oxford: Oxford University Press, 2000.

Intergovernmental Panel on Climate Change. *Climate Change 2007: The Physical Science Basis, Working Group I Contribution to the Fourth Assessment Report*. Cambridge, UK: Cambridge University Press, 2007.

Jacques, Martin. *When China Rules the World*. New York: Penguin, 2012.

Kissinger, Henry. *On China*. London: Allen Lane, 2011.

Kynge, James. *China Shakes the World*. London: Phoenix, 2009.

Lai, Karyn L. *An Introduction to Chinese Philosophy*. Cambridge, UK: Cambridge University Press, 2008.

Lao Tzu. *Tao Teh Ching*. Translated by John C. H. Wu. Boston: Shambhala, 2003.

Leonard, Mark. *What Does China Think?* London: Fourth Estate, 2008.

Li Zhisui. *The Private Life of Chairman Mao*. London: Arrow Books, 1994.

Lovell, Julia. *The Opium War: Drugs, Dreams, and the Making of China*. New York: Picador, 2012.

MacFarquhar, Roderick, and Michael Schoenhals. *Mao's Last Revolution*. Cambridge, MA: Harvard University Press, 2008.

Mitter, Rana. *A Bitter Revolution: China's Struggle with the Modern World*. Oxford: Oxford University Press, 2004.

Morellon, Mario, et al. "Climate Changes and Human Activities Recorded in the Sediments of Lake Estanya." Springer Link, 2009.

Nolan, Peter. *Capitalism and Freedom: The Contradictory Character of Globalisation*. London: Anthem Press, 2008.

———. *China and the Global Economy*. London: Palgrave, 2001.

———. *China at the Crossroads*. Cambridge, UK: Polity, 2004.

———. *Crossroads: The End of Wild Capitalism*. London: Marshall Cavendish, 2009.

———. *Is China Buying the World?* Cambridge, UK: Polity, 2012.

North China Herald. 1837–61, various sources.

Peyrefitte, Alain. *The Collision of Two Civilisations: The British Expedition to China, 1792–4*. London: Harvill, 1993.

Plimer, Ian. *Heaven and Earth: Global Warming, the Missing Science*. London: Quartet, 2009.

Salisbury, Harrison. *The New Emperors: Mao and Deng: A Dual Biography*. New York: HarperCollins, 1992.

Schell, Orville, and John Delury. *Wealth and Power: China's Long March to the Twenty-first Century*. New York: Little, Brown, 2013.

Shapiro, Judith. *Mao's War Against Nature*. Cambridge, UK: Cambridge University Press, 2001.

Short, Philip. *Mao: A Life*. London: Hodder & Stoughton, 1999.

Snow, Edgar. *Red Star Over China*. London: Victor Gollancz, 1937.

Spence, Jonathan D. *God's Chinese Son: Taiping Heavenly Kingdom of Hong Xiuquan*. New York: HarperCollins, 1997.

———. *Mao*. London: Weidenfeld & Nicolson, 1999.

————. *The Search for Modern China*. New York: Norton, 1990.

Sun Tzu. *The Art of War.* Translated by Thomas Cleary. Boston: Shambhala Dragon Editions, 1988.

————. *The Art of War.* Translated by Samuel B. Griffith. Oxford: Oxford University Press, 1963.

Svensmark, Henrik. *Experimental Evidence for the Role of Ions in Particle Nucleation under Atmospheric Conditions*. London: Royal Society, 2007.

Svensmark, Henrik, and Nigel Calder. *The Chilling Stars*. Thriplow, UK: Icon Books, 2007.

Terrill, Ross. *The White-Boned Demon: A Biography of Madame Mao*. New York: William Morrow, 1984.

Vogel, Ezra F. *Deng Xiaoping and the Transformation of China*. Cambridge, MA: Belknap Press, 2011.

Yan Xuetong. *Ancient Chinese Thought, Modern Chinese Power.* Princeton, NJ: Princeton University Press, 2011.

Zhang De'er. *Evidence for the Existence of the Medieval Warm Period in China*. Beijing: Chinese Academy of Meteorological Sciences, 1994.

Zhang Weiwei. *The China Wave*. Hackensack, NJ: World Century, 2012.

AUTHOR'S NOTE

This book is essentially a plea to take China more seriously. Its involvement in world affairs is critical to solving the four core problems that confront humanity: war, financial instability, poverty, and man's impact on the environment. We have much to learn from China. That does not mean that we should blindly accept its ways any more than China should just mimic the West. We should engage in honest debate so that each side might benefit from taking some of the more successful parts of the other's experience and apply it in their own different contexts. So far, China has been more proactive in that regard than the West. It's time for all of us to "up our game" on China—not just so that we can cooperate better but also in order to compete.

In writing this book, I have been helped immensely by Jenny Lawrence, Ian Maskell, James Kynge, Rowan Zhao-Pease, Jim O'Neill (to whom I dedicate the First Rule), Alastair and Jo Michie, Nicky Hansell, Alex Pearson, Margaret Black, Frank Li, and Robin Sunley. I know that reading unedited manuscripts is a labor of love, so I am deeply grateful for your precious time, your comments, and your suggestions. It has been a real pleasure to have Hollis Heimbouch as publisher. Her intuition and lightness of touch transform dull sentences or poorly expressed ideas in a way that leaves one feeling, How come I never thought of that?!

I have learned more about China from Peter Nolan than from any other individual. His insights into the current dilemmas facing the Chinese state—and the world—are both deeply moving and inspiring and I feel that it is a privilege to spend time with him and to read his books.

I would also like to thank Toby Eady and Jennifer Joel. They both believed in the idea behind this book and shaped it from the start. It would never have been finished if they had not put their own energies behind it and I am deeply grateful for their interest and professionalism. No one knows the business better.

I would also like to thank Peter Yates, Australian entrepreneur turned philanthropist, who fit in the time to chair our business in China while at the same time leading numerous other organizations, including the Australian Royal Institution. His Deng-like common sense made the process of investing other people's money much safer for all of us and we all benefited greatly from his ideas and experience.

Jamie Russell was the first person who was willing to take the time to explain to a complete novice the complexities of the international carbon trading system. Nearly ten years on, I am lucky to count him as a friend and supporter.

I would also like to record my gratitude to the late Nick Robinson, without whose support I would never have been a published writer.

Finally, I would like to thank Jerry St. Dennis for his fundamental fairness, Elaine LaRoche for her time and interest when we were just getting started, Jeannemarie Gescher for putting me in touch with Mina in the first place, and finally, of course, Mina herself. No one I have met in business has quite the same drive and energy; it has been a roller-coaster ride but it was more colorful in your company and more endurable with your support.

Finally, if anyone thinks that dealing with China sounds like a challenge, they should try a family of four that skis directly off cliff faces, argues furiously about anything from Christopher Hitchens to partial differentials, and is renowned for unauthorized parties. But then how could we live without you?

Tim Clissold
Haute Savoie, France
小寒, 2014

ABOUT THE AUTHOR

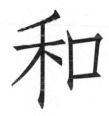

TIM CLISSOLD has lived and worked in China for more than twenty-five years and traveled to almost every part of the country. After graduating in physics and theoretical physics from Cambridge University and working in London, Australia, and Hong Kong, he developed a fascination for China. He spent two years studying Mandarin Chinese in Beijing before joining a private equity group that invested more than $400 million in China in the mid-1990s. Since then he has spent time with Goldman Sachs recovering distressed assets and set up a business that invested in greenhouse gas emission reduction projects in China through the United Nations Clean Development Mechanism. His first book, *Mr. China*, has been translated into twelve languages. It is being made into a film in mainland China and was an *Economist* Book of the Year. He is now working on a project to create English-language teaching materials on Chinese civilization for high school students around the world.